rabbi M

Rabbi
Esriel Hildesheimer
and the Creation of a
Modern Jewish Orthodoxy

JUDAIC STUDIES SERIES

Leon J. Weinberger, General Editor

Rabbi Esriel Hildesheimer
and the Creation of a Modern Jewish Orthodoxy

David Ellenson

The University of Alabama Press
Tuscaloosa and London

Copyright © 1990 by
The University of Alabama Press
Tuscaloosa, Alabama 35487–0380
All rights reserved
Manufactured in the United States of America

The paper on which this book is printed meets the minimum
requirements of American National Standard for Information
Science-Permanence of Paper for Printed Library Materials,
ANSI A39.48-1984.

Library of Congress Cataloging-in-Publication Data

Ellenson, David Harry, 1947–
Rabbi Esriel Hildesheimer and the
creation of a modern Jewish orthodoxy / David Ellenson.
p.   cm. — (Judaic studies series)
Includes bibliographical references.
ISBN 0-8173-0485-1 (alk. paper)
1. Hildesheimer, Esriel.   2. Rabbis—Berlin (Germany)—Biography.
3. Orthodox Judaism—Germany—History—19th
century.   4. Berlin
(Germany)—Biography.   I. Title.   II. Series.
BM755.H445E55   1990
296.8'32'092—dc20
[B]   89-20554
CIP

British Library Cataloguing-in-Publication Data available

0-8173-1272-2 (pbk: alk. paper)

For My Parents
Samuel Ellenson, z"l,
and
Rosalind Stern Ellenson z"l
With Love and Gratitude

Contents

Preface

Nineteenth-century German Jewry experienced notable departures from the established patterns of the past. The century witnessed a veritable revolution in the legal status, occupational distribution, cultural habits, and religious beliefs and behavior of central and western European Jewry. Under the impact of Enlightenment and emancipation, Judaism underwent a transition—not everywhere uniform in shape and intensity—from European traditionalisms to the modern era of contemporary Judaisms. Modern varieties of Judaism, each a response to the changing time, emerged in Germany during the 1800s. Each deserves study for its attempt to adapt and modify Judaism to this new challenge in Jewish history, as well as for its effort to maintain a link to the past.

No group in nineteenth-century Germany is more representative of this effort than modern Orthodoxy. As one apologete, Hermann Schwab, has written, "German-Jewish Orthodoxy was Sinai Judaism." Yet in talking of German Orthodoxy, even Schwab is forced to concede that "some of its characteristics could be traced to its German surroundings."[1] The German Orthodox were not one with the antimodernist Hungarian rabbi the Hatam Sofer (1762–1839), who was eager to endorse a total rejection of the contemporary, cosmopolitan world. In Germany, the reaction of such spokesmen as the Frankfurt rabbi Samson Raphael Hirsch (1808–1888) was to make peace, as far as possible, with many aspects of modernity and the transformations it wrought in Jewish status and culture. Simultaneously, they insisted on the eternality of the Oral Law. Hirsch saw Western culture as a positive good and became a master of it, "reformulating" his conception of Orthodoxy to permit himself and his adherents to participate in the modern world and its culture. German-speaking Orthodox Jews faced a similar, if not identical, problem as did their more liberal brethren of the Reform and Positive-Historical schools. In one respect, however, their dilemma was perhaps more acute than that of their liberal peers. For they had to confront the tensions and ambivalences which innovation and change posed to continuity with a past regarded as both sacred and, in the realm of Jewish law, immutable.

The tale of the modern Jewish Orthodox response to the changing society of nineteenth-century Germany has most often been told through the life and works of Samson Raphael Hirsch. Yet modern Jewish Orthodoxy had other exponents, men whose visions of modern Orthodoxy diverged from Hirsch's in several ways. Rabbi Esriel Hildesheimer (1820–99) of Berlin championed an enterprise Hirsch rejected—*Wissenschaft des Judentums*, the painstaking academic study of Jewish sources. Hildesheimer was the founder of the Rabbiner-seminar, the first modern Orthodox rabbinical seminary to be established in Germany. In this institution, erected in Berlin in 1873, critical study of Jewish sources was combined with an allegiance to the principle that the Torah, both written and oral, constituted direct revelation "from the mouth of the Almighty." Hildesheimer and Hirsch agreed in discarding such medieval vestiges as traditionally distinctive Jewish garb in favor of conventional Western clothing. But Hildesheimer went further; in the institutions he guided not only was the *Hochdeutsch* vernacular spoken instead of Yiddish but the academic study of Judaism was assiduously pursued. The former innovation earned him the enmity of traditional conservative elements within the Orthodox camp, and the latter separated him from Hirsch. But like the Hatam Sofer and unlike Hirsch, Hildesheimer called for the reinstitution of the *Bet Din*, the rabbinic civil court. Hildesheimer was also a master *posek*, a Jewish legal authority, who issued hundreds of responsa (Jewish legal decisions) in his lifetime.

Hildesheimer attempted to mediate between the pull of tradition and the demands of modernity. Indeed, his efforts make him a paradigmatic practitioner of the dialectical interplay between tradition and change that characterizes modern Jewish Orthodoxy.[2] Hildesheimer displayed a rich mixture of tradition and innovation, testifying to the complexity of the evolution of contemporary Jewish religion and society from the traditional patterns of medieval central European Judaism. An examination of Hildesheimer's life and work demonstrates the necessity of focusing on the manifold varieties and variations in the relationship between traditional forms and new institutions and values. His example provides a lens through which to understand the transformations modernity wrought in Judaism and the contemporary development of modern Jewish Orthodoxy.

The goals of this book are thus twofold. One is to demonstrate that modern Jewish Orthodoxy, as it emerged in nineteenth-century Germany, was not a monolithic entity confined to the prescriptions of Samson Raphael Hirsch. An account of the work of Esriel Hildesheimer will show that a pluralistic modern Orthodox Judaism also arose in that time and place.

A second goal is to highlight the blend of and dissonance between tradition and modernity which Hildesheimer's version of Orthodoxy displays. Indeed, it is this interplay between the old and the new, the tensions and the congruities, that indicates Hildesheimer's capacity to respond to the realities of the contemporary world while simultaneously affirming a commitment to traditional Jewish values. Of course, Hildesheimer was forced to make certain intellectual accommodations in order to live in two sometimes contradictory cultural worlds. The task here goes beyond a description of what Hildesheimer did to a portrayal of how he dealt with the conflicts created by such an attempt. This analysis hopes to uncover how Hildesheimer, as a self-conscious exponent of Orthodoxy within the nineteenth-century German milieu, created a modern Jewish response to the developments of the contemporary era.

The primary documents consulted for this study are published editions of Hildesheimer's literary works. These works can be divided into three major categories.

Hildesheimer's letters constitute the first category. His letters, in both German and Hebrew, are found in the *Rabbiner Esriel Hildesheimer Briefe,* edited by Professor Mordechai Eliav of Bar-Ilan University and published by the Leo Baeck Institute in 1965. In the last several decades, other letters have been published by the literary executors of Hildesheimer's papers in journals such as *Sinai* and *HaMaayan.*

Hildesheimer's responsa and interpretations of Jewish law are the second major primary documents consulted in this work. This legal literature represents Hildesheimer's responses to questions of belief and practice presented to Jewish Orthodoxy in the nineteenth-century context. The contours of Hildesheimer's Orthodoxy are especially well revealed through an examination of these sources. They appear in two volumes, in Hebrew, entitled *The Responsa of Rabbi Esriel*, and were issued in Tel Aviv in 1969 and 1976. An additional volume, *The Novellae of Rabbi Esriel on Tractates Yevamot and Ketubot*, appeared in 1984 in Jerusalem.

Hildesheimer's polemical and popular essays, primarily in German, have also been surveyed. They appeared in the newspapers and journals of his day. His most important essays have been collected in his *Gesammelte Aufsätze*, published in Frankfurt in 1923. They, too, reveal Hildesheimer's responses to many of the major issues of his time.

Although it may be possible for scholarship to be objective, the values that lead persons to pursue a particular subject are not. My own interest in Hildesheimer is proof of this, for much of my life has been spent in an effort to examine the same problem that confronted him: how to live in two different cultural worlds. Of course, the problem is not unique to either of us. It has confronted almost all Jews in Western countries during the last two centuries. Nevertheless, by tracing one particular response to this dilemma, I have attempted to gain a deeper insight into my own being and the challenges that confront me. My answer to this problem diverges from that of Hildesheimer. Yet, through this study, I have come to see much of his problem as my own and to admire his efforts to resolve it. I acknowledge my highly personal interest in studying Hildesheimer and his efforts at creating a viable and authentic form of modern Judaism.

I expected that this study would focus primarily on the philosophy of Jewish Neo-Orthodoxy as put forth by Hildesheimer. As I encountered the sources, however, I soon realized that such an approach would not be fruitful. Hildesheimer's fundamental interests were not philosophical. He did not attempt a systematic definition of Jewish ideology. Rather, he articulated his vision through the practical tasks of institution building. His ideology found its foremost expression through the institutions he created, not through formal philosophical treatises. Moreover, in assessing Hildesheimer's work, his institutions emerged as his most important contribution. Thus an account of Hildesheimer and his significance had to center on the institutional responses he issued to problems such as religious authority, Jewish religious pluralism, and education; they made up the essential elements of the modern Jewish Orthodoxy he established.

I wish to express my gratitude to the many people who have taught and nurtured me. To two of my undergraduate professors at The College of William and Mary in Virginia, Ed Crapol and James Livingston, I offer special thanks. Professor Crapol initially introduced me to the spirit of intellectual excitement and creativity that can mark the academic enterprise at its best. Professor Livingston convinced me that the academic study of religion was a field unparalleled in intellectual depth and moral significance. Both of these men inspired me to enter university life and modeled its importance and beauty for me. I was also fortunate to come under the tutelage of Professors David Little and Alan Lettofsky when I began my graduate studies in religion at the University of Virginia. Professor Lettofsky's knowledge and erudition, as well as his kind and nurturing manner, inspired me to continue my studies in Judaica. David Little introduced me to the sociology of religion, a field I continued to pursue with Gillian Lindt at Columbia University. Their intellectual influence is, I believe, evident in the way many of the problems in this book are addressed.

Stanley Chyet, Arnie Eisen, Daniel Landes, Robert Levine, Ismar Schorsch, Michael Signer, Fredelle Spiegel, and Ellen Umansky all read either parts or the whole of this manuscript. I greatly appreciate the support and friendship they offered throughout its writing. I have discussed numerous intellectual problems raised by this study with each of them and have benefited from their comments. Paula Hyman deserves a special word of thanks for her constant encouragement and her unfailing support. I also am grateful for the suggestions made by the anonymous readers for The University of Alabama Press and the thorough editing job performed by Trudie Calvert.

I wish also to thank Professor Mordechai Eliav of Bar-Ilan University in Israel. His publication of many of the primary sources used in this study and his own writings on the nineteenth-century German-Jewish world made my work possible. Furthermore, he kindly read the entire manuscript and offered many suggestions and corrections which I incorporated into the final version. I feel fortunate to stand on the shoulders of such a giant.

My community at the Hebrew Union College–Jewish Institute of

Religion has been unfailingly supportive. As a student at the New York school, I was fortunate to be taught by knowledgeable and caring teachers, and as a faculty member on the Los Angeles campus I have been blessed with stimulating and sympathetic colleagues. Lee Bycel, dean of the Los Angeles school, and Uri Herscher, executive vice-president of the college-institute, not only have provided the financial support necessary for the completion of this book, they have also been wonderful and caring friends. I thank them and my colleagues on the faculty not only for their help on this book but also for making the campus one on which I feel privileged to teach and study. I would also like to thank Phil Miller and Harvey Horowitz, librarians at the college-institutes in New York and Los Angeles, for bibliographical assistance in locating sources necessary for this study. Further, I acknowledge the support of Alfred Gottschalk and Eugene Mihaly to this project.

I also thank the National Foundation for Jewish Culture and the Memorial Foundation for Jewish Culture for their generous financial support.

Two persons who played special and prominent roles in helping me write this book are no longer alive: Professors Joseph L. Blau and Fritz Bamberger. Professor Blau was my initial sponsor at Columbia University. He believed in the importance of this project from the beginning and devoted much time and effort to helping me complete it. Fritz Bamberger, too, was a source of strength and encouragement. He provided me with insights and knowledge which only a veteran authority in this field could bring. Professor Bamberger will always stand for me as my *rav*, a title he himself would never have claimed, but whose virtues he nevertheless embodied. I am only sorry that he and Professor Blau did not live to see this volume in print.

Finally, I thank Helaine Ettinger, who read and discussed every page and issue of this manuscript with me. Her editing skill and her ability to define the significant amid a morass of detail helped to clarify and strengthen every argument I present. I thank her for her appropriate and gentle prodding of me at various stages of this task. Whatever merits this book has are certainly due, in large measure, to her as well as to the others I have mentioned. The shortcomings, of course, remain my own. To all these people, as well as to my wife, Jackie, and my children, Ruth, Micah, Hannah, and Naomi, I say thank you.

Beyond all the persons mentioned above, I owe my greatest debt of gratitude and love to my parents, Rosalind Stern Ellenson and Samuel Ellenson, to whom this book is dedicated. They nurtured me with warmth and kindness from an early age, and they instilled in me a love of scholarship, Judaism, the Jewish people, and humanity. I am grateful to have been raised in their home, and a day never passes that I do not think of them. I miss them and hope that this book is in some way a tribute to their memory. Their love truly remains a blessing.

Rabbi
Esriel Hildesheimer
and the Creation of a
Modern Jewish Orthodoxy

1

The Man and the Challenges of His Times

$\mathbf{T}$he year 1820 was a time of transition for German Jewry in an era of ferment for Judaism. The medieval order of central European Judaism had been for some time in the process of dissolution, confronted by the new society and the new economy which had been taking shape throughout the eighteenth century. The parameters of new structures of Jewish life and religion, however, had yet to emerge. On May 11 of that year, Esriel Hildesheimer was born in Halberstadt, a small town in Saxony. Halberstadt had been annexed by Prussia in 1815 in the wake of the defeat of Napoleon's armies by the conservative forces of Europe.[1] Hildesheimer was destined to be both a product of the ferment of his time and a major force in shaping new directions for Jewish life and religion in the years ahead.

Hildesheimer's life spans almost the entire nineteenth century (1820–99); his career embraced two nations—Hungary and Germany; and his reputation extended throughout Europe. He was educated in the first Orthodox school in Germany to add secular subjects to its curriculum. He continued his studies with Jacob Ettlinger and Isaac Bernays, rabbis noted for their traditional observance and knowledge as well as their receptivity to contemporary thought. Both men encouraged Hildesheimer's interest in secular studies, and under their influence he went on to study at the two finest universities in Germany, Berlin and Halle. He received a Ph.D. from the latter in 1846 for a study of the Septuagint. He emerged from this education a staunch opponent of Reform Judaism and a major proponent of the position that secular studies and traditional rabbinic scholarship were fully compatible.

Hildesheimer's first opportunity to realize his ambitions for the creation of a "cultured Orthodoxy" came in 1851, when he became the rabbi of the Jewish community in Eisenstadt, Hungary. There he established the first yeshiva in the modern world to have a secular component in its regular course of study. This innovation earned Hildesheimer the wrath of many Orthodox traditionalists in Hungary. As a result, he returned to Germany in 1869 and there became the rabbi of Berlin's separatist Orthodox congregation Adass Jisroel. In 1873, with the opening of the Orthodox Rabbinical Seminary in Berlin, Hildesheimer fulfilled his dream of a school that would train rabbis committed to both Jewish Orthodoxy and *Wissenschaft des Judentums* (the modern scholarly study of Judaism). This institution gained Hildesheimer a position of leadership among Orthodox Jews in his own day and marks him as a major architect of modern Jewish Orthodoxy in our own.

Like his medieval rabbinic predecessors, Hildesheimer was committed to a belief in the divine sanction for and authority of halakha (rabbinic law). But the medieval worldview that undergirded this belief and the cultural system and communal structure that had supported its authority were shattered by events of the eighteenth and nineteenth centuries. To appreciate fully the significance of Hildesheimer's efforts and achievements, one must understand the nature of that earlier world, especially the pervasive influence of the traditional rabbinate and the implicit and explicit educational systems that nurtured it. Likewise, it is important to analyze the changes that transformed the nature of both the rabbinate and the community in Hildesheimer's day. With this understanding, the trials facing Hildesheimer and other Jewish religious leaders become clear and one may assess the substance, uniqueness, and commonality of the response formulated by Hildesheimer and his circle.

The institution of the rabbinate, its power, and its authority were based on Jewish religious tradition as sustained by the organizational structure of the medieval German society. The Jews, as a group within the corporate structure of the medieval body politic, were granted internal authority in political and cultural affairs by the rulers of the localities in whose midst they dwelt. Thus the Jewish sphere of influence was determined largely by the governing institutions of the state, whether secular or ecclesiastical.[2] The Jewish community was able to maintain itself and its political and cultural autonomy as long as the corporate structure and rabbinic authority of medieval society persisted.

The overwhelming majority of Jews during this period were effectively segregated from non-Jewish society in central and western Europe. They regarded themselves as living in *Golus* (exile) and, as Jacob Katz has commented, in their view, "complete segregation from the outside world would have been desirable."[3] Despite shifts that occurred within the Jewish community, either because of those exceptional individuals who penetrated the non-Jewish world or those movements from within that challenged the existing community organization, the community remained intact. As both Katz and Salo Baron have contended, the medieval Jewish community was essentially united and able to withstand any threat of disintegration.[4]

Within this largely autonomous and insulated German Jewish world, the rabbis functioned as religious leaders and civil magistrates. The rabbi was usually called upon to preach but twice a year, and he seldom engaged in pastoral functions.[5] His principal responsibility was to decide questions of law, either ritualistic or civil, for the members of his community. He, along with lay leaders (*parnasim*), administered and governed the community; together they held complete judicial authority within the community. They were charged with preserving peace and order; providing assistance for the poor; maintaining the community's educational system; supervising building construction within the confines of the Jewish quarter; overseeing Jewish cultural activities; fulfilling all communal and individual religious needs from the erection of the synagogue to the rites of passage that marked the Jew's journey from cradle to grave; and, most important, vis-à-vis the host society and its rulers, collecting taxes imposed on the Jewish community by the gentile authorities at whose pleasure the Jews were permitted to remain in a specific territory.[6]

The rabbis and lay boards exercised virtually all-embracing control over the community. Further, the rabbis were empowered with police authority to punish deviations from the norms they established. They could enforce their policies through methods such as fines, stripes, or incarceration. The rabbis and their lay cohorts (generally with rabbinical permission) could and did employ forms of excommunication to squelch dissent and ensure discipline within the community. Of all the disciplinary means at the disposal of the rabbinate, this weapon was, as Baron puts it, "the most effective punishment and method of enforcement wielded by Jewish communal organs." For not only did *herem*, the ban, remove the individual from the synagogue and force him to suffer social and economic boycott, but it denied his wife and children admission to religious ceremonies and schools.[7]

More significantly, the rabbi's power was legitimated through the community's shared beliefs and values. Among all strata of Jewish society the ancient commitment to halakha as divinely sanctioned was reinforced and served to fortify the authority and respect due the rabbi as the official interpreter of God's commands. The day-to-day life of the community reflected the traditional rabbinic ethos. Thus, for example, one finds a distinctive sense of religious and cultural unity pervading the home and the synagogue. Within the family the child was introduced to customs regarding the Sabbath, benedictions before and after meals, the Passover Seder, and other religious ceremonies. Similarly, almost every Jewish boy had attended the synagogue often enough to have learned the prayers by rote even before the age of bar mitzvah. Through such informal means the Jews of medieval Europe created a strong sense of ideological agreement.[8]

These values and beliefs were transmitted within the educational institutions of the community. Jewish law obliged every community to provide an elementary school, a *heder*, which all boys could attend. Nearly every community seems to have fulfilled this obligation. Most boys, except the very poorest, attended at least through age thirteen. The curricula of all these schools were essentially uniform, and the course of study included only Jewish subjects.

The first three months were spent mastering the Hebrew alphabet, after which both the Bible and the traditional commentary of Rashi and the synagogue service would be studied. Theoretically, the student could progress by the age of ten to the study of the earliest code of Jewish law, the Mishnah, and if he were exceptionally talented, could continue with Gemara at the age of fifteen. Although it lacked any real systematization and comprehensiveness, as Katz has remarked, "from the viewpoint of social function, this education fulfilled its purpose."[9] Such practical knowledge as one might need to engage in business was to be acquired through experience. Indeed, the German rabbis of the fifteenth through seventeenth centuries discouraged secular learning. Even into the eighteenth century, a rabbi such as Pinchas Horowitz of Frankfurt, the

Baal Haflaah, who was the teacher of Esriel Hildesheimer's father, absolutely forbade his students to engage in secular studies. Far from being neutral toward secular knowledge, the rabbis of Germany in the centuries immediately preceding Esriel Hildesheimer's birth were openly hostile to such study.[10] The *heder*, with its exclusive focus on Jewish subjects, was thus an effective instrument for the dissemination of traditional rabbinic values and beliefs among all the members of the community.

The medieval Jewish child who experienced this education quickly became familiar with the rudiments of Jewish religious tradition and, perhaps more important, became imbued with a belief in the importance of its study. The community assigned its highest priority and honor to those individuals (rabbis) who could claim to have mastered such study. The power, prestige, and authority of the rabbinate and of Jewish learning were thus reinforced through the formal and informal educational processes in Jewish society.

To see a Machiavellian stratagem on the part of the rabbis would be an error. The rabbis were religiously motivated; they, too, were cultural products of their society and were infused with the scholarly ideal of becoming masters of Jewish tradition and learning. Theirs was a divine mandate legitimated by Scripture and reinforced by social, cultural, and political realities.

The ideal of the rabbinic scholar reached its zenith in the yeshiva, the educational institution that trained rabbis and scholars. Jacob Katz has observed: "A thorough knowledge and preoccupation with the Talmud, although acquired only by the minority, constituted a value of supreme importance to society as a whole. The educational aims which applied to the entire people—a basic knowledge of Judaism and observance of its precepts—were considered only byproducts of its ultimate goal, the rearing of scholars."[11] The *Rosh Yeshiva*, head of the yeshiva, was a living embodiment of this ideal of scholarship. He was required not only to have mastered rabbinic literature but also to be able to offer novel interpretations of the material. The *Rosh Yeshiva*'s reputation attracted students from both neighboring and distant communities to come and study. For communities with a rabbi eminent and scholarly enough to establish a yeshiva, it was a matter of great local pride both to support the yeshiva and to have resident in their midst such a famous personage.

Only rabbinic literature was taught in the yeshiva, as the *heder*. Secular subject matter was not permitted to intrude. Unlike the *heder*, the yeshiva focused exclusively on the Talmud and codes of

Jewish law. The study was carried on at a very advanced level and was intellectually rigorous. The rabbis who studied there benefited in the prestige emanating from their association with it and simultaneously became socialized through it—internalizing the ideal of the rabbi-scholar and the belief in the rightness of the political system and cultural ethos in which their positions of status and authority were rooted. The yeshiva served as the most fundamental expression of the values of medieval central and western European Jewish society.[12]

Girls were not taught in the educational institutions of the community. The average girl of this period might have known a bit of Hebrew, and special books were written for her in the vernacular (Yiddish or Judeo-German) so that she could understand the Bible and a few other Jewish tales and legends. Otherwise, her duties were concentrated in the home. Her public authority, in contrast to the power she might wield in the home, was minimal.[13] The position of women became an issue later in the nineteenth century, as Hildesheimer and other religious leaders supported formal education for girls along with boys in the elementary schools of the Jewish community.

Jewish society in Germany throughout the Middle Ages until the beginning of the eighteenth century can broadly be described as a traditional society, characterized by common religious and cultural values and circumscribed by the political structure of the organized community so as to create a definable worldview and an institutional structure. The social and political experience of the Jews in this civilization remained largely constant during the entire era. Any internal threats to Jewish unity that arose were ultimately dissipated so long as the institutions of Jewish communal life remained stable. At the heart of this civilization lay the rabbinate, which served as the highest real authority and the greatest symbolic repository of the community's values.

Hildesheimer was a descendant of several generations of rabbinical scholars. His grandfather Rabbi Moses Galia was a student of Rabbi Lev Eger, the uncle of the famed Rabbi Akiva Eger (1761–1837). Esriel's father, Rabbi Lev Galia, was a student of Rabbi Pinchas Horowitz of Frankfurt from 1780 to 1785. Horowitz was also the teacher of the Hatam Sofer. Esriel Hildesheimer was thus linked to several of the greatest personages of traditionalist Jewry in central Europe during the first part of the nineteenth century. After serving as a *dayan* (judge) of the rabbinical court in another community,

Rabbi Lev Galia moved to Halberstadt and taught talmudic lessons (*shiurim*) in the community yeshiva.

Testimony to the quality of his father's and grandfather's rabbinic scholarship is offered in the literary legacy—rabbinic novellae on Yebamot and Ketubot—they left to Esriel. Esriel's appreciation of their work is reflected in a statement he made about his father's scholarship: "And the merit of my father, the righteous one famed for his goodness and scholarship in all the cities of his native land, has aided me." His father's commitment to rabbinic learning is like-wise revealed in an anecdote preserved by the Hildesheimer family. It is said that on the day after his wedding, Esriel's father took a goodly portion of the dowry money and purchased classical rabbinic texts. When asked where he would find the money to buy bread in the future, he replied, "Bread I will need tomorrow. However, *sefarim* [holy books] I already need today."[14]

As the scion of a rabbinic family whose roots stretched back into this period, Esriel Hildesheimer assumed many of the attitudes characteristic of this essentially medieval Jewish civilization.[15] He was born in the nineteenth century, however, and currents of his own time helped mold his character and outlook. These elements led to a virtual revolution of Jewish life in nineteenth-century Germany.

The rise of nationalism in western and central Europe challenged the old corporatism of the medieval centuries. As the nation-state, with its ideal of individual citizenship, began to emerge during the eighteenth and nineteenth centuries, the Jewish community was progressively deprived of its autonomy. This loss led to a transformation of Jewish communal organization, and for the rabbinate it posed an unprecedented crisis. During the medieval period the rabbinate could employ limited legal sanctions and methods of coercion to compel obedience to its will. The specific powers granted the rabbis by the secular rulers in combination with the general nature of the medieval body politic often made the rabbis powerful political figures in their local communities. Over time the dual role of civil magistrate and religious leader was stripped from the rabbis. The change in the political status of the Jew and the Jewish community, along with other cultural and educational transformations, altered the nature of the rabbinate.

Although the authority and prestige of the rabbinate had begun to decline from the beginning of the 1700s, it was increasingly diminished in the late eighteenth century through the influence of the Haskalah, the Enlightenment—an intellectual emancipation that preceded the political one by at least half a century. The rabbis frequently issued bans against the Maskilim, the advocates of the Haskalah, but because most rabbis failed to understand the nature of the changes then at work in their community, the bans were ignored. Further, the rabbinate was ridiculed for issuing bans.[16] Eventually, structural changes in the German corporate system led the secular authorities to remove the weapons of coercion formerly at the rabbis' disposal. These changes in the political life of the Jewish community did not occur all at once but went through several transitional stages. The final result, however, was the dismemberment of the medieval structure of the Jewish body politic. Disabilities that had applied specifically to Jews were removed by law, and Jews were granted all the rights and duties of German citizenship.

The process leading to Emancipation was long and bitter, lasting in Germany from the 1780s until the passage of the law on Jewish equality by the North German Confederation on July 3, 1869, and its extension, with the ratification of the constitution, to the new Hohenzollern-ruled German Empire on April 14, 1871. Theoretically, the ideology of the western European Enlightenment, with its emphasis on reason and egalitarianism, carried the inherent logic that the Jews should be enfranchised as rapidly as any other group in society. It was not until March 11, 1812, however, that the Jews were granted full rights and privileges as citizens of the French-influenced Prussian state. These rights and privileges were annulled some years later by the Prussian legislature when conservative rule was restored in post-Napoleonic Europe. Thus more than fifty years elapsed from the time the measure was initially passed until the Jews were granted full rights as citizens of the imperial German state in 1871.[17]

The traditional jurisdiction of the rabbis was abolished long before political emancipation came to all Jewish residents of the German states. As early as the 1780s, secular authorities in certain localities forbade the rabbis to issue bans of excommunication. In 1811 the rabbis were stripped of their judicial authority in all the German states. Only in Altona-Schleswig-Holstein, which was under Danish rule until 1864, was a Jewish *Bet Din* (court) empowered by the state to adjudicate civil disputes.[18] Hildesheimer studied at the yeshiva of Rabbi Jacob Ettlinger of Altona from 1837 to 1842. He perfected his knowledge of Jewish civil law and actually adjudicated civil disputes as a *dayan* (judge). Hildesheimer was thus privileged to experience firsthand the autonomy of the medieval Jewish community in the postmedieval period. His early life mirrors the halting nature of the transition in the political status of the individual Jew and his community leader. With this one exception, the rabbis could no longer enforce obedience through political means to what they regarded as God's law. Instead, to persuade individuals to accept their authority, they had to resort to the same methods of propaganda and education as the other religious leaders in nineteenth-century Germany.

This does not mean that the structure of the community was totally destroyed. Indeed, the community continued to exist as a corporation of public right in all the German states, entitled to administer its own religious life and educational institutions and retaining some measure of autonomy in matters relating to social welfare. Jews in each community were required to pay taxes for the support of these institutions and activities regardless of their religious affiliation or lack of it within the community. Thus in Berlin, for example, the individual members of the Reform Temple were a part of the local Jüdische-Gemeinde and were legally bound to pay a tax to support general Jewish communal organizations in addition to voluntary contributions for the support of their own Reform synagogue. Similarly, in communities where the Orthodox were in the minority, they were compelled to support the community's institutions. Even freethinkers who rejected Judaism as a religion (*Konfessionslose Juden*) were obligated until 1876 to pay a tax to support the religious and philanthropic structure of the Jewish community. In that year the Reichstag passed a law permitting Jews to secede from the general Jewish communal organization of a given city on the basis of religious conscience. It is not surprising that this bill was introduced by a Jewish member of the Reichstag, Eduard Lasker, under the influence of certain elements of the Orthodox Jewish community and certain politically unattached Jewish freethinkers.[19]

The German Jewish community in the nineteenth century cannot be viewed as a voluntary association of like-minded religious individuals, along the lines of an American model. The community functioned as a corporation of public right with limited powers of taxation. This state-sanctioned political structure, combined with the force of centuries of tradition, helped to create a strong sense of community for many Jews throughout the nineteenth century. Nevertheless, the loss of political autonomy which the community experienced at this time was a pivotal factor in the development of modern Judaism. The Jews now received their political and civic identity (at least in theory) from the outside world and not from the community itself. This innovation heralded the deathblow for an unmodified medieval rabbinic Judaism in Germany.[20]

Intellectual changes accompanied the political changes. The Haskalah stressed rationalist ideals and the universality of man. In its view Jewish teaching was no more than "a special supplement for the education of the Jew"; the worth of education was "dependent on the prior mastery of the foundations of universal knowledge."[21] Acquisition of secular knowledge supplanted the medieval stress on rabbinic literature and tradition. Moses Mendelssohn (1729–86), a towering figure of the German Haskalah, translated the Bible from Hebrew into German in an effort to encourage his coreligionists to improve their knowledge of the latter. In addition, Mendelssohn influenced his students to publish articles of general interest in Hebrew periodicals so that Jews could increase their awareness of the intellectual currents in the larger society. Indeed, his stress on the use of Hebrew over Yiddish reflected an attempt to wean his fellow Jews away from that mode of expression into the broader realm of German-language discourse.[22]

The drift toward secular education was combined with an attitude of indifference to halakha. Many Jews no longer regarded the traditional sacred texts of Judaism as subjects worthy of study or the *mitzvot* (commandments) as binding, and not a few Maskilim rejected them altogether. Jewish society no longer sought to legitimate all changes and innovations on the basis of the Jewish past, that is, Torah. Rabbinic authority weakened under the pressure of such conflicting opinions and was diluted further by the Maskilim's successful efforts to create educational institutions completely removed from the aegis of religion. The Maskilim often failed to include any religious instruction in the curricula of their schools. They sought to release the hold of traditional religious values on the consciousness of the community so that individual Jews could participate in a broader intellectual life. Their educational institutions helped foster changes that undermined the established unity of normative Jewish religious life.

The rabbinate initially failed to understand that the rise of the Maskilim and of individuals such as Mendelssohn signaled a new era for Judaism. They tended to believe rather that any Jew who considered secular studies significant was a deviant. They were unable to grasp the radically changed circumstances inside and outside of their community. They resorted to the old weapons of excommunication and invective to prevent Jews from sending their children to the schools of the Maskilim or from engaging in secular learning.[23] Moses Sofer placed a ban on the writings of Mendelssohn.[24] Teachers such as Pinchas Horowitz banned secular learning altogether. Other rabbis went so far as to proclaim anyone who spoke or wrote German a heretic for having denied the fundamental principles of Torah.[25] These rabbinic protests were largely ineffectual. The ever-growing demand for knowledge among the laity created pressure to establish German and secular studies as a central part of the school curriculum. The thirst for such knowledge was so great that the rabbis were unable to discourage parents from sending their children to the schools of the Maskilim, and in the case of wealthier families, from hiring Maskilim as tutors.[26] The relentless push for the acquisition of secular knowledge, combined with the unceasing and harsh attacks of the Maskilim on the traditional religious curriculum of the yeshiva, caused the more perceptive among both the rabbis and the laity to seek some sort of accommodation with the spirit of the time.[27] Rabbi Samuel Landau of Prague was among the first to propose an ideological basis for such compromise.

Rabbi Landau (d. 1834) was the son of the famous Rabbi Ezekiel Landau, the great halakhist and author of the *Noda Bi-huda,* who was vehemently opposed to Mendelssohn, the Maskilim, and all secular learning. Samuel Landau, however, wrote that it was an "obligation to teach one's son German and the manners of the state." He employed the term *Torah im Derekh Eretz* to describe the consideration he felt was necessary between religious studies (Torah) and secular learning (*Derekh Eretz*). The phrase was to be popularized by Rabbi Samson Raphael Hirsch later in the nineteenth century. Landau thus prefigured the "enlightenment Orthodoxy" that would enable the educational activities of Hirsch a half-century later and was to become the hallmark of modern German traditionalism.[28] His departure from the teachings of his father is indicative of the tumultuous and transitory nature of this era.

It was certainly clear to Hildesheimer, as to any discerning Jewish religious leader in nineteenth-century Germany, that the ideological unity of the medieval Jewish community was doomed to extinction. The acculturated, pluralistic world of the current German Jewish society no longer favored such insular communities. The strongest supporters of Orthodoxy itself during this century in Germany were highly acculturated and successful businessmen, bankers, entrepreneurs, doctors, and lawyers.[29] Rabbinic authority could thus no longer expect to legitimate itself solely through an appeal to tradition. Pluralism within the community was a reality, and the rabbinate had to confront competing brands of religious Judaism which claimed legitimacy for their interpretations of the tradition. In addition, in the nineteenth century there arose the novel problem of how to deal with sizable numbers of Jews who were irreligious and not governed by traditional religious norms. Relations with the gentile world had to be approached in a new way, for Jews no longer resided as "a nation within a nation." Instead, Emancipation and the aspirations it inspired within the Jewish community made the Jews eager to redefine their relationship to their gentile neighbors, as they did not necessarily see themselves as residing in *Galut*. Finally, the transformation in the educational and cultural values of the Jewish community meant that the relationship between Jewish tradition and secular learning also had to be redefined. Once these definitions were arrived at, institutions that accorded with these values had to be established—both for the laity and for the rabbinate.

Judaism, under the impact of Enlightenment and Emancipation, underwent a transition—not everywhere uniform in shape and intensity—from the medieval tendencies of central and western European traditionalisms to the modern era of contemporary Judaisms. Modern varieties of Judaism emerged in Germany during the 1800s. For the liberal movements, however, the advent of religious pluralism within Judaism did not pose the ideological problem it did for Orthodoxy, which saw itself as the only rightful bearer of the tradition. Consequently, no group in nineteenth-century Germany is more representative than modern Orthodoxy of the struggle both to adapt and to modify Judaism to the new challenges of the time and to maintain a link to the past.[30] Hermann Schwab might speak of German Orthodoxy as "Sinai Judaism," yet even he was forced to concede that a number of its characteristics "could be traced to its German surroundings."[31] All German-speaking Jews, the Orthodox as well as their liberal peers, had to confront the tensions and ambivalences which ongoing change now posed to continuity with the past. All, including Hildesheimer, stood between the Scylla and Charybdis of tradition and innovation.

In 1795, Zvi Hirsch Katzlin, a wealthy and religiously observant Jewish philanthropist and businessman, left ten thousand thalers in his will for the creation of a school that would combine Jewish learning with a secular curriculum and would prepare students for occupations in general German society. Like other Jews of his economic class who were eager to receive the benefits proffered by the French Revolution, Katzlin was an enthusiastic proponent of the Emancipation. He was convinced that the acquisition of one's "equal rights" depended on a mastery of the German language, as well as a knowledge of general subjects and professions. In this sense, his views were typical of other Maskilim of his day. Yet unlike the more secular Maskilim, he did not abandon belief in the importance of traditional rabbinic scholarship. Katzlin was particularly concerned that poor Jewish families might send their children to Christian schools so they would receive the advantages of a modern education. He feared that in these schools they would abandon Jewish knowledge and, ultimately, Jewish identity. As a result of Katzlin's bequest, Hasharat Zvi was opened in Halberstadt in 1796. It was the first school among German Jews to employ an educational philosophy of "Torah im derekh eretz."[32]

The language of instruction in the school was German, and secular subjects designed to prepare Jewish youth for jobs and professions in the general society were integral to the curriculum. French and Latin were taught to prepare the more gifted students for examinations that would allow them to enter the *Gymnasium* after completing elementary school. Religious instruction was also important. Six hours a day were devoted to the study of traditional Jewish sources—Bible, Commentaries, and Talmud. Students thus left the school with a thorough grounding in Hebrew, Bible, and traditional Jewish law and lore. Indeed, the school's motto was "A blending of eternal religious verities with popular enlightenment in accord with the spirit of the time." By 1825, Hasharat Zvi had attained such prominence in the community that it became the central elementary educational institution for the Jewish population of Halberstadt and, significantly, in 1827 the school opened classes for girls.[33]

Esriel Hildesheimer's father, a resident of Halberstadt and a famous rabbinical scholar, was evidently not a rigid traditionalist, for when his son reached the age to begin formal elementary school instruction, he was enrolled in Hasharat Zvi. In this respect, Esriel's father diverged from his own teacher, Rabbi Pinchas Horowitz. Esriel's father obviously supported the spirit of accommodation with the intellectual currents of the day as reflected in the educational philosophy and curriculum of the Halberstadt school.[34] Esriel's attendance at this school inculcated within him from a young age a positive attitude toward secular learning which continued throughout his career. From this experience, moreover, he learned that traditional religious learning could be combined with a secular education in such a way that the blend of the two appeared natural and without tension. Indeed, his experience as a boy in a coeducational classroom foreshadowed the liberal attitude he would take later in his life toward the formal education of women.

This positive view of secular learning was also penetrating the world of the central European yeshiva. Rabbi Jacob Ettlinger (1798–1871) of Altona—who was to have a profound influence on the course of Orthodox Judaism in Germany during the nineteenth century through the efforts of two of his students, Esriel Hildesheimer and Samson Raphael Hirsch—was a product of the changing times. Ettlinger's yeshiva provided instruction only in the traditional religious subjects, but he himself had attended a German university and, unlike many of his rabbinic peers, preached in the vernacular, not in Yiddish. Later in his career he advocated the creation of a modern seminary for the training of rabbis. After the death of their father when Esriel was twelve, his brother Abraham became his guardian and, when Esriel reached the age of seventeen, enrolled him in the yeshiva of Jacob Ettlinger. In so doing, Abraham not only exposed Esriel to one of the great rabbinical scholars of contemporary Europe but also, given Ettlinger's attitudes, reinforced the approach to secular learning Esriel had gained as a child. The young Hildesheimer's respect for Ettlinger was unbounded; he always referred to Ettlinger as his "outstanding teacher."[35] Hildesheimer's letters indicate that he consulted with his teacher both on private matters and on public issues throughout his life.[36] Ettlinger seems to have returned Hildesheimer's deep respect and high esteem, for he more than once described Hildesheimer as his "outstanding student" and even referred to him as "my son" in one legal responsum. Most important, Ettlinger granted Hildesheimer permission to attend the philosophical lectures delivered in German by Rabbi Isaac Bernays (1792–1849) of Hamburg while Hildesheimer was still a student.[37] Rabbis like Ettlinger and Bernays, who were simultaneously bastions of Orthodoxy and receptive to a modernist intellectual temper, are further evidence that traditional German Jewry was in a state of transition during this era.

At the urging of both of his rabbinical masters, particularly Bernays, Hildesheimer determined to study for a Ph.D. He decided that

Orthodox Judaism could acquire status and prestige in the eyes of Jews and gentiles only if Orthodoxy had champions trained in and devoted to academic pursuits. Consequently, in 1843, Hildesheimer went to the University of Berlin for two years to study Semitic languages, philosophy, history, physics, and analytic geometry.[38] When he left Berlin in 1846, he continued his studies at the University of Halle, another of Germany's prestigious universities. That same year he received his Ph.D. from Halle for a dissertation entitled "The Correct Way to Interpret Scripture." The manuscript of the dissertation has been lost, but an article that appears to be a section of it appeared in the *Literaturblatt des Orient* in 1848 under the title, "Material for an Investigation of the Septuagint."[39] Evidence concerning his professors' attitudes toward him is not available. Nevertheless, in earning the Ph.D., Hildesheimer became one of the few Orthodox rabbis in Germany up to that time to receive a secular doctorate.

The receptivity to the dominant intellectual currents of the time that was beginning to manifest itself in the circles of rabbis such as Ettlinger and Bernays did not overshadow the highest priority these men assigned to traditional Jewish learning. The medieval ideal of the *matmid*, the scholar constantly engaged in the study of Talmud and related rabbinical literature, still occupied a central position within their value scheme. Stories and legends about Hildesheimer as the dedicated *matmid* reflect this attitude. Hildesheimer garnered a reputation as a brilliant Talmudist during his years of apprenticeship with Ettlinger. His peers said that even if there were twenty-five hours in a day, Hildesheimer would find an additional one for the study of rabbinic sources.[40] Hildesheimer himself wrote concerning his years in Ettlinger's yeshiva, "When I studied with my master in Altona, although I was not so far from my mother's home, still I did not visit my mother until the end of four and a half years. And my mother, my teacher, did not request this from me earlier."[41] Perhaps these reports of Hildesheimer's fervor for his studies are somewhat exaggerated (they do appear rather apocryphal). Still, they seem reliable in indicating that he was a devoted student and that the Hildesheimer family placed the highest priority upon rabbinic studies in keeping with the traditional religious value assigned the study of Torah.

It should be emphasized that within the yeshiva the method employed to study Talmud was one which hearkened back to the medieval period. Hildesheimer studied *derekh hapeshat,* as was the custom of his teacher Ettlinger. This method, which demanded an analytical study of the Talmud text along with the traditional legal commentaries on it, was opposed to the more fanciful mode of talmudic study then dominant in the yeshivot of Hungary.[42] Indeed, this method of study might even be termed one of "halakhic rationalism." Though not identical to a *wissenschaftlich* approach, it did require a close and careful exegetical reading of the Gemara. Hildesheimer's education thus prefigures the trends of his later career. He lived in the world of the traditional yeshiva while at the same time imbibing the values of the German university system through his doctoral studies there. With one foot in each of two worlds, the medieval-religious and the modern-secular, he was to forge a new path. Throughout his career, he strove to achieve a unique balance between the demands of his heritage and the demands of his day in his efforts to affirm an authentic Jewish identity in the modern world.

The struggle for Hildesheimer, as for his peers, was to develop an authentic Jewish lifestyle in harmony with the times. This required cultivating a new understanding of Jewish identity to compensate for the reduced definition of Jewish status. *Status* in this case is taken from the Latin word meaning *standing* and refers to the condition of a person in the eyes of the law. When employed in regard to a person's relationship to a group, the person's own definition of that relationship may be totally irrelevant. Authorities either external to the group or within the group itself may well make status designations with absolutely no regard for the individual's own sense of self-definition. In sum, *status* is essentially a legalistic term.

Identity, in contrast, embraces a more subjective and personalistic component. Its etymological root derives from the Greek *idios* meaning *private* or *individual.* When the term *identity,* as opposed to *status,* is used to refer to a person's relationship to a group, it may simply signify the psychological orientation of that individual toward the group. It indicates the individual's autonomous understanding of who he or she is. Identity does not address the issue of the Jewish legal relationship that obtains between an individual and the Jewish community. Rather, identity reflects a personal definition of self in reference to a group.

Within the context of a medieval political order, Jewishness involved a corporate status. Individual citizenship in a nation-state, as a modern Western model would have it, was essentially unknown.

Furthermore, the Jewish community was either politically autonomous or semiautonomous in governing the lives of its members. The Jewish community provided its members with a sense of cultural and political as well as religious status and identity. There was thus little or no dissonance between public and private spheres, individual and collective realms.

With the advent of "modernity" in the West, the situation began to change. Modernity, through such political and ideological events as the Emancipation and the Haskalah, largely transformed the matter of Jewishness from a question of status to one of identity. As the status definition of the Jews and the Jewish community became ever more diminished, consideration of Jewish identity became paramount. Changes in the political and religious realms reduced the community from its previous position as a political corporation possessing legal authority over its membership into what ultimately became a pluralistic and voluntaristic association. Because the political structure and authority of the community were dismantled, no one denomination within the community could legally impose its definition of Jewishness upon the entire community. As Peter Berger has phrased it:

> In the situation of the ghetto . . . it would have been absurd to say that an individual *chose* to be a Jew. To be Jewish was a taken-for-granted given of the individual's existence, ongoingly reaffirmed with ringing certainty by everyone in the individual's milieu. . . . There was the theoretical possibility of conversion to Christianity, but the social pressures against this were so strong that it was realized in very few cases. . . . The coming of emancipation changed all this. For more and more individuals it became a viable project to step outside the Jewish community. Suddenly, to be Jewish, [and how to be Jewish], emerged as one choice among others.[43]

Hildesheimer's Orthodox colleagues were aware of this threat, albeit tacitly so, and devised strategies to meet the challenge of preserving Judaism.

Samson Raphael Hirsch, Hildesheimer's contemporary, provides one example of an Orthodox religious leader's response to these changed circumstances. Hirsch, like others of his day, was filled with the new spirit of universalism and enthusiastically welcomed Emancipation and Jewish emergence from the ghetto. Emancipation permitted the Jews to observe the Torah in freedom, not oppression, and consequently led to the spiritual purification of Israel. Hirsch wrote: "We must become Jews, Jews in the true sense of the word imbued with the spirit of the law, accepting it as the foundation of life, spiritual and ethical. Thus Judaism will gladly welcome Emancipation as affording a greater opportunity for the fulfillment of its task."[44]

Hirsch, unlike the Reformers, clung to the traditional belief in the divine sanctity of the Oral Law and was opposed to the "scientific"—*Wissenschaftlich*—study of Judaism. Other aspects of his thought and actions, however, reveal that his response to the conditions imposed upon Judaism by its nineteenth-century German milieu was remarkably similar to the liberals'. Though he did not reform the liturgy and would not permit organ music, he did improve the aesthetics of both the service and the synagogue building by delivering a sermon in German, adding a male choir, donning clerical robes, and insisting on contemporary German standards of beauty and decorum. His positive attitude to secular education, as indicated by the educational curriculum he designed for his Frankfurt school and by his allowing coeducation in the elementary grades of his institution, reveals the great similarity between his attitudes and those of the Reformers.[45] Hirsch, no less than the Reformers, may be described as having created a philosophy of Judaism designed for a rising burgher class eager to participate in the life of nineteenth-century German civilization. Ismar Schorsch provides the following analysis of the challenge common to Hirsch and the Reformers:

> Like the spokesmen for reform, Hirsch dropped all demands for judicial autonomy and continuance of Jewish civil law. He insisted upon the wholly religious character of Judaism, reduced the significance of periods of Jewish national independence, and divested the messianic concept of political overtones. With a rationalism and Hegelianism that he fully shared with the reformers, whom he detested, Hirsch too emphasized the ethical content and universal mission of Judaism. Without a doubt, his vigorous defense of the divine character and origin of Jewish law infuriated the Reform, but one should not lose sight of the substantial agreement in the area of theology imposed by the same external pressures.[46]

Although Hirsch asserted the continuity and immutability of Jewish law to demonstrate the coherence of medieval and modern Judaism, the thrust of his thoughts and actions, like those of his liberal contemporaries, indicate a movement away from the closed world of medieval Jewish self-sufficiency and communal autonomy and toward a full cultural and intellectual participation in the larger world.

Only a strict sectarian could avoid the pressures of change and choice. Rabbi Moses Sofer of Hungary died early in the century, in 1838, but his attitudes toward modernity continued to dominate Hungarian Orthodox circles throughout the nineteenth century. Sofer opposed Emancipation in both its political and cultural manifestations because, as he saw it, it provided an opportunity for Jews to slip away from the moorings of traditional Jewish society and made them aspire to be part of Western culture. Sofer was himself a native of Frankfurt and well aware of the changes the Haskalah and political reorganization had wrought in the German Jewish community. Consciously, then, he proscribed secular education for his followers and, though he himself knew the languages of his native and adopted lands, he forbade either German or Hungarian to be spoken in his traditional yeshiva at Pressburg. To try to eliminate social intercourse with Christians, he labeled them halakhically as "idolaters," harking back to an earlier trend in Jewish legal literature. Sofer also elevated custom to the position of immutable sanctity. He summed this up by appropriating the halakhic statement *"Hadash assur min hatorah*—Innovation is forbidden according to the Torah" to forbid the introduction into community life of even the slightest innovation, even one that could be shown to be halakhically justifiable.[47] By choosing to eschew totally all manifestations of the contemporary world, Sofer was not simply being obdurate; he was displaying, from one point of view, a great deal of sociological acumen. For while the Reformers and Neo-Orthodox in Germany chose to adopt a posture of accommodation with the larger world, Sofer and his group maintained only the minimal relations necessary for economic and political survival. The merest additional concession to the outside world was deemed by Sofer a major deviation. He feared that once a crack in the wall of tradition appeared, once the smallest acquiescence to modernity was made, it might not be possible to prevent the tradition from being relativized and, eventually, collapsing. Indeed, Sofer's sociological instinct to protect the world of medieval Judaism by resisting all change indicates a reasoned sectarian posture which a religious leader might, and Sofer did, adopt toward a changed social, cultural, and political milieu. The great benefit of this posture is that membership in the Jewish community continued to be presented as a matter of both status and identity for Sofer's followers.

Of course, Sofer and his adherents were dependent for their success on the degree to which they could motivate individuals to be sectarians and to the extent to which they could impose their own discipline on Hungarian Jewry in the nineteenth century. These efforts were bound up in many nonreligious factors beyond their control. Although Hungary was close to Germany, the town of Pressburg where Sofer lived was relatively isolated.[48] Sofer's great charisma, combined with his determination to erect a yeshiva that would be socially and culturally aloof from the influence of modernity, enabled him to leave his impress on the Orthodox elements in his own community and throughout all of Hungary. Hildesheimer was well aware of and sensitive to Sofer's stance. Yet it was not his, and that is cause for further investigation.

2

The Quest for Religious Authority

In its quest for authority, religious leadership often has to perform a delicate balancing act. If they want their authority to be viable, religious leaders must adapt to changing situations while nevertheless appearing to retain the sanctions of the past. Only then can they be perceived as authentic. Joseph Blau, in describing this phenomenon, has written: "Not the least of the elements of paradox that enter into the very nature of religion is the necessity that lies upon it, in its organized and institutionalized forms, to change while both seeming changeless and protesting its changelessness."[1]

This was the problem that confronted Rabbi Esriel Hildesheimer in his attempt to legitimate Orthodox religious authority in the Jewish community of nineteenth-century Germany. The abrogation of rabbinic civil authority throughout most of the German states in 1811 plunged the rabbinate into an unprecedented crisis of authority.[2] Stripped of their political power, the German rabbis of the nineteenth century had virtually lost what sociologists Jerome Carlin and Saul Mendlovitz have labeled "imperative authority." In its place they had to adjust to what Carlin and Mendlovitz have identified as "influential authority."[3] For, as Alexander Altmann has noted, the German rabbi "would not give up his claim to authority."[4] To exercise it, however, he now had to persuade others to obey his directives through "the imposition of unorganized diffuse sanctions."[5] He could no longer use coercive sanctions to compel others to follow his lead. The rabbi had to strive to establish legitimations that would make his authority appear deserved in the eyes of his followers. Such legitimation enabled the rabbi to exercise effective influential authority.

Ismar Schorsch has noted that "a rich and flexible legal tradition served as sole authority . . . within the Jewish community [of the Middle Ages]."[6] But by the nineteenth century, the supremacy of that legal tradition had become "dethron[ed] . . . in broad sections of the community."[7] Religious leaders were compelled to acknowledge and deal with novel cultural and religious as well as political developments. As the German Jewish community increasingly internalized Western cultural values and judged Judaism in light of them, the old ideological sanctions that had supported medieval rabbinic authority were either ignored or proved insufficient to maintain the authority of the modern rabbi.

Hildesheimer and his Orthodox rabbinical colleagues had to acknowledge the cultural and political discontinuities that distinguished the medieval from the modern era. They could neither base their right to authority on traditional grounds alone nor legitimate their claims to authority solely through the medium of traditional rabbinic literature. To have done so would have condemned Orthodox Judaism to a cultural isolation that would have rendered it uninfluential and thus undermined their efforts to attain authority.

Hildesheimer's task, as an Orthodox rabbi, was to compose a response that would take account of the transformations in the community while simultaneously affirming the eternality and unchanging divine nature of halakha. Or, as Schorsch might put it, he had to have the halakha and belief in its divine sanction serve as the foundation for Orthodox religious authority while allowing nineteenth-century German cultural, social, and academic forms to act as the medium through which that authority could be realized. His response involved a use of both traditional and contemporary justifications in the quest to establish religious authority. His example represents a Modern Orthodox attempt to grapple with one of the greatest challenges presented to Judaism by modernity.

Scholars have noted that mid- to late nineteenth-century German Jewish Orthodoxy had three great rabbinical leaders—Samson Raphael Hirsch, Seligman Baer Bamberger, and Hildesheimer.[8] Among the three, Hildesheimer was unique. He was neither a traditional *rav* like Bamberger nor a prototypical nineteenth-century German *rabbiner* like Hirsch. Instead, Hildesheimer strove to combine, not without tension, stances common to both worlds. His distinctive response to the dilemma of religious authority was anchored in the singularity of his position.

Bamberger, unlike his two colleagues, received little formal secular education. As a youth he did not know German, and it was only through the tutelage of his wife that he learned to speak it as an adult. He seldom wrote in German. The few German publications he did compose generally appeared in Hebrew characters. He did, however, write traditional rabbinic commentaries and novellae in Hebrew on the Talmud and Jewish codes of law. He issued responsa in the traditional style that had characterized this genre of rabbinic literature for the previous thousand years. Bamberger corresponded frequently with leading rabbinical authorities in central and eastern Europe and enjoyed a reputation among them as an outstanding scholar. Bamberger chose to speak to those who were imbued with the culture and outlook of medieval rabbinic traditionalism. By totally eschewing the world of German culture and letters, opting instead for the literary modes and language of traditional rabbinic civilization, Bamberger was consciously affirming these sanctions as both necessary and sufficient for establishing rabbinic authority. He represented, in Mordechai Eliav's words, "the old model of German rabbinical leadership."[9]

Hirsch was at the other end of the spectrum. He seldom wrote in Hebrew. He composed no major commentaries in the traditional rabbinic style on the Talmud and Jewish codes of law. He issued so few responsa in Hebrew that, according to Eliav, "a child could count them." Instead, Hirsch, as a product of German secular education, wrote prolifically in German and addressed himself to Jews immersed in German culture.[10] His numerous articles and books on the Bible and prayerbook, as well as his expositions of Judaism, reflect the impact of G. W. F. Hegel, Friedrich Schleiermacher, and other German thinkers. Thus the substance of his thought in addition to the literary genres he employed marks a break between the medieval and modern periods of Jewish history. Although Hirsch defended the traditional notion of the divinity of the Oral Law, he did so as a man of Western culture. His efforts at legitimating religious authority emanated, in Jacob Katz's words, "from a new set of concepts . . . which distinguished him from the religious leaders of the older generation."[11]

Hildesheimer embodied attributes common to both of these men. Like Hirsch, Hildesheimer was a man of German culture. He received a Ph.D. from an outstanding German university and wrote several books and numerous articles in accepted German academic style.[12] German was his first language and, as his daughter Esther Calvary reports, Hildesheimer loved German literature and classical music. In her memoirs she writes: "On *Yom Tov*, between *Mincha* and *Maariv*, when no students were present, [father] would seat himself in the large armchair in the living room; we children around him. (I remember him placing his feet on the footstool, Levi and Aaron standing beside him, mother and the little ones on the sofa.) Then father would sing to us German *lieder*, among them his heart's favorites. And each time for us, his children, the high point was [when he sang] *Die Zwei Grenadiere* ["The Two Grenadiers"] of Heine."[13] Hildesheimer also dressed in contemporary German attire, which irritated many of his Orthodox rabbinical colleagues when he lived in Hungary.[14] The vernacular always served as the language of instruction in his yeshivot, and he authored many popular/polemical articles on the issues confronting the Jewish community of his day in such German-language publications as *Der Orient* and *Der Israelit*.[15] He established *Die Jüdische Presse* in 1870 as a vehicle for disseminating his views to the German-reading Jewish public.[16] Hildesheimer was clearly conscious of the efforts needed to make Orthodox Jewish authority viable in his nineteenth-century German context.

Yet, like Bamberger, Hildesheimer also immersed himself in the world of rabbinic culture. His involvement is evident in several ways. Hildesheimer was equally prolific in his authorship of Hebrew rabbinic responsa, commentaries, and novellae on the Talmud and Jewish codes of law as he was in contemporary German writings.[17] His decision to use traditional literary forms and his choice of Hebrew align him with those possessing the worldview of the medieval rabbi. Further, they provide an important insight into how Hildesheimer attempted to establish his authority as a rabbi in the changed social, cultural, and political milieu of his time and place. As Ellis Rivkin has pointed out, an analysis of literary structure and language may reveal stability as well as change in the historical continuum.[18] By employing these traditional medieval forms of the Jewish literary genre, Hildesheimer affirmed more than a sense of continuity with the Jewish past. In effect, he asserted that the traditional claim of divine sanction for rabbinic authority—in spite of the transformations that marked the Jewish community of Germany during the nineteenth century—was still feasible and, in fact, neces-

צורת הרב המופלא הגאון פאר הדור נשיא בא"י
מדה"ר **עזריאל הילדעסהיימער** זצ"ל
שהיה אב"ד ור"מ בק"ק אייזענשטאדט ח"י שנים משנת תרי"א
עד שנת תרכ"ט, ואח"כ נתקבל לרב בקהל עדת ישראל בע"ם
בערלין ויסד בה"מ לרבנים בשנת תרל"ג
וננגנז הארן ביום ב' ד' תמוז שנת תרנ"ט לפ"ק:

Rabbi Esriel Hildesheimer (From the Collection of Hebrew Union College,
Skirball Museum, Los Angeles, Lelo Carter, Photographer)

sary for establishing claims to rabbinic authority. Hildesheimer's adoption of traditional Jewish literary genres and his writing in Hebrew are, in one sense, more important than what he wrote or substantively decided in these writings. For these writings symbolize his efforts to establish traditional rabbinic norms and methods as means to legitimate Jewish religious authority in the modern age.

If his dress reflected his modern sensibilities, his relationship with his teacher Jacob Ettlinger reproduced a traditional consciousness. Ettlinger, recognized as one of the outstanding talmudic authorities in nineteenth-century Europe, took great pride in Hildesheimer's scholarship. He felt that Hildesheimer possessed a rare ability to investigate and decide Jewish legal matters with "depth of understanding and great erudition."[19] Hildesheimer reciprocated these feelings of respect and admiration. In a responsum he wrote to a former student, Isaac Bing, in 1862, Hildesheimer stated that his own ruling on a particular matter stood only if Ettlinger concurred with it.[20] A direct communication reveals Hildesheimer's attitude toward his master most clearly. Ettlinger had asked Hildesheimer's view on a Jewish legal issue and Hildesheimer, after expressing his opinion, concluded, "All this I have written as a pupil who rules before his teacher and it is understood that I will cancel my opinion should you disagree, in deference to your greater knowledge."[21]

The mutual love and respect between Hildesheimer and Ettlinger was not characteristic of the formal student-teacher relationships of the nineteenth century. Jacob Katz has pointed out that the yeshivot of the Middle Ages fostered this special bond between student and teacher. The stereotypic pattern, according to Katz, was for boys gifted in rabbinic learning to spend their adolescent years away from home in a yeshiva. There they came to "revere the head of the yeshiva as their instructor and mentor." As a result, a "close personal link came to be forged" between rabbi and pupil.[22] The great devotion between Hildesheimer and Ettlinger conforms to this pattern.[23]

Hildesheimer's firm attachment to the world of rabbinic traditionalism and the position of honor he held in it are likewise reflected in the relationships he enjoyed with leading eastern European rabbinical figures. Rabbi Elijah Levinson, a leader of the *Musar* (pietist) movement in eastern Europe, referred to Hildesheimer as "a great man." Rabbi Israel Lipkin from Salant, one of the greatest of all *Musar* leaders, maintained very cordial relations with Hildesheimer and praised the Hildesheimer seminary in Berlin along with Hildesheimer's efforts there.[24] Rabbi Judah Aszod and Maharam Schick, two Hungarian rabbinic authorities, not only had close personal relationships with Hildesheimer during his years in Hungary (1851–69) but paid him the tribute of sending their sons to his yeshiva in Eisenstadt.[25]

The surest testimonial to the extent and erudition of Hildesheimer's mastery of traditional Jewish learning can be seen in the acknowledgment of that scholarship on the part of representatives of that world. The Ktav Sofer, son of Rabbi Moses Sofer of Hungary and the leader of Hungarian Orthodoxy after his father's death, invited Hildesheimer to serve as the second rabbi in Pressburg, Sofer's home community, in 1851. Thus the two sons continued the connection between the Hildesheimer and Sofer families. Although Hildesheimer declined the offer, that it was tendered him bespeaks the degree to which he had earned fame as a master of traditional Jewish sources, as well as the high esteem in which he was held by a leading rabbinic authority.[26] Hildesheimer's eminence in the traditional world of rabbinic learning is also evidenced by the Jewish legal correspondence he conducted with Rabbi Isaac Elchanan Spektor of Kovno. Spektor was the leading rabbinical authority in Russia and eastern Europe during the nineteenth century. Spektor indicated his high regard for Hildesheimer by consulting him on several Jewish legal matters. Furthermore, in his correspondence with Hildesheimer, Spektor used terms of hyperbolic praise typically reserved in rabbinic literature for persons and scholars of great achievement. Once, for example, Spektor identified Hildesheimer as "the crown of Torah" and in another instance called him "the famous *Tzaddik* [righteous one], the glory of Israel, and its holiness."[27]

Although he is more closely identified with Samson Raphael Hirsch than with Seligman Baer Bamberger, Hildesheimer falls in between these two colleagues on the spectrum of nineteenth-century German Orthodoxy. He held a strong affinity to both the traditional rabbinic world and the contemporary Western one. He constantly found himself mediating between these two realms, drawing upon and combining elements from both in his efforts to achieve Orthodox religious authority in the Jewish community of his day. Events in his hometown of Halberstadt in 1847 illustrate Hildesheimer's earliest attempts in this direction and present a paradigm that he was to follow for the rest of his life in Jewish communal affairs.

The Hildesheimer family had long played a prominent role in the public affairs of the Halberstadt Jewish community. Esriel's father had been a leading rabbinical scholar there, and his older brother Abraham had served as secretary to the community until his death in 1844. It was natural, therefore, that, upon the completion of his doctorate in 1846, Esriel should return to Halberstadt to assume the position that had been vacant since his brother's death. For the first time, Hildesheimer assumed a public role in Jewish communal affairs. He also now had an opportunity to display his intellectual and political talents before a public audience.[28]

The traditional nature of the community was beginning to change, and Reform Judaism was making its presence felt just about the time that Hildesheimer arrived in Halberstadt. Ludwig Philippson (1811–89), the editor of the *Allgemeine Zeitung des Judentums*, was arguing vigorously on behalf of Reform in the pages of his journal and was making his views known throughout Saxony. Philippson's influence was first felt in Halberstadt in 1847. On March 3 of that year, a law had been passed permitting Jews to come before secular authorities for permission "to secede from the community to which they are attached." In reaction to this law, eight Jewish citizens went before the secular authorities of Halberstadt and asked for permission to leave the Orthodox-controlled organized Jewish community. Hildesheimer believed they had been encouraged by Philippson.[29] The action precipitated a crisis for the leadership of the Halberstadt community—Hildesheimer and Rabbi Mattathias Levian—and they were determined to combat these Reformers. An analysis of the different counteractions taken by Levian and Hildesheimer to meet this challenge will indicate the distinctive way in which Hildesheimer attempted to invoke traditional and modern sanctions to maintain Orthodox religious authority in the town.

Levian, originally from Poland, served as the rabbi in Halberstadt from 1824 to 1863. He was the rabbi during Hildesheimer's childhood, and Hildesheimer regarded him as one of his teachers. Levian was not fluent in German. When he spoke in the synagogue, teachers from the community school would come and translate for the congregants, undoubtedly an index of Halberstadt Jewry's level of acculturation. It is not surprising that Levian, in responding to these men, issued a Jewish legal decision attacking them and proscribing their activities.[30] They were, he wrote, "apostates [*mumarim*] to the entire Torah."[31] They had decided to sever their ties to the community, he charged, because they intended to convert to Christianity and thereby gain more rights than the other Jewish citizens of Halberstadt, who were, in Levian's words, "downtrodden in [their] bitter exile." Levian held that even if they did not formally convert to Christianity, they were, by virtue of their rejection of the Oral Law and traditional rabbinic authority, "like gentiles." Consequently, Levian maintained that these men could not be married in a Jewish wedding ceremony, could not be counted as Jews for purposes of a prayer quorum, and could not receive a Jewish burial. Moreover, he forbade them to be called to a public reading of the Torah, and they were not allowed to recite the traditional mourner's prayer on behalf of deceased relatives.

Levian's authorship of a traditional responsum in Hebrew as his means of resolving this situation reveals the limitations of his capabilities. He framed the issue as one of apostasy. He was not prepared to engage—nor, apparently, could he even envision—the larger challenge modernity presented to Judaism. His response was comprehensible only to those knowledgeable in Hebrew and learned in Jewish law. Such Jews, however, were likely already to sympathize and agree with Levian's opposition to the Reformers. In composing this responsum, Levian was, in effect, addressing those who already agreed with him. To maintain Orthodox religious authority in Halberstadt, Levian needed to speak to the gentile authorities who had the power to adjudicate this case. He needed, equally, to be able to speak to the acculturated Jews, who, because of their affirmation of Western culture, were likely to be disaffected with Levian's leadership. Yet by writing in Hebrew, by referring derisively to the Reformers as being "like gentiles," and by identifying Germany negatively as a land of "bitter exile," Levian composed an argument that would only have alienated both of these groups.

Levian's responsum was that of a traditional rabbi who did not grasp the full dimensions of the struggle in which he was engaged. He responded as if his rabbinic decisions in mid-nineteenth-century Halberstadt carried the force of law, when in fact they were merely religious-moral exhortations. He did not possess the imperative religious authority. His community was no longer culturally monolithic, and the rabbinic view of Judaism was no longer seen as the sole legitimate expression of the Jewish tradition by members of that community. Moreover, he was unable to grasp that rebellion against rabbinic authority was not necessarily tantamount to apostasy. In this first major struggle between Reform and rabbinic tradition in Halberstadt, Levian understood and reacted by playing by the "old rules"—rules that were no longer functional in the Halberstadt of 1847.

Levian did not act alone, however. Because he was cognizant of his linguistic deficiencies in German, he was pleased to have his former student, Hildesheimer, carry on the public battle against the Reformers. Thus it was Hildesheimer who directly addressed the governing board of the Halberstadt municipality, which had the ultimate power to make a decision on the matter. And it was Hildesheimer who tried to persuade the acculturated Jews in the community that continued Orthodox rule in internal communal affairs was desirable. Prompted by this event, Hildesheimer wrote a pamphlet in German, *Verwaltung der Jüdischen Gemeinde Halberstadt,* to present the case for continued Orthodox domination before both these groups. In this work, Hildesheimer traced the administration of the Halberstadt Jewish community historically and argued that the Orthodox had competently managed the affairs of the community both before and after the turn of the century. By writing this piece in accordance with the standards of the day, Hildesheimer was demonstrating to the gentile authorities, who were interested primarily in preserving order among Halberstadt's Jewish citizenry, that the best means to achieve this end was to leave the administration of internal Jewish affairs in the tested and proven hands of the Orthodox authorities. Any attempt to diminish their authority—such as permitting a group of Jews to secede from the community without Orthodox approval—would, he implied, be a mistake. To the acculturated Jews in the community, Hildesheimer's work indicated that the Orthodox were capable of adapting themselves to the cultural currents of the day. For the time being, Hildesheimer had silenced those critics in the Jewish community who claimed that the Orthodox were obscurantist and too tied to tradition to confront the challenges of administering the Jewish community in the contemporary world.[32] His work, both in substance and in style, reflected his keen perceptiveness concerning the problems posed to Orthodox authority by the rise of Reform. It also indicated that he was capable of devising an effective stratagem in keeping with the demands of the time and place to combat the Reformers. This ability, as well as the distinctions between Hildesheimer "the modernist" and Levian "the traditionalist," stand out even more clearly in the Hebrew responsum which Hildesheimer wrote on this same issue.

It was imperative that Hildesheimer, as an Orthodox rabbi, respond to this crisis by writing a traditional responsum; for the ultimate legitimacy of his stance rested on the fact that he spoke in the name of an unchanging religious tradition. Consequently, it was incumbent upon Hildesheimer, if he did not want to undercut his claim to authority, to speak as rabbis had spoken for the previous millennium. The Hebrew responsum was more than a stratagem Hildesheimer employed to attain Orthodox authority in this situation; it was the foundation upon which this authority rested.

Hildesheimer's responsum combines an effective Orthodox position with an awareness of modernity. Unlike Levian, Hildesheimer was able to recognize that a decision to reject the traditional basis of Jewish faith need not be accompanied by a desire to convert to Christianity. He observed that these men, in their official pronouncement, claimed that they wished to secede because they disagreed with a majority of the community on matters of Jewish faith. They did not speak of converting to Christianity. Hildesheimer felt this was crucial for the traditionalists to understand; otherwise a proper stratagem to combat the Reformers could not be adopted. Simply to engage in wild invective, as Levian had done, was unwise, "for a judge can rule only on what the eyes see and the ears hear."[33]

This last point applied both to the gentile authorities and to Hildesheimer and Levian, who had to determine the Jewish legal consequences of these men's actions. In the responsum he indicated that he had testified orally before the communal governing board regarding them but that he did not charge them with apostasy. To have done so would have been imprudent, for it could have been interpreted as an attempt to infringe on their right of free conscience. Hildesheimer was aware of the potentially counterproductive results of such a charge for his efforts to attain influential authority. Therefore, he stated that these men wished to secede not because of faith, which the state had no right to coerce, "but only to escape paying communal taxes." The men were thus portrayed as wishing to evade their civic duty. The controversy was thereby taken out of the realm of conscience and put in terms that could appeal to both the gentile authorities and the acculturated Jews of Halberstadt.[34]

Hildesheimer responded similarly to Levian's assertion that these Reformers wanted more civil rights than their fellow Jews. He questioned both the prudence and the accuracy of the charge, "for in this generation, with the mercy of the Most High, may He be blessed, there is no need for this alienation from our Father in heaven in order to attain this goal [of civic equality]." Hildesheimer did not perceive Germany as a land of "bitter exile." The Jews of Halberstadt, he claimed, lived under no threat of "subjugation or persecution." Here it is obvious that Hildesheimer opposed Levian's negative references to Germany for reasons of diplomacy and because of his personal feelings for his homeland. He possessed a positive attitude toward political developments in nineteenth-century Germany which Levian did not share. Hildesheimer demonstrated that even in the context of a Jewish legal responsum, his consciousness was that of a contemporary German Jew. Therefore, the argument against the Reformers had to be made in a manner that would be inoffensive to nineteenth-century German-Jewish sensibilities.

Hildesheimer legitimated this stance from a Jewish legal point of view on the grounds that the Reformers' desire to secede from the community was not an effort "to destroy God's covenant with Israel at Sinai." These Reformers, as "Deists," were not "apostates to the entire Torah." Rather, they were "ones who separated themselves from the ways of the community," a serious but lesser offense. As a result, Hildesheimer ruled along with Levian that these men could not be included in a Jewish prayer quorum, nor could they be buried in a Jewish cemetery. In addition, they could not be called to a public reading of the Torah and they were not to be permitted to recite the traditional mourner's prayer on behalf of deceased relatives, unless there was no one else to do so. Hildesheimer did not address the question of whether these men could be married in a Jewish wedding ceremony. The conclusions of Hildesheimer's responsum were thus the same as Levian's. The reasons for these sanctions, however, were different despite their common grounding in the traditional soil of rabbinic responsa.

Hildesheimer's efforts were successful. The governing board of the community was persuaded by Hildesheimer's arguments and refused to permit the Reformers to secede. The formal religious unity of the Jewish community was preserved because Hildesheimer, through a skillful use of traditional and modern writings, symbols, and ideas—a combination that accurately reflected his emerging persona—was able to address all the involved parties on their own terms. Already as a young man, Hildesheimer understood that traditional Judaism had to be expressed in a variety of ways if it were to be transmitted forcefully in the modern world. He demonstrated the ability to exercise influential religious authority. And yet there were tensions inherent in his position, as an episode later in 1847 reveals.

On September 15, 1847, at the instigation of Ludwig Philippson, the governing board of the Magdeburg Jewish community issued an invitation to all the Jewish communities in Saxony to come to the town of Magdeburg for a provincial assembly.[35] Hildesheimer, along with his brother-in-law Joseph Hirsch, represented Halberstadt at the mid-October conference. Ostensibly, the meeting was called to discuss the implications of a communal reorganization bill that had gone into effect on July 23. But it soon became clear to Hildesheimer and the other traditionalists that discussion of the recently passed law was not the real reason for the gathering. Hildesheimer wrote, in speaking of himself and his brother-in-law, "As Halberstadt's representatives, we were not lulled by these . . . unparliamentary tactics," advanced, quite obviously, by the Reform forces.[36]

The true purpose of the conference became apparent early on when Philippson delivered a keynote address to the assembly. He asked all of those in attendance to come together in a spirit of peace and harmony, and he made several concrete proposals. Two of these items assumed particular significance in the eyes of Reformers and traditionalists alike. The first was a proposal that the delegates pass a resolution recommending the adoption of "an alteration and adjustment of the divine service" to be used in the synagogues of Saxony. In effect, Philippson was asking the gathering to acknowledge the principle of religious reform as a legitimate element in Judaism. Philippson was surely aware that his proposal would be controversial and would stir up Orthodox resistance. The Orthodox, as he well knew, did not recognize reform as a legitimate component of Judaism and, consequently, Philippson could not seriously have expected the Orthodox delegates to approve the adoption of these proposed changes for the Jews of the province. He must not have been surprised when Joseph Hirsch rose to speak for postponing consideration of this proposal by the convention; in so doing, Hirsch was clearly expressing his opposition to it.[37]

Philippson's second request—that the assembly pass a resolution asking that the "synagogue community" in each town be formally separated from the "total community"[38]—was much more threatening and posed a profound dilemma for the Orthodox. The Reformers were still the minority in most of the Jewish communities of Saxony. Therefore, the Orthodox majority, which controlled the Jewish communal institutions, was able to check changes submitted by the Reformers in almost every community. Philippson was proposing the establishment of an autonomous foundation for the development of Reform synagogues in each town apart from the inhibiting checks provided by a dominant Orthodox majority. He was asking, as he might have phrased it, for the convention to grant Reform and the Reformers the right to create a Judaism in keeping with their own interpretation of the Jewish religion. In making this proposal, Philippson was simply asking the delegates to affirm the principle of religious freedom. This proposal did not ask, or even necessarily imply, that the convention or the Orthodox recognize Reform as a legitimate religious expression of Judaism. Philippson had succeeded in placing the traditionalists in the uncomfortable position of either having to accept his proposal and thereby pave the way for the growth of Reform or reject it and appear to be opposing religious freedom. Philippson had turned the tables on Hildesheimer, who only a few months earlier had transformed the struggle between Orthodox and Reform in Halberstadt from a matter of religious conscience into one of civic duty.

Hildesheimer, Hirsch, and several other traditionalists responded to this confrontation by leaving the convention. Hildesheimer later wrote a series of articles in *Der Orient* explaining the traditionalists' stance. Hildesheimer claimed that the delegates had been brought to Magdeburg under false pretenses and therefore he and the other traditionalists felt that they could not, in good conscience, participate in the voting. In addition, Philippson's proposals called upon the assembly to violate the elementary principles of democracy for the delegates, in Hildesheimer's opinion, were not truly representative of their communities and, in voting for these resolutions, were guilty of attempting to force their views on the communities of the province.[39]

Here Hildesheimer was clearly arguing on contemporary nineteenth-century grounds. Presenting his case before a Jewish community wedded to the ideology of the Enlightenment which had made a long-desired Jewish Emancipation possible, Hildesheimer did not want to appear opposed to notions of religious freedom. It was imperative that he transform the issue from one of religious freedom into another question entirely. When Hildesheimer charged the Reformers and Philippson with deceit in calling the convention and claimed that the assembly had violated the fundamental rules of representative democracy, he effectively refused to respond to the issue as one of religious freedom. Moreover, the implication to be drawn from the episode by the reading public was plain—the Reformers, not the Orthodox, were guilty of violating the canons of nineteenth-century parliamentarianism. A good case had been made before the acculturated Jews of Saxony to continue Orthodox religious authority in Jewish communal affairs.

Hildesheimer went on, however, to argue against the Reformers on traditional religious grounds. He claimed that the representatives were ignorant Jewishly and, as laypersons, were not endowed with the authority to act on the proposal set before them.[40] The issue was not really one of democracy, then, but of proper religious authority. For even if all the Jews in Saxony had favored these proposals, it would not have been proper for them to pass the resolutions in the absence of suitable rabbinic sanction. Hildesheimer's arguments derive from both a nineteenth-century German *Weltanschauung* and traditional rabbinic values. He was obliged to appeal to both worlds to be effective. His attempts to effectuate Orthodox religious authority in this situation reveal that the relationship between the values of traditional Judaism and modernity are not always congruent.[41] Hildesheimer may well have taken the only path open to him— drawing upon both the traditional and the modern to support his position—as an Orthodox religious leader attempting to achieve influential religious authority in nineteenth-century Germany. He may not have been aware of the tensions intrinsic to this position. Yet as twentieth-century observers, we can see the intellectual bind in which he was placed. His efforts reveal something of the dilemma confronting Judaism in the modern world and the inherent struggles between continuity and discontinuity.

Although he was unsuccessful in this fight against Philippson and the Reformers, the Magdeburg episode demonstrates Hildesheimer's pattern of combining traditional and modern justifications in his attempt to exert influential religious authority. Hildesheimer remained committed to exercising Orthodox religious authority over all sectors of the Jewish community. This unyielding position was to be altered by his experiences in Hungary and Berlin later in his life. There it became apparent to him that the Orthodox would not be able to be the dominant Jewish religious force in the community.

Through the events of 1847, Hildesheimer secured his reputation as a defender of Orthodoxy in the minds of the German and Hungarian Jewish public. Hildesheimer concluded his articles against Philippson in *Der Orient* by stating, "It is the holy duty of anyone who has the weapons in his hands to protect the Jewish community from these destructive movements."[42] Moses Menachem Mendel of Frankfurt, the uncle of Rabbi Samson Raphael Hirsch, wrote Hildesheimer to congratulate him on his articles and to applaud him as a vigorous champion of Orthodoxy.[43] The most impressive sign of the eminence he had achieved, however, was that in 1851 the community of Eisenstadt, Hungary, invited him to "fill the chair" of their rabbinical office.[44] Hildesheimer accepted the post and, along with it, a host of different challenges to his ability to forge modern religious authority.

Well versed in rabbinics, armed with a secular doctorate, and now famed as a fighter against Reform, Hildesheimer was esteemed by many in the Orthodox world. By 1851 he was viewed as a religious leader capable of meeting the challenges of a changing age. According to a letter Hildesheimer received, the community of Eisenstadt was "one of the most important in Hungary" and consisted of approximately 150 families.[45] It has been a center of Talmud study during the eighteenth century and the home of the Hatam Sofer's wife, the daughter of the famed Rabbi Akiva Eger.[46] Although Eisenstadt "remained in the Orthodox camp" in the nineteenth century, its proximity to Vienna led to infiltration of external cultural influences.[47] The rabbinical post in Eisenstadt had been vacant for eleven years before it was tendered to Hildesheimer.

The community was apparently composed of Orthodox traditionalists who were hostile to secular culture, a few Neologues, the name given to the Reform party in Hungary, and modern Orthodox Jews receptive to the cultural spirit of the day. The conservative elements in the community opposed Hildesheimer's election to the office because they feared the coming of a rabbi with a secular education. They were overruled by the majority of leaders, who decided that an Orthodox rabbi such as Hildesheimer was essential if the Orthodox were to maintain their hegemony in the community and survive the onslaught of liberalism.[48]

Hildesheimer agreed with them. He felt that Orthodox religious authority could be maintained in Hungary and western Europe only if rabbis capable of mediating between the demands "of Torah on the one hand and the needs of the time on the other" were available.[49] As Hildesheimer sorrowfully observed throughout his years in Hungary, few Jews in Europe acted in accordance with Jewish law.[50] Indeed, "in a time and period like this, where many sins are committed,"[51] the creation of rabbinical leaders like himself, who were armed "with all the necessary stratagems of war which are required at the present time,"[52] was to be accorded top priority.

Hildesheimer's sentiments resonated in the community. He was instructed to devote his major efforts in Eisenstadt to the field of education, an area that "was currently neglected," according to communal leaders.[53] Indeed, when the community hired Hildesheimer, they agreed to provide food and lodging for ten yeshiva students, in addition to Hildesheimer's salary.[54] Like Hildesheimer, the leaders firmly believed that the continued existence of Orthodox religious authority in the Jewish community depended on a basic revision of the educational curriculum of the yeshiva. Hildesheimer deemed it essential that students be steeped in rabbinic texts and also capable of transmitting these texts to the general Jewish populace.[55] Without such transmission, influential religious authority could not be realized.

To accomplish this goal, Hildesheimer planned carefully the curriculum for the new yeshiva. Knowledge of the vernacular was assigned top priority. All courses were taught in German, not Yiddish. Thus, upon his arrival in 1851, Hildesheimer founded the first yeshiva in the Western world to include both secular subjects and traditional religious instruction in its curriculum. Hildesheimer's yeshiva grew and prospered throughout the 1850s and 1860s.[56]

These major innovations were not met with equanimity by all members of the Eisenstadt community. Soon after Hildesheimer opened his yeshiva, a group of Orthodox extremists appealed to the government to close the school. They asserted that it posed a revolutionary danger to both Judaism and the government because of the secular subjects in the curriculum, the instruction in German, and the modern pedagogic methods. Hildesheimer was able to convince the government to overturn the decision. The school was closed for only twenty-four hours. The incident served to foreshadow tensions and disputes that were to surface later in the Hungarian community.[57]

Pleased with his success and confident of his ability to meet the demands of the era, Hildesheimer stated, "Schools alone will assure the future."[58] It appeared to him that his policy of combining secular learning with religious instruction was working. In 1860 he wrote to Wolf Feilchenfeld (1827–1913), a German rabbi and close friend from his student days in Berlin, describing his life in Hungary: "Here there is still Torah and respect for Torah. Here there is still an authentic Jewish life, and many communities properly honor and respect their rabbis, something one cannot find in Germany except for Frankfurt. Here one can be a teacher of Torah. Here there is a life that is a true pleasure."[59]

The exact contents of his curriculum as well as the nature of his educational philosophy will be discussed more fully in a later chapter. There is no doubt, however, that Hildesheimer's policy of employing German as the language of instruction in his yeshiva and his insistence that students master secular subjects were designed to train leaders to spread Orthodoxy (and hence Orthodox religious authority) among acculturated segments of the Jewish community. Hildesheimer aimed to enable his students to "fight the war on behalf of Torah and her commandments,"[60] in order to gain them the respect of both "their congregants and their opponents."[61] Hildesheimer was engaged in a war. He was fighting for the survival of Orthodoxy in an era that witnessed the destruction of Jewish communal autonomy and rabbinic hegemony, convinced that Orthodoxy's only chance for effectuating continued religious authority was to adapt to the cultural standards of the new age.

These convictions expressed themselves in spheres other than the educational. As he had done in Halberstadt, Hildesheimer continued to urge Orthodox cooperation with the secular authorities. In 1856, for example, Hildesheimer sought to unite the Orthodox to engage in public political action on behalf of Hungarian Jewish soldiers. Jewish soldiers' religious needs were not being met, nor had yeshiva students attained exemption from their military service as yet. His colleagues, much to his sorrow, would not join with him in such public activity.[62]

On another occasion, in July 1860, a group of zealous youth in Amsterdam entered an assembly of the Shochrei Deah, a Reform group, and stoned the liberal rabbi Dr. M. Chronik, almost killing him. The authorities punished the culprits, but the incident caused a great stir.[63] Hildesheimer, writing about the affair, condemned it as a "profanation of God's name." More important for purposes of this study, Hildesheimer realized that such acts could damage the Orthodox cause in the larger community and lead to further deterioration of Orthodox religious authority. He stated, "There is no way to tell of the great damage which will come to the believers in all places and lands if the majority of [Orthodox] rabbis do not gather together to denounce this action before the Jewish people." Hildesheimer therefore circulated a petition for Orthodox rabbis in various lands to sign. The petition stated: "We, the undersigned, have read with great sorrow the announcement about the unrestrained disturbance in the synagogue in Amsterdam. Albeit that the report springs from a one-sided source, we declare that this sad episode, which is perhaps understandable from a psychological point of view, is opposed to the commandments of Judaism."[64]

It is unclear whether this petition was published, and it is uncertain how his Orthodox colleagues reacted to it. Both Rabbis Ettlinger and Bamberger supported it.[65] Whatever the fate of the petition, Hildesheimer's initiation of it indicates his awareness that Orthodoxy had to conform to nineteenth-century standards of decorum and civility or risk consigning itself to the role of a small sect within contemporary Judaism. The old weapons of invective and coercion were not appropriate in the open climate of the 1800s.

Hildesheimer's petition demonstrates in addition that he was firmly entrenched in the Orthodox camp. He understood that influential religious authority, if it was to be effective, had to be expressed in ways consonant with the cultural values of the times. Yet, as an Orthodox rabbi, he could not refrain from condemning the source (*Allgemeine Zeitung des Judentums*) of the story or sympathizing with the psychological motives that led the perpetrators of the crime to desire the destruction of Reform. Although he had a positive attitude toward modernity and the benefits Emancipation offered to the Jewish people, when Jewish law and modernity clashed, preference had to be given to the law. His commitment to halakha as understood and interpreted by the Orthodox authorities was absolute. Hildesheimer's position regarding the primacy of rabbinic sources of Judaism is summed up in the following statement, "We . . . have no immutable validity, as only Jewish law according to its source [is fully authoritative] and we can have no other authority than this."[66] Hildesheimer recognized that the halakha could permit a variety of interpretations, but no compromise could be made with the principle that the "Torah had been revealed from the mouth of the Almighty" to Moses.[67] Hildesheimer felt that this was the ultimate source of his own authority as an Orthodox rabbi. In Hungary, just as in Halberstadt, he remained wedded to this belief.

Yet this conviction only caused the Neologues to attack him more severely. Indeed, the fury of the liberals against the *Neuorthodoxie* was unrestrained. Fearful, no doubt, that the modern Orthodoxy, unlike the *Altorthodoxen* of Sofer and his followers, might appeal to acculturated segments of the Hungarian Jewish community, liberal Jewish newspapers referred to the *"Pest der Neuorthodoxie"* and attacked modern Orthodox leaders such as Samson Raphael Hirsch with articles entitled *"Die Pseudoorthodoxie des Samson Rapael Hirsch und dessen Clique in Osterreich."* Among the modern Orthodox villains, none was deemed greater than Hildesheimer.[68] Every effort was made to diminish his influence, and thus his authority, with the acculturated segments of the Hungarian Jewish community. The Neologues, eager to gain total control in the community, searched for ways to disparage Hildesheimer. They felt that his educational attainments, his inclusion of secular subjects in the yeshiva's curriculum, and his use of secular methods of disputation when dealing with either the secular authorities or the general Jewish community obscured his religious rigidity. His attempts to mediate between general enlightenment and religious traditionalism further aroused their ire. It is no wonder that Leopold Löw, the leading non-Orthodox rabbi in Hungary and editor of the Reform journal *Ben Chananjah*, constantly attacked Hildesheimer in the pages of his journal.[69] The most severe attacks were directed against Hildesheimer's yeshiva because it was the major weapon Hildesheimer used to combat the Neologues. It was also the major source of his prestige in the eyes of the acculturated in the community. Evidently, Löw felt that if he could discredit Hildesheimer's school, he could considerably weaken Hildesheimer's influence and authority in the community at large. Löw claimed that Hildesheimer's yeshiva did not match the standards of the Breslau seminary directed by Zacharias Frankel (1801–75). He charged that Frankel was far superior to Hildesheimer in scholarship and contended that Hildesheimer's knowledge of Hebrew was inadequate. Finally, Löw stated that the general standards of the Hildesheimer yeshiva were low and the students' secular educational backgrounds poor.[70]

Hildesheimer replied to the charges concerning his scholarship and his learning in comparison to Frankel's. He did not feel that Löw's attack on his knowledge of Hebrew even merited a reply.[71] Hildesheimer did concede that the level of secular studies in his yeshiva was not on a par with that of the Breslau seminary, and he acknowledged the correctness of Löw's critique of the educational background of his students. Hildesheimer felt, though, that a major purpose of his yeshiva was to remedy his students' deficiencies in secular studies, and thus he did not discriminate against those students who came to him with insufficient secular educations. Indeed, these were among the students he cherished most. They provided him with material he could mold to meet the challenges posed to Orthodox religious authority in his day. And though Hildesheimer acknowledged the weaker level of secular instruction in his yeshiva, he argued that the standards in rabbinic instruction were at least equal to, and probably better than, those of the Breslau seminary.[72]

Hildesheimer felt the sting of the Neologues' assaults in other areas as well. In 1864, Hildesheimer criticized an article written by Heinrich Graetz, the famed Jewish historian and faculty member at the Breslau seminary. Graetz earned Hildesheimer's enmity because he claimed that Isaiah 52 was written by a second Isaiah who lived during the time of Ezra. Moreover, in the same article Graetz stated that the "servant of the Lord" passages referred not to a personal messiah who would arise from the House of David but to the people of Israel.[73] Hildesheimer's response set forth as a basic belief of the Jewish faith the coming of a personal messiah as referred to in that Isaiah passage. To deny this belief, Hildesheimer stated, was akin to denying God's revelation at Sinai. The Neologues seized on the opportunity to ridicule Hildesheimer for his refusal to accept the findings of contemporary biblical scholarship.[74] The Neologues hoped to paint Hildesheimer as a "fundamentalist" and thereby impugn his integrity in the world of academic scholarship and in the opinion of those who valued *wissenschaftlich* study.

Hildesheimer's counterattack recalls the earlier stratagems he employed in his battle to gain Orthodox religious authority. Hildesheimer presented the issue as one of "heresy." He asserted that Graetz's interpretation of the "suffering servant" passages in Isaiah did not raise an issue of controversy over scholarship. Rather, Graetz's stance involved a question of authentic religiousness. Hildesheimer's argument echoed the position articulated by Rabbi Moses Sofer a generation earlier in his polemics against the Neologues. Sofer had maintained, in an effort to win both traditional Jewish and Christian sympathies, that anyone who had abandoned traditional Judaism had, in reality, deserted not just Judaism but religion altogether.[75] Hildesheimer found Sofer's polemic of utilitarian value in his fight against the Neologues, despite the obvious differences in their outlooks. Implicitly building on Sofer's authority to realize his own, Hildesheimer managed once more to center the dispute between the Orthodox and non-Orthodox on that part of the issue designed to give Orthodoxy maximum leverage.

Nonetheless, by 1860 Hildesheimer had begun to realize that Orthodox hegemony over the entire community was a dream. Before his years in Hungary he had worked to achieve Orthodox religious authority among all sectors of the Jewish community. He had succeeded in Halberstadt early in 1847. His experiences in Hungary taught him that the strength of liberalism and secularism was too powerful to be dismissed. Now he was prepared to speak only to those among the acculturated in the community who would affirm the principles of an emerging modern Orthodoxy—an Orthodoxy that confirmed the worth of secular culture while simultaneously clinging to the belief of *"Torah Min HaShamayim."* In short, Hildesheimer came to acknowledge that his Orthodoxy prevented him from exercising influential religious authority in all segments of the community. In choosing not to apologize for his "fundamentalism," Hildesheimer was, in effect, serving notice that Orthodox Judaism was prepared to exert influential religious authority over only a part of a clearly divided community.

Several responsa written by Hildesheimer at this time reflect his awareness of the effect of the Neologues' attacks on him. Once he allowed their criticism to be a factor in a Jewish legal decision he rendered. In 1867, Hildesheimer was asked whether it was permissible for a charity to make public the names of its contributors and the amounts they had donated. Though slightly uncomfortable with such a procedure, Hildesheimer did admit, "We are not able to deny that by publishing names, contributions are increased." He reluctantly gave his permission. But when he justified the publicity, he added that if the names were not published, "the Neologues will claim that we keep our ways secret."[76]

In short, Hildesheimer was fully cognizant that the Neologues hoped to diminish his prestige and undermine his authority in both the Jewish and gentile worlds. Their critiques, however, offered a particular challenge because both they and Hildesheimer were interested in appealing to Jews who affirmed the worth of secular culture. Thus Hildesheimer could not ignore attacks that were essentially addressed to these same people. Ludwig Philippson stated that modern Jews desired to join with "the rest of the world in all intellectual, social, and material [dimensions of life] . . . with the exception of religious and group association—*Glaubens und Stammesgenossenschaft."*[77] His words reflect the analogous hopes of Löw or of Hildesheimer. Each man sought to enhance the "intellectual, social, and material" integration of the Jewish people into the rest of the world. Each man believed he was best preserving "religious and group identity." On one hand, the similarity between the goals and resolutions of a Löw and those of a Hildesheimer meant that the boundary between the two could be difficult to discern. On the other hand, as an Orthodox rabbi, Hildesheimer's absolute commitment to the halakha meant that on some issues the break between himself and other Jews in the community would be unequivocal. The contours of Hildesheimer's final policy were still in the process of being defined. Tensions within the Orthodox camp would, in time, put his policies to the test.

The challenge presented Hildesheimer by the Hungarian liberals in his quest for religious authority was mild when compared to the tasks confronting him among the Hungarian Orthodox. The dominant forces in the Hungarian Orthodox Jewish community rejected the worth of Western culture altogether and regarded the slightest change in Jewish culture as a major deviation from Jewish tradition. Thus, despite the respect he enjoyed among some elements of Hungarian Orthodoxy, he was ultimately subjected to scorn and derision, and his attempts to effectuate influential religious authority ended in dismal failure.

From the very beginning of his stay in Eisenstadt, the overwhelming majority of Orthodox rabbis in Hungary distrusted this German Ph.D. who introduced secular subjects into the yeshiva curriculum. Hildesheimer's daughter Esther Calvary reports that Hildesheimer wore modern garb and occasionally corresponded in German with other Hungarian rabbis, thus setting himself apart from them.[78] His most serious deviation, in their view, though, was the decision to include secular studies in the curriculum of the yeshiva. As a result, some Orthodox rabbis furiously attacked Hildesheimer and his yeshiva. Rabbi Akiba Yoseph Schlesinger pronounced a ban of excommunication upon Hildesheimer and charged that only sinners who caused others to sin emerged from the Eisenstadt yeshiva.[79] The most virulent personal attack was issued by Rabbi Hillel Lichtenstein, Schlesinger's father-in-law and one of Moses Sofer's outstanding pupils. Lichtenstein wrote: "[Hildesheimer] is a man of deceit, a liar, out only for monetary gain, wrapped, so to speak in a garb of righteousness which outwardly justifies his deed, like a pig that stretches forth its hoofs . . . so that many are caught in his net. . . . His every tendency uproots Torah and fear of God and plants in their stead apostasy and heresy in Israel. The city and its surroundings, which before were like the Garden of Eden, have been left after him as a wilderness destroyed by foreigners." Quoting Rabbi Haim Sofer, Lichtenstein continued: "May God have mercy over this land because the wicked man Hildesheimer is the horse and wagon of the evil inclination. His strength and success have not come in a natural way, but the demon of Esau rides on him. . . . Were it not that God left us a small remnant, all of Hungary would have been turned to heresy by him and his evil agents."[80]

Hildesheimer, of course, regarded these men as hopelessly myopic and felt that their approach to Judaism would not only prevent Orthodoxy from achieving a role of authority in the general Jewish community but would result in its eventual destruction. Of the Hasidim in particular he wrote, "They act as if piety was given to them alone. . . . Yet, they are often among the greatest sinners in Israel."[81] Reflecting a rationalism he shared with the German Reformers, Hildesheimer considered the Hasidim "superstitious" and saw them as practicing a "false Judaism."[82] In speaking of his other Hungarian Orthodox colleagues, he acknowledged, "My way is not their way. There is no hope [for the Jewish future] except in the creation of a seminary." Although he recognized that his intention was the same as that of his Orthodox rabbinical peers,[83] he knew that his stratagems for achieving Orthodox religious authority were an anathema to the other Orthodox in Hungary. Foremost among his plans was the creation of a seminary employing modern pedagogic techniques and a systematized curriculum to provide students with the best possible secular and religious instruction. Although Hildesheimer's yeshiva combined the study of religious subjects with secular instruction, it did not merit the title of seminary. *Wissenschaft des Judentums* was not stringently practiced within its walls, and the secular educational backgrounds of the students did not permit advanced secular or academic study at the level of the Breslau seminary. Nevertheless, these deficiencies made the establishment of a modern seminary all the more desirable in Hildesheimer's eyes.

Hildesheimer, however, was not the only person urging the establishment of a rabbinical seminary in Hungary. The Neologues were as well, and herein lay one of the keys to the Hungarian Orthodox objection to the creation of any modern seminary. In an article published in 1862 entitled "A Few Words about the Use of the Hungarian School Fund," Hildesheimer noted that after the revolution of 1848 the Hungarian government imposed a tax on the Jewish community because of its participation in the revolution. In September 1850, King-Emperor Franz Joseph decreed that the money (1 million gulden) could be used by the Jewish community for educational purposes. The Neologues wanted to use the money to establish educational institutions, or perhaps a rabbinical seminary, in the spirit of the Haskalah. The Orthodox were opposed to the creation of such a seminary as much for their suspicion and condemnation of secular culture as for their hatred of the Neologues who had proposed it. Hildesheimer, in suggesting that this money be employed to endow a modern seminary, was alone among all the Orthodox rabbis in Hungary.[84] Despised already by the Neologues, Hildesheimer became increasingly estranged from his Orthodox peers throughout the 1850s and 1860s over these issues.

In the year 1864 the singular position Hildesheimer occupied among the Orthodox of Hungary was made embarrassingly public. A delegation of seven Orthodox rabbis met with the king-emperor on April 11 to protest the establishment of a seminary under liberal auspices. Earlier in the year, the Neologues had gathered in Budapest to lobby for government recognition of the proposed liberal seminary. Hildesheimer had responded by criticizing the Neologues' program in an article in *Der Israelit*. He feared that the Neologues would be successful and, consequently, must have felt that his public warning had, at least in part, prompted the Orthodox decision to send a delegation to Franz Joseph. Yet he was excluded from the group that went to speak with the monarch. The exclusion by his Orthodox colleagues embarrassed and embittered Hildesheimer. When asked to comment on the meeting, he wrote, "What was discussed and agreed upon privately was totally unknown to me, as I did not take part in the discussion."[85]

Hildesheimer's rift with the other Orthodox rabbis deepened in 1865. Hildesheimer's close friend Rabbi Judah Aszod and other Orthodox rabbinical leaders in Hungary circulated a petition among the Orthodox rabbinate of Hungary protesting the establishment of a modern rabbinical school because they feared that the government would not heed their earlier protests. The petition stated, "Even if a seminary is established which is guarded on all matters religious, in the end it will be transformed into neology which will lead Hungarian Jewry into the path of religious reform." The petition was sent to Franz Joseph and was published by Leopold Löw in the liberal newspaper *Neuzeit*. Hildesheimer had not seen the petition, but when it was published by Löw, he learned that his name had been among the 121 attached to it. Hildesheimer was certain that Löw had signed his name to the petition to humiliate him. Thus he wrote to Judah Aszod: "Last week I heard that *Ben Chananjah* published a petition of the Orthodox rabbis in Hungary in the paper *Neuzeit* . . . and that my name was included among the [signatories.] . . . Yet, I am not opposed to the establishment of a seminary if it is in the hands of pious Jews."[86]

Hildesheimer went on to register his protest against the content of the petition. He reiterated his previous position regarding the establishment of a seminary and reaffirmed his support for the establishment of a modern Orthodox rabbinical school. Indeed, as Hildesheimer wrote to Rabbi Pinchas Stein: "So far we have only seen the fruit of a seminary which has sinners at its head. However, if a seminary will be established which has God-fearers as its leaders, there will be a sanctification of God's name."[87]

Aszod replied to Hildesheimer's letter by stating that the petition had been signed only by the seven men who were in the delegation that went to see the emperor in 1864. The other 114 names had been added, Aszod wrote, to make the strength of the Orthodox party felt in government circles. Aszod explained that he, not Löw, was responsible for attaching Hildesheimer's name. He apologized to Hildesheimer but had honestly assumed that Hildesheimer, as an Orthodox rabbi, supported the cause adopted by every other Orthodox rabbi in Hungary. Indeed, Aszod urged Hildesheimer not to withdraw his name publicly from the list because to do so would embarrass the Orthodox before Franz Joseph and delight the heretical Neologues. Aszod closed by advising that since the deed was done, Hildesheimer should accept the judgment of the other rabbis, and he cited the verse from Proverbs 3:5, "Do not rely upon your own understanding," to indicate that Hildesheimer should not take any public action against the petition.[88]

Hildesheimer replied to Aszod immediately. He wrote: "The truth is that it is no small matter to me that my name was signed to a petition which contained the opposite of what I had said, and not only privately, but publicly." Hildesheimer felt an obligation to express himself publicly once again in support of a seminary, for, he told Aszod, he owed it to his supporters not to confuse them. He realized that this set him apart from the other Orthodox rabbis in Hungary, but he felt strongly on the issue. He informed Aszod that he intended to write letters to both *Der Israelit* and *Jeschurun* disassociating himself from the petition and reaffirming his earlier publicly expressed support for the establishment of a seminary. He hoped that the other rabbis would not take offense at this action but believed he had no other choice.[89] This episode symbolizes Hildesheimer's dilemma vis-à-vis the Hungarian Orthodox. As an acculturated Jew and proponent of Western culture, Hildesheimer was their opponent in spite of his Orthodoxy. Compromise on matters of religion could not be tolerated, and so Hildesheimer's program to achieve Orthodox religious authority in Hungary could not be accepted by his rightist colleagues.

They quickly took offense at his opposition to them over the matter of the seminary. Another old friend, Maharam Schick, warned Hildesheimer not to write any more in support of a seminary and told him that he was obligated to accept the decision of the majority of rabbis in Hungary. If he continued to aid those who wanted to establish a seminary, Schick warned, then Hildesheimer would, "in the future, have to give a strict accounting,"[90] presumably before both his Orthodox colleagues and God.

Hildesheimer responded once more by calling on the Orthodox to wage a "positive war" against the Neologues, although he knew he was alone in this view. Although Hildesheimer acknowledged that it would be "smarter not to swim against the stream, I have my duty to cast my minority vote." Otherwise, he added, "My conscience will give me no rest."[91]

The open and extreme hostility between Hildesheimer and the Orthodox leadership in Hungary emerged fully in 1866, when Hildesheimer publicly criticized the Orthodox rabbinate of Hungary for resolutions they had passed at an assembly convened in Mihalowitz earlier that year. The convention, led by Rabbi Hillel Lichtenstein—one of Hildesheimer's most vocal Orthodox critics[92]—and Rabbi Haim Sofer of Budapest, was held because the Neologues were making rapid advances in many Hungarian Jewish communities. The Orthodox felt it would be wise to establish guidelines to instruct communities as to the reforms they should resist. The social utility of such guidelines is obvious. By designating certain practices as unacceptable, the convention provided the Orthodox community with clear boundaries for permissible behavior, thereby bolstering a threatened Orthodox group identity. Sixty-seven rabbis signed a petition calling for the conference. It is interesting that three of the leading talmudists of the community—Rabbis Samuel Sofer of Pressburg, Maharam Schick, and Abraham David Deutsch—did not sign the petition.[93] Hildesheimer chose not to attend.

The conference, true to its intent, passed a series of nine resolutions in which the rabbis detailed their objections to particular reforms which the liberal elements in Hungarian Jewish life had introduced into their communities. The first resolution called for a ban against preaching in a non-Jewish language and ruled that if such a sermon was delivered, a Jew must immediately absent himself from the synagogue. Second, it was forbidden to enter a synagogue where the *bimah* (prayer platform) was not in the center. It was also forbidden to erect a synagogue with a tower, and neither rabbis nor cantors were allowed to don clerical robes similar to those worn by officiants of other religions. The rabbis ruled that the *mehitza* (separation) between men and women in a prayer service was ritually acceptable only if the men could not see the women. Separate seating, where men could see women, was not acceptable, and if it occurred, a Jew was directed to leave the synagogue and not pray there. (Separate seating was still the custom among the non-Orthodox in Hungary.) The rabbis prohibited Jewish entry into a synagogue where there was a choir (even if the choir was all male) and forbade Jews from going into a synagogue that had an organ, even if the organ was not played on the Sabbath. Indeed, they remarked that it was better to enter a church than such a synagogue. Finally, they stated that a wedding could only take place outdoors, not inside the synagogue, and ruled that it was forbidden to change any custom or synagogue practice handed down from their ancestors. It would be better to pray alone than to worship at a synagogue that violated even one of these rules.[94]

Hildesheimer responded that he understood the necessity of taking extraordinary measures to halt the anarchy the Neologues had introduced into the community. Moreover, as an Orthodox rabbi, Hildesheimer emphasized that in their own communities his colleagues had the right to establish these decrees. But they were applicable only to the communities under their jurisdiction. Elsewhere they carried no authority. Hildesheimer, on sound Jewish legal grounds, wished to pacify his colleagues while simultaneously asserting that he did not feel bound by their strictures.

Hildesheimer continued by questioning the Jewish legality of the measures. He contended that they fell under the category of *lemigdar milta* (extraordinary measures to check lawlessness). As such, they should not be regarded as normatively binding. In other words, Hildesheimer recognized that the Neologues threatened the stability of Orthodox communal life in Hungary because of the changes they had introduced into Hungarian Jewish life. He knew that if boundaries were not drawn, chaos would result and the cohesion of the Orthodox community would be endangered. He obviously empathized with the efforts of his Orthodox colleagues, but he departed radically from them on where these boundaries should be drawn.

Hildesheimer dissented from these decisions not only on Jewish legal but on practical grounds as well. In a petition he authored to protest the Mihalowitz resolutions, Hildesheimer stated, "Not only is the majority of the public unable to abide by these measures, but a much, much greater loss than reward will spring from them."[95] Again, sociological considerations undergirded by talmudic principles are evident in his deliberations.

Nevertheless, for Hildesheimer to assert his authority among the Orthodox members of the Hungarian Jewish community, he had to express his dissent in formal Jewish legal terms. Consequently, he investigated each of the nine items in the Mihalowitz resolutions and subjected them to Jewish legal scrutiny. To have done otherwise in this instance would have been to surrender his claim to Orthodox religious authority.

Hildesheimer stated that the prohibition against delivering or listening to a sermon in a non-Jewish language was absurd and had no foundation in Jewish law. His own teachers, Ettlinger and Bernays, whose piety was unquestioned, had preached in German. To make absolute a custom against preaching in the vernacular when there was no authority for it in the Talmud or the Jewish codes of law was, in Hildesheimer's opinion, akin to idolatry. The only genuine source for Jewish authority, as Hildesheimer saw it, "was the law according to its [talmudic] source." Here Hildesheimer was disputing the substantive decisions of these rabbis by employing their shared criterion for authority.[96] Since no such prohibition against preaching in a non-Jewish language existed in Jewish sources, Hildesheimer felt that Orthodox rabbis had an obligation to preach in the vernacular. Only then could they speak to the public against "the temptation of the destructive party, i.e., the Neologues."[97]

Hildesheimer agreed that the prayer platform should be in the center of the synagogue. On at least two other occasions Hildesheimer had written responsa stating that the *bimah* should not be placed at the front of the synagogue.[98] In one instance, Rabbi Moshe Lev Engel had complained to Hildesheimer that his community had moved the *bimah* from the middle of the congregation and, in accord with nineteenth-century aesthetic standards, placed it next to the Holy Ark at the front of the synagogue. Engel realized that there was a dispute in the codes of Jewish law over this issue[99] and wondered whether he should raise it as a matter of importance with his congregation. Hildesheimer responded by saying that the position of the *bimah* in the synagogue was more one of custom than law, inasmuch as the law admitted of two interpretations. He quickly added, however, "It will certainly be regarded as a commandment to observe this custom just as other customs are obeyed. This is not a matter about which the phrase, 'silence is better than speech,' should be applied." Hildesheimer felt that Engel had an obligation to reprove the congregation and urge them to observe the ancient custom. His reasoning in this case was similar to that of the Orthodox at Mihalowitz, for he added, "Until now I have seen this change made only in synagogues where a group of Neologues had appeared."[100]

Nonetheless, in his dispute with the rabbis of Mihalowitz, Hildesheimer felt that there was no justification for the view that Jewish law prohibited entry into a synagogue where the *bimah* was not in the center. Although he favored placing it there, particularly in light of the Neologue practice of placing it next to the Holy Ark, it was not a legal requirement to insist upon such placement. In Hildesheimer's opinion, it was a grave error on the part of the rabbis in Mihalowitz to make this demand in absolutely every community, for in certain locales, he knew that it would alienate people from Orthodoxy.[101]

Hildesheimer agreed that a tower should not be erected on a synagogue for fear that it might appear to be a church. Yet he added, "Architecture does not make the synagogue what it is, but the genuine Jewish spirit which resides in those who attend it." He also felt that officiants at Jewish religious services should not wear clerical robes and acknowledged that Rabbi Moses Isserles (1530–72), the great legal authority of Ashkenazic Jewry, was opposed to marriages being performed inside a synagogue. As with the placement of the *bimah*, however, Hildesheimer claimed that these issues admitted of honest difference of opinion between observant Jews.[102]

Hildesheimer regarded the ban against choirs as totally unfounded from a Jewish legal perspective.[103] He wrote in an earlier responsum that the introduction of the choir in the synagogues of the nineteenth century was clearly the work of the Neologues. Nevertheless, Hildesheimer cited precedent for such a practice in the Middle Ages and noted that by 1857 this custom had been accepted even among the "observant and God-fearing." Recognizing social reality once again, Hildesheimer stated that even if opposition were desirable, "We have no strength to stand against the general community on this matter."[104] In the absence of any definite Jewish legal prohibition against any of these innovations, and because insistence on their observance would weaken the ability of the Orthodox to exercise influential authority in the general Jewish community, Hildesheimer felt it was ridiculous to split the community and weaken

Orthodox authority by taking a stringent stand in regard to any one of them.[105]

On two issues, however, Hildesheimer was in total agreement with his Orthodox colleagues. It was forbidden to enter a synagogue where men and women, in spite of a *mehitza*, could see one another, he maintained. Similarly, he applauded the prohibition against the organ. Hildesheimer wrote in a letter that it was forbidden to enter a synagogue where an organ was permitted on the Sabbath or holidays and declared that no rabbi who permitted an organ in the synagogue could be called Orthodox.[106] In one special case, Hildesheimer had noted that there was no "explicit prohibition against entering such a synagogue."[107] He delivered this opinion in a case in which a *shohet* (Jewish ritual slaughterer) would have lost his position had he not attended a service in such a synagogue. Hildesheimer reasoned that if the community dismissed the *shohet*, the replacement might not be as scrupulous in his religious observance and, consequently, the community might no longer have kosher meat. Outside of this one case, Hildesheimer was adamant that a Jew not attend a synagogue where there was an organ. This prohibition was of biblical origin and was based on Leviticus 18:3, "Thou shalt not walk in their ways."[108] Even more significantly, Hildesheimer added that he banned entry into such a synagogue to avoid "imitation of the apostates."[109]

Hildesheimer concurred with his Orthodox colleagues on the need to establish Orthodox boundaries against the Neologues on this particular issue. In taking this stance, Hildesheimer clearly identified himself with the Orthodox camp and attempted to deemphasize the differences that separated him from the less acculturated Orthodox rabbinate in Hungary. Despite these efforts, the fact that he was forced to write such an article indicates the futility of Hildesheimer's position in Hungary. Too great a distance separated him from his Orthodox colleagues—both in his views of Judaism and in his stratagems to achieve Orthodox religious authority—for the gap to be breached. Hildesheimer acknowledged this difference in a letter to the Ktav Sofer. He recognized an attitudinal contrast which he felt distinguished him from them. The majority of the Orthodox rabbis in Hungary were, in his opinion, negative: "It seems to me there is a great danger in always shouting 'No! No!'"[110] Hildesheimer believed that the Orthodox had to discover "a way which finds assent and favor in the eyes of the majority of the people," if Orthodox religious authority were to be realized.[111]

The following May, Rabbi A. D. Deutsch wrote to Hildesheimer to suggest a meeting between Hildesheimer and the more conservative Orthodox leaders of Hungary. Deutsch hoped to prevent a split in Orthodox ranks and to restore Hildesheimer to a position of respect in the Hungarian Orthodox community. In his letter to Hildesheimer, Deutsch added that the Orthodox were adamantly opposed to the idea of a seminary as well as the inclusion of secular subjects within an elementary or high school Jewish curriculum. Hildesheimer refused to yield. "Even though our common goal is to magnify Torah and make it great," Hildesheimer wrote, "our means of arriving at this goal are as far removed as is the East from the West. . . . And I say frankly that in the coming days, [the challenge facing Orthodoxy can be met] only by the establishment of a seminary." Hildesheimer defiantly continued: "Our only hope is to create schools in which our children learn—besides the chief subject of the Holy Torah—secular subjects as well, which is just what occurs . . . in the schools of the leftists and the Neologues. . . . It seems to me that there is a great danger in always . . . fighting what others propose instead of proposing what we in truth want."[112] Hildesheimer understood, by this point in his career, that rapprochement with his Orthodox colleagues was impossible. And rather than argue with them again, he declined Deutsch's invitation to attend the meeting.

The pressure on Hildesheimer to succumb to his Orthodox colleagues escalated during the next few months and years. As the situation between the Orthodox and liberal parties in Hungary deteriorated, relations between the two camps degenerated into constant warfare. In Budapest, a small group of Orthodox Jews openly opposed the liberal orientation of the majority of the community. This group, called the Israelitische Kultusgemeinde, wrote to the cultural minister of Hungary and asked that a central organization for all Hungarian Jewry be created to administer the affairs of the entire community. Obviously they were confident that a majority of Hungarian, if not Budapest, Jewry was still Orthodox. The eventual result of this proposal was the convening on December 14, 1868, of the Hungarian Jewish Congress. Representatives of all segments of Hungarian Jewry were in attendance, and the congress lasted through February 23, 1869.[113]

Before the congress met, two hundred Orthodox rabbis assembled in Pest to assure a united Orthodox delegation. Hildesheimer felt that the purpose of this meeting was to achieve a compromise between himself and the other Orthodox, and so he decided to attend the meeting. But when the conference chose to contest both the creation of a modern seminary and the inclusion of any secular subject in the curriculum of a yeshiva, he decided to leave the conference.[114]

Sigmund Krauss, a merchant and lay leader of Hungarian Orthodoxy, subsequently wrote to Hildesheimer and assured him that he believed only Hildesheimer's program would ultimately save Hungarian Orthodoxy from decay and stagnation. Yet Krauss contended that Hildesheimer's program was premature. In view of the importance of the forthcoming congress, he beseeched Hildesheimer to abandon his program, which Krauss said had little, if any, chance of success at the congress. Otherwise, he implored, "all will be lost."[115] Unity among the Orthodox, Krauss maintained, had to be assigned top priority. Hildesheimer, as was to be expected, responded bitterly.

Painfully aware of his isolation after these many years, Hildesheimer complained that the Orthodox in Hungary resisted all innovation, even that which was permissible under Jewish law. He told Krauss that he regarded the Mihalowitz convention in 1866 as a personal attack and lamented that he was caught between the Neologues on one hand and the Orthodox on the other.[116] Indeed, Hildesheimer was uncomfortable with the Orthodox antagonism toward himself and his program. He confessed to Judah Aszod that his isolation from the Orthodox camp wounded him deeply and personally.[117] Yet Hildesheimer's policies and his unwillingness to abandon them made such a position, in Hungary, inevitable.

At the Hungarian Jewish Congress, Hildesheimer attempted to offer a moderate position between the Neologues on one side and those whom he considered the extreme Orthodox on the other. Only thirty-five people supported him. All the proposals he offered and every position he represented were roundly defeated. The extremists in both parties dominated, and the Congress concluded with an official split of the Hungarian Jewish community along emergent Orthodox-liberal lines.[118] In a report on the Congress, Hildesheimer complained about the extremists in the Hungarian Orthodox camp and the hegemony they enjoyed in it.[119]

In summary, Hildesheimer's efforts to effectuate his brand of Orthodox religious authority in Hungary were a dismal failure. His approach of combining traditional and modern symbols and ideas into a single system remained unappreciated and unheeded. He was doubly censured. The Neologues, his professed enemies, condemned him as an antiquarian. They strove to undermine his credibility and authority with the acculturated members of the Hungarian Jewish community, for whose allegiance they both competed. The Orthodox, his supposed allies, were inhospitable to his religious and cultural views. They were ultimately committed to an ideology that promoted resistance to cultural change and innovation. Hildesheimer was rendered powerless on all fronts. He had foreseen that his enemies would despise him. He had not expected his colleagues to divorce him.

By 1869, Hildesheimer realized that a united Jewish community was impossible. His hopes for achieving religious authority among the entire community, a cause he had championed so successfully in Halberstadt two decades earlier, were no longer viable. Nevertheless, Hildesheimer remained convinced that if Orthodoxy wished to avoid being reduced to a small and insignificant sect in the total Jewish community, efforts had to be extended to express Orthodox Judaism in nineteenth-century cultural terms. He was not prepared to surrender either his views of Judaism or his policies for realizing Orthodox religious authority in the larger community because of developments during these eighteen years in Eisenstadt. In a letter dated December 31, 1867, Hildesheimer wrote again to his close friend Wolf Feilchenfeld about the conditions in Hungary. Unlike 1860, when he described his life in Eisenstadt as a "genuine pleasure," Hildesheimer now complained, "I live in a very small, uncultured place."[120] Certain that, as a product of "cultured Orthodoxy," he would be able to expose his ideas to a more receptive audience in Germany, Hildesheimer retained enough confidence in himself to accept the invitation tendered him by Congregation Adass Jisroel in Berlin. In 1869, he returned to Germany to become their spiritual leader. Hildesheimer made Berlin the major arena of his life's work. There, at last, he found a place where his approach to Judaism and the problem of religious authority could flourish.

With a population of approximately forty thousand, the Berlin Jewish community was the largest in any German city by the 1860s. The population had increased nearly fivefold in the twenty years since Hildesheimer had studied there at the university. In 1864 the death of Berlin's leading Orthodox rabbi plunged the community into bitter controversy. Liberals and traditionalists argued over the appointment of a successor for Michael Sachs, who had affirmed the importance of secular culture. The liberals, who were successful in this struggle, put forth Joseph Aub, a moderate Liberal, as their candidate. Aub, from Mainz, favored the adoption of a prayerbook that would omit mention of the ancient Hebrew sacrificial system as well as the prayers for a Jewish return to Zion. In addition, Aub advocated the playing of an organ in synagogue services and favored several other modifications in the choreography of the prayer service. All these positions made him unacceptable to the Orthodox.[121]

The traditionalists quickly petitioned the board of the community to appoint a second rabbi to serve with Aub. They hoped the community would elect a rabbi to supervise dietary regulations and service the needs of faithful Orthodox Jews. The board postponed acting on this request until 1868, at which time a public ballot was held. The vote was powerfully contested and very close, but the Reformers prevailed by 150 votes in this community of 40,000 and no rabbi was appointed.[122]

The Orthodox continued to fight for their demands. Thus, when Elchanan Rosenstein, one of the two remaining private Orthodox rabbis in Berlin, died in 1869, eight hundred of the more conservative members of the community petitioned the communal board to appoint another rabbi. They sought someone who had a university education, a thorough knowledge of Talmud, and a commitment to a traditional Jewish way of life. The petition made no impact on the board. When the decision to elect a new rabbi was made, Abraham Geiger was selected. The chairman of the communal board was quoted as saying, "Orthodoxy is legally extinct among us."[123]

At this point, the Orthodox decided to organize and look for a new rabbi whom they would pay out of private, not communal, funds. Hence in June 1869, several prominent families in the Berlin Jewish community established Congregation Adass Jisroel. Among the founders were Dr. L. Sternheim, J. Marcuse, Jacob Bamberger, Jacob Israel, Benjamin Lieberman, A. H. Heymann, Moritz Bab, Johann Hoff, M. Kempner, J. Simon, and D. Struck. All of these individuals came from established Berlin Jewish families, and their ties to the general Jewish community, notwithstanding their decision to create their own "religious society," were firm and secure. They had no intention of striving for a secession from the general Jewish community. They wanted only to have their own religious needs met.[124]

It was to Hildesheimer that these men turned in their search for a religious leader. During his years in Hungary, his fame as a champion of religious Orthodoxy and a master of modern culture continued to grow among the traditional, acculturated Jews of Europe. Two years earlier, in fact, the board members of the Beth Hamidrasch Verein in Berlin had asked Hildesheimer to come from Eisenstadt to Berlin to become the head of their institute. The school, in 1867, had only ten or fifteen students, and its course of study was exclusively talmudic. The board wanted to revive the institute and overhaul the curriculum. They were aware that the traditional form and content of instruction preserved there could no longer attract the acculturated Jews of contemporary Berlin. Hildesheimer's appointment was seen by the board as a means "to regenerate Orthodox life in Berlin."[125]

Hildesheimer responded to this offer on February 14, 1867. He wrote: "I know that Germany has claims on me and, in view of its cultural level, I should be able, though perhaps on a smaller scale, to achieve more than I do here where I find very little understanding of my principles."[126] But he was still too attached to his yeshiva in Eisenstadt to accept the Berlin post. Despite all his difficulties in Hungary, his yeshiva had grown to 150 students (the second largest yeshiva enrollment in Hungary), and he was reluctant to leave it for an obviously struggling school in Berlin.

Despite the problems and frustrations he experienced, Hildesheimer's renown as a master of two cultures continued unabated. After the Jewish Congress in 1868–69, Hildesheimer's disenchantment with his constricted position in Hungary grew. Yet a surprising faith in his ability to exercise influential religious authority, even in Hungary, is contained in a request sent to Hildesheimer by Rabbi Solomon Ganzfried, author of the *Kitzur Shulhan Aruch*. Ganzfried headed some of the most extreme Orthodox elements at the Hungarian Jewish Congress and had attacked Hildesheimer not only at the congress but often throughout his years in Hungary.[127] Just a few months after the congress, Ganzfried addressed Hildesheimer as the "famous *Gaon* [genius]" and requested Hildesheimer's help on a problem confronting the community of Ungvar.

Ganzfried reported that the Reformers in Ungvar had seceded from the general community because they felt that it had neglected to represent them at the recently completed congress. They subsequently erected their own temple and appointed their own cantor and preacher. Most significantly, they appointed their own *shohet*. Ganzfried was, of course, upset on religious grounds over these developments. He was most concerned, however, over the Reform designation of a *shohet* because it also had serious practical ramifications.

The *shohet* paid a tax on a part of his revenues into the community treasury. Indeed, the majority of the community's budget came from this source.[128] The appointment of a Reform *shohet* thus had serious implications for the financial welfare of the Orthodox-dominated general community. Each time someone purchased meat from the Reform- rather than from the community-sanctioned *shohet*, the communal treasury lost revenue.

When the Reform-sanctioned *shohet* decided to slaughter meat without the permission of the Orthodox rabbi of the community, Ganzfried and several Orthodox rabbis had proclaimed all of his meat *tref* (ritually unfit for consumption). Yet members of the community refused to heed their ruling and were purchasing meat from this man. Ganzfried reported that the attitude of the community members was that "rabbis who have no secular education issued this prohibition and, consequently, they have no confidence in them." Ganzfried continued, "The people claim these rabbis act only to obstruct progress." Ganzfried thus found himself in the unusual position of seeking help from Hildesheimer. Ganzfried wrote: "The leaders of our community request your help, your Excellency, as you are renowned for both your religious and secular knowledge. The people have confidence in you. . . . Render a judgment unto us in the case of this *shohet*." The letter concluded by asking Hildesheimer to reply quickly. Hildesheimer answered on April 5, 1869, just two months after the congress and five months before his arrival in Berlin. The letter is remarkable for its muted tone. Hildesheimer seems to have resisted the impulse to speak harshly. He acknowledged that though he was "more comfortable with those who walk in the spirit of the times" than were other Orthodox colleagues, it seems clear that he doubted whether his agreement with their stance would carry much weight with the Reformers in the community.[129] Hildesheimer's view, though still in a nascent stage, was beginning to crystallize. Effective Orthodox religious authority could no longer be exercised over the entire Jewish community—a view Ganzfried was still unwilling to accept. Hildesheimer did imply that his opinion might be valued by those traditionalists in the community who also approved of secular culture, though he stated that Ganzfried would do better to seek the support of other Orthodox colleagues in the area. Although he did not say so, Hildesheimer must have savored this exchange as vindicating his belief that Orthodoxy in Hungary must eventually produce leaders who had the ability to present the tradition in contemporary cultural terms.

In any event, that Ganzfried turned to Hildesheimer in this instance indicates that, by mid-1869, his reputation as the outstanding modern Orthodox rabbi in Hungary was secure.

In view of all these developments, it is surprising neither that Hildesheimer was invited by the acculturated leaders of Adass Jisroel to become their rabbi nor that he decided to accept their offer. Unlike Samson Raphael Hirsch, he did not already occupy a well-established modern Orthodox pulpit in a cosmopolitan German city. The Berlin position meant that he could at last come to a thriving metropolis with a large Jewish population receptive to his notions of a modern acculturated Orthodoxy. He would be able to provide his own children with the finest education available in Europe and take them to the Berlin Museum.[130] At last, as the leader of an exclusively Orthodox community, Hildesheimer could develop his program for achieving Orthodox religious authority unhampered by Reform. This is not to say that he was unaware of or ignored Reform during his years in Berlin. Indeed, he cooperated with Reformers, and also fought against them, in many communal activities. In some instances, he appears to have won their respect.[131] Nevertheless, since they were no longer part of his constituency as they had been earlier in his career, he did not need to struggle to realize authority over them. Likewise, the Orthodoxy that dominated the Hungarian community was virtually nonexistent in Berlin. Thus he had no need to combat Orthodox extremists who would look askance at his program of combining secular and religious cultures. Adass Jisroel was elated with its choice of spiritual leader. Hildesheimer was the ideal candidate to lead a revival of Orthodox Jewish life in the Prussian capital. Hildesheimer now had the forum he had so long desired to actualize his program for religious authority.

Hildesheimer arrived in Berlin on September 2, 1869. One month later, on October 10, he established an elementary religious school for both boys and girls.[132] The establishment of such a school, which never could have been created in an Orthodox community in Hungary, bespeaks the radically different cultural atmosphere Hildesheimer had entered. This school embodied Hildesheimer's conception of modern Orthodoxy, an Orthodoxy he defined as combining a "faithful adherence to traditional teachings with an effective effort to keep in touch with the spirit of progress."[133]

Such a modern Orthodoxy, however, required more than elementary schools to flourish. Cultured Orthodox leadership needed to be trained. The necessity for the creation of a modern Orthodox rabbinical seminary was more pressing than ever. Hence, two years after arriving in Berlin and securing his position there, Hildesheimer turned to confront the task that was to provide the crowning moment of his life—the building of a modern Orthodox rabbinical seminary. The details of Hildesheimer's educational philosophy and the nature of the curriculum taught in the seminary will be discussed in a later chapter. It is vital to emphasize that Hildesheimer viewed the seminary as his primary means for achieving religious authority among the Jews of Germany and western Europe. As Hildesheimer wrote, the seminary would permit the Orthodox "both to combat the destructive ambitions of the Reformers and to answer the demands of the time."[134]

In a letter dated 4 Iyaar, 5632 (1872), Hildesheimer addressed ten prominent Jews throughout Germany, telling them of the need for the creation of an Orthodox seminary and urging them to donate money for its support.[135] Hildesheimer also sought contributions from Jews living outside Germany and, according to David Hoffmann, succeeded in raising a considerable amount from them. In less than eighteen months, Hildesheimer had obtained the necessary funds, and on October 22, 1873, the seminary was founded. Hildesheimer now had the means to produce "rabbis imbued with Torah and the fear of God," who would also "be armed with science." The "Reformers and academic heretics" could now be contested effectively in their own parlance, and traditional Judaism could meet the demands of the age.[136]

Hildesheimer could now spread influential religious authority among those acculturated Jews in Germany and throughout Europe who still clung to an observance of Jewish law and tradition. Yet Hildesheimer had no illusions that the formation of the seminary would permit his religious authority to be exercised among all segments of the contemporary Jewish community. Three major episodes indicate that Hildesheimer was content to accept limitations on his influential authority. Hildesheimer felt that a self-imposed restraint on reaching out to the entire Jewish world was the wisest course of action for the modern Orthodox to pursue at that time. For any effort to establish modern Orthodoxy among all the members of the community was likely to prove futile.

In one episode, parents from a Jewish school in Vienna asked Hildesheimer whether it was permissible for boys in the school to study with uncovered heads. The school was sponsored by the community, and the board forbade head coverings in 1881 "on sanitary grounds." Hildesheimer recognized, naturally, that the ostensible reason given for the prohibition of the head coverings was ridiculous. He assumed that the majority of the board that had issued such a ruling was either Reform or secular. Although he admitted that skullcaps were not mandated by Jewish law, he also stated that it was traditional for males to wear them when praying, eating, or studying holy texts. Elsewhere he commented that the wearing of a head covering helped the wearer to achieve a sense of piety and reverence while studying.[137] Further, since the wearing of a head covering by the man was a universally observed Jewish custom at this point in Jewish history, it should be observed. In the end, whether or not the boys wore a head covering was not Hildesheimer's primary concern. He maintained that the issue that concerned him most as a result of this inquiry was that Orthodox children were obviously attending a school where the majority, or at least a sizable minority, of students were non-Orthodox and nonobservant. He feared the influences such children would have on the Orthodox children and contended that it would be better, if possible, for the Orthodox parents to remove their children from such a school.

Hildesheimer clearly believed, by this point, that the modern Orthodox would be better advised to focus their energies on consolidating their strength within their own community rather than reach out to the larger one. This does not mean that he opposed all Orthodox efforts at cooperation with the non-Orthodox world. Rather, it reveals his comprehension of the boundaries of modern Orthodox religious influence in the general Jewish community in which he lived.[138]

This interpretation is underscored by another event three years later. On October 25, 1884, a committee of *Hovevei Tsiyon* (Lovers of Zion) in Warsaw sent Hildesheimer a telegram entreating him to attend their forthcoming convention across the German frontier in Kattowitz, Silesia, on November 6. Hildesheimer had long been sympathetic to the cause of building up the Jewish settlement in Eretz Yisrael (Land of Israel). The committee felt that Hildesheimer's attendance at the conference would aid them in gaining both financial and ideological support from Orthodox and German Jews.[139] In spite of his sympathy for their cause, Hildesheimer refused their invitation. In a letter to Leon Pinsker, he claimed that his advancing age and heavy work load made his attendance impossible, but it seems clear that religious factors also dictated his nonattendance at the conference. Hildesheimer objected because the conference was being cosponsored by the B'nai B'rith in Kattowitz. Although Hildesheimer was a member of the Berlin lodge,[140] he claimed that the members of the Kattowitz chapter were blatantly antireligious. Moritz Moses, a Kattowitz merchant who was a major figure in the organization, was particularly notorious for his nonobservance, in Hildesheimer's opinion. As he saw the rebuilding of the Land of Israel in religious terms, Hildesheimer considered it inappropriate for him to lend formal support to this gathering at Kattowitz. Pinsker could not even persuade him to become an honorary member of the committee.[141]

It is apparent that Hildesheimer made this decision partly based on a judgment he made about his ability to exercise influential religious authority. For Hildesheimer pointed out to Pinsker that his influence among the great bulk of German Jews on such an issue was minimal. His support of the committee and its work would not aid significantly in securing either additional financial or intellectual support for the Zionist organization. He wrote to Pinsker, "You are certainly wrong if you believe that my influence on this question is, in general, effective with my coreligionists."[142] Hildesheimer accepted this fact with equanimity. Rather than feel disturbed by his inability to exercise broad influential authority on this matter, Hildesheimer thought it best not to lose prestige and thus influential authority among those eastern European rabbis who valued his friendship and respected his opinion. For when he wrote to the Warsaw committee that had invited him to attend the meeting, Hildesheimer noted that Rabbi Isaac Elchanan Spektor, Saul Rabinowitz, and David Gordon—all leading eastern European Orthodox figures—would be upset with him for appearing on a committee with people who were nonobservant.[143] Thus he thought it best not to lend the meeting his support. In approaching this matter, Hildesheimer was content not to strive to realize his authority among all elements in the Jewish community. He chose instead to garner a position of respect among the Orthodox. Such a stance indicates a shift from the stratagems he had employed years earlier to realize his religious authority and simultaneously demonstrates his determination to affirm his place in the Orthodox camp.

Finally, Hildesheimer's view that Orthodox religious authority could effectively be achieved by concentrating primarily on the Orthodox members of the community can be seen in his changed position regarding secession. By accepting the post of rabbi of Congregation Adass Jisroel in 1869, Hildesheimer revealed his belief that it was advisable for the Orthodox to create their own religious institutions, such as this "synagogue community," apart from the Reform-dominated Grossgemeinde. Additionally, in 1875, Hildesheimer supported Rabbi Samson Raphael Hirsch in his efforts to have the Prussian parliament pass a Law of Secession that would permit Orthodox Jews in Prussia to secede from and thereby no longer pay taxes to the general Jewish community. The law passed on July 27, 1876, and Hildesheimer was one of those instrumental in its passage.[144] Hildesheimer's activities on behalf of the bill, as well as his ascension to the pulpit of a "separatist" Orthodox congregation in Berlin, testify to his conviction that the Orthodox could best achieve authority by focusing on their own community.[145] In this way, Orthodox religious authority could be established unencumbered by the potential obstacles posed by a Reform majority.[146]

Hildesheimer's experiences in Hungary from 1851 to 1869 convinced him that Orthodoxy could not maintain its hegemony over the total Jewish community in central Europe during the latter half of the nineteenth century. In fact, his own brand of modern Orthodoxy was destined to be uninfluential among other Orthodox groups who rejected the worth of secular culture. Accordingly, Hildesheimer considered it best to appeal to those elements in the Jewish community which simultaneously affirmed both tradition (as interpreted by the modern Orthodox) and the value of Western culture. Such a movement represents a significant shift in his thinking and a pragmatic (albeit honestly held) approach to the problem of effectuating influential religious authority.

By his final years, Hildesheimer had attained a position of stature and respect in the German and European Jewish communities. He was asked by his coreligionists in both Germany and Russia, as well as other places, to adjudicate disputes within the community and to represent the community in relations and dealings with secular authorities in various lands.[147] His students were constantly sought by communities throughout Europe, and by 1884 he could boast that he did not have enough graduates to fill the requests for rabbis that came to his seminary.[148] Even non-Orthodox Jews came to Hildesheimer for advice, and many clearly saw him as the leading Jewish legal authority in all of Germany.[149] Perhaps one of the major indexes of the position of eminence he had earned can be found in remarks Samuel Montagu made about Hildesheimer in a letter he addressed to Benjamin Hirsch, Hildesheimer's nephew, on December

8, 1877. Montagu was one of the most prominent and wealthy Jews in England. In 1890 he established a philanthropic foundation bearing Hildesheimer's name. He wrote: "I had the pleasure of seeing your esteemed uncle, Dr. Hildesheimer, several times. I was glad to make the acquaintance of so worthy a man and so renowned a scholar. I was pleased to find that he holds such liberal ideas in secular matters at the same time being perfectly Orthodox in religion and strictly observing all our holy laws."[150] Such testimony reflects Hildesheimer's persona and explains why he succeeded so well in his program to achieve Orthodox religious authority among certain segments of German Jewry.

In spite of his conviction that Orthodox authority could not be realized in the total community, Hildesheimer remained sensitive to the appeal of both traditional and modern sanctions in his quest for influential religious authority. He continued to combine elements from both in his efforts to achieve that authority and would emphasize one or the other as the situation warranted. For example, Hildesheimer alone among the Orthodox rabbis of Germany in the nineteenth century urged Jews to resolve their civil disputes by coming to a *Bet Din* (Jewish court) for settlement. Hildesheimer's position reflected an attitude common to leaders of the "old Orthodoxy," who, as Ismar Schorsch has described them, "attempted to salvage as much of the judicial autonomy and separatism of the medieval Jewish community as was possible under an unwelcome emancipation." In contrast, Samson Raphael Hirsch "dropped all demands for judicial autonomy and continuance of Jewish civil law." Hirsch, however, in his writings, argued on behalf of the morality inherent in Jewish law.[151]

Hildesheimer, too, saw Emancipation as "desirable." Yet his defense of the traditional institution of the *Bet Din* in civil disputes is an important index of his commitment to tradition. It is significant that his defense of the *Bet Din* is nevertheless couched in modern terms.[152]

Hildesheimer began his defense of this proposal by arguing for the superiority of the *Shulhan Aruch*—the code of Jewish law of which one section, the *Hoshen Mishpat*, is devoted to civil matters—to the German code of law. Prejudice against the *Shulchan Aruch* was unfounded, he argued, because Jewish law remained flexible enough to adjust to the unique circumstances of particular eras. Indeed, this genius of Jewish law made it ideal for application in the contemporary period. Furthermore, if Jews employed this law to settle their civil disputes, they would no longer need to take unnecessary and oftentimes humiliating oaths in secular, gentile courts.[153] Hildesheimer also argued pragmatically that in cases involving only minor costs, the dispute could be handled more quickly and efficiently in the *Bet Din* than in the secular courts. Appealing to Jewish moral sensitivities, Hildesheimer added that, in cases adjudicated by the *Bet Din*, the money normally siphoned off in court costs could be donated to charity. The restitution of the *Bet Din* in civil disputes would raise the esteem of Judaism in the eyes of Jew and gentile alike and would avoid the possible spectacle of "a profanation of God's name" taking place in the secular courts.[154] These arguments on behalf of the *Bet Din* and Jewish law reveal Hildesheimer's receptiveness to his environment and his ability to employ contemporary justifications in defense of a traditional institution. In this sense, his essay in defense of the *Bet Din* is prototypical of the stratagems Hildesheimer employed to achieve Orthodox religious authority.

Hildesheimer's singular awareness of the environment and the weight he assigned it colored his policies and programs for achieving influential authority. In July 1884, the governing board of the Jewish community in Basel asked the local school authorities to excuse Jewish schoolchildren from school attendance on the high holidays and the three pilgrimage festivals (Passover, Shavuot, and Succot). The request was not granted, and the committee decided to design another petition with reference to laws in other lands. Because of his prominence, Hildesheimer was asked about regulations on this matter in Berlin and northern Germany. In a letter dated July 27, 1884, Hildesheimer replied that agitation for the passage of such a law had begun in Prussia in 1869, but the law permitting Jewish pupils to be excused from school on these holidays had not passed until 1884. Even then, the school officials stated that they would not be responsible for any adverse consequences or disadvantages to the Jewish students as a result of their absences. Hildesheimer related that Prussian policy did not permit the schoolteachers to force the Jewish students to write on either the Sabbath or holidays.[155] His letter thus reveals that Jewish students were attending school on these days (including the Sabbath) and that such attendance was a social reality Orthodox Judaism had to contend with during these years.

The universality of this custom of Jewish school attendance on the Sabbath and holidays throughout Germany can be seen in other samples from Hildesheimer's correspondence. Moses Bamberger, the son of Seligman Baer Bamberger and his successor as rabbi in Würzburg, wrote to Hildesheimer in 1882 about the issue of Jewish children exercising in German schools on the Sabbath. Bamberger was concerned both because the matter was of practical import for his community and because he had heard from a rabbinical colleague that Hildesheimer forbade such physical activity. In reply to Bamberger, Hildesheimer admitted that the reason for the prohibition was merely a *shevut* (a rabbinically, as opposed to biblically, proscribed activity on the Sabbath or holidays). He added, however, that the spirit of the Sabbath was such that this physical activity was inappropriate to the Sabbath day. The justification for his stance was thus firmly embedded in rabbinic traditionalism. Nevertheless, Hildesheimer quickly added that he had refrained from issuing an absolute prohibition (*issur*) publicly proscribing it because he was not certain such a ban would be obeyed. Hildesheimer consciously chose not to create a situation in which Jews would knowingly violate this ruling. By refusing to make it into a public issue, Hildesheimer avoided two adverse situations: his authority was not tested, and those Jews who did exercise on the Sabbath in these schools were not guilty of intentionally violating the Sabbath. He asserted that the Jews of Germany had painstakingly gained acceptance from school administrators and that now Jews were not compelled to write in the schools on the Sabbath. He feared that if calisthenics were made into a major issue, that gain might be lost and the Jewish student who told them of this additional prohibition would appear as a "lunatic." As a result, both the individual pupil and the Jewish people would be held up to scorn and derision.[156] The social and cultural environment of nineteenth-century Germany clearly had a decisive impact on Hildesheimer's ruling on this matter and caused him to measure carefully the boundaries in which his authority could be effective.

This issue of Jewish school attendance on the Sabbath exacted Hildesheimer's greatest concession to the German milieu in the form of an innovation he instituted in Congregation Adass Jisroel. So many of Hildesheimer's congregants were attending school on the Sabbath that he ruled that a Torah reading, with the traditional seven Sabbath readers, be held in the afternoon on Saturday. Following the Torah reading, the *Musaf* (additional) service was to be chanted, followed by the regularly prescribed *Minha* (afternoon) service. As the Torah reading and the *Musaf* service were traditionally read in the morning, this constituted a major change in the liturgical life of the congregation. Hildesheimer justified this innovation as an "emergency measure" designed to prevent the Torah "from being forgotten in Israel." He made no attempt to legitimate it from a traditional Jewish legal point of view. A generation later, Rabbi David Hoffmann, Hildesheimer's successor as the head of the Rabbiner-Seminar, when asked to comment on the propriety of this continued practice, admitted that it was of dubious legality. Hoffmann immediately cited the verse employed by rabbis for centuries to justify extraordinary measures in times of stress: "Because it was a time to work for the Lord, they have made void Thy Law" (M. Berachot 9:5) and contended, "An elder has already decided" to defend the legitimacy of the practice.[157] Hildesheimer's rulings in all these cases involving Jewish school attendance on the Sabbath reveal that he was prepared to accommodate his interpretation of Jewish law to the reality of the German social environment. Yet it is equally significant that he legitimated this innovation and his leniencies by an appeal to particular elements in the Jewish legal tradition and not by an outward appeal to the "spirit of the times." Thus, unlike his essay on behalf of the reinstitution of the Bet Din in the civil life of German Jewry, an effort in which he employed primarily modern rationales in support of a traditional institution, here Hildesheimer used traditional considerations found in the halakha to legitimate an innovation in the religious life of German Jewry.

When the community of Isserlohn was considering the adoption of a Reform prayerbook, Hildesheimer justified his opposition to it on both traditional and contemporary grounds. In a letter dated July 9, 1884, Hildesheimer noted that the prayerbook had removed certain sections from the traditional siddur. Consequently, Hildesheimer opposed it. Responding to a matter that was obviously troubling the Jews of Isserlohn, Hildesheimer also stated that selections in the traditional prayerbook referring to Zion and Jerusalem should be understood literally, not metaphorically. The Land of Israel, Hildesheimer wrote, "is our homeland and especially during a time of anti-Semitism our only hope." He noted that there were already about twenty Jewish colonies established in Palestine and that hopes for a Jewish settlement there continued to grow. These realities, combined with his recognition of German anti-Semitism and his disenchantment with the unrealized promises offered by the universalism of the Emancipation, prompted Hildesheimer to respond as he did. In writing about the prayers relating to sacrifice, however,

Hildesheimer did opine that these prayers should be seen partially as a spiritual ideal. The Reformers also objected to these prayers, yet Hildesheimer was not afraid to take his audience and his own views into consideration to reach a similar conclusion. He commented that the prayers relating to sacrifice should be taken literally only insofar "as repentance is a necessary component of sacrifice."[158] Here again, as was the case in his argument for reinstating the *Bet Din*, moral considerations derived from the worldview of the dominant culture played an important role in the formulation and presentation of his views. Indeed, even if the point could be made that ethical concerns were derived from the tradition, it is also correct to assert that such views dovetailed nicely with the views of morality his acculturated Jewish community would have received from the writings of Kant and Hegel. As such, they were particularly effective in aiding Hildesheimer in his quest for authority in the community.

The positions and attacks of the Reformers remained a serious consideration for Hildesheimer during his years in the German capital. His responsa reflect this consciousness. He disapproved of the irreligiousness of his generation. Typically, he wrote in 1885, "We have a great deal to lament and complain about in this orphaned generation in which many of our brothers in the household of Israel make permissible what the Mishnah specifically identifies as transgressions against the Jewish religion." It was not uncommon to find even Jewish religious officiants violating what Hildesheimer regarded as essential elements of Jewish religious observance. For example, he noted that a *mohel* (ritual circumciser) in a given community had a wife who went out in public with her head uncovered. Such an act, in Hildesheimer's opinion, constituted a violation of Jewish law on the wife's part and indicated that the *mohel* lacked sufficient "awe of heaven." Such a man, he felt, ought not to serve in a religious office. But he refused to declare the man unfit for his office and stated that such a decision depended on local conditions, that is, perhaps the Reformers would replace this man with an even less observant Jew. As a result, Hildesheimer ruled that the continued use of this man in this job depended solely upon "discretion [shikul daat]." That is, the local rabbi, in light of local conditions, had to decide whether such a man should be employed in the office of *mohel* by the community.[159]

Another responsum addressed to Rabbi Salomon Carlebach in 1879 testifies to Hildesheimer's sensitivity to Reform and its challenge to religious authority. Rabbi Carlebach had told Hildesheimer that too few Jews were coming to the synagogue early on Saturday morning for there to be a prayer quorum for the *Shaharit* (morning) service. Therefore, the *Shemoneh Esreh* prayer in the morning service could not first be prayed silently by the congregation and then repeated aloud, as was the custom in Orthodox synagogues. One possible solution which Carlebach suggested was for the cantor to recite the prayer out loud without having the congregation pray silently beforehand. Yet, because this was the custom in most liberal synagogues in Germany, both Carlebach and Hildesheimer feared that the Reformers would cite it as a precedent for their custom. Hildesheimer eventually assented to this suggestion but emphasized that the reasons for the change should be carefully noted so that it could not be interpreted as a general sanction for change. "Yet who knows, God forbid, what the Reformers will do?" Hildesheimer wrote. "Our only obligation is to be as careful in our warnings as possible." Again, Hildesheimer contended that common sense in situations such as this must serve as the Orthodox Jews' guide.[160]

Several other halakhic decisions demonstrate Hildesheimer's singular approach to the question of authority in light of the nonobservance and Reform that marked the German Jewry of his day. He stated that it was permitted to eat in the home of a Jewish woman whose husband profaned the Sabbath. In fact, Hildesheimer claimed that—assuming the woman herself was observant—a Jew was obligated to do so. Otherwise, the Orthodox would be guilty of "repelling her with both hands" and, consequently, might be the cause of her nonobservance.[161] The pressures of the age figured in another decision rendered in a separate episode. A woman had deserted her husband for a lover and was nowhere to be found. It was unclear whether she desired a divorce from her husband. The husband, however, had met another woman in the meantime and desired to marry her. A civil divorce had been granted, and he had now come to a Jewish court to initiate proceedings for a *get* (Jewish divorce), which would permit him to marry again in a Jewish religious ceremony. The problem was that Jewish law stipulated that a woman could not be divorced without her consent, and consequently—in light of the first wife's absence—the Jewish court was reluctant to grant the husband the divorce. The man threatened that he would marry the second woman in a civil ceremony in the event that the *Bet Din* would not issue a *get*. Hildesheimer acknowledged that the situation was a difficult one but maintained that "on account of the pressure of the age . . . it is better to grant him a religious divorce than to permit him to marry a second wife [in a civil ceremony]."[162]

Hildesheimer was obviously unhappy over the lack of imperative authority the Orthodox could exercise in nineteenth-century Germany. Still, he accepted the reality of the situation and felt that the utmost should be done, when Jewish law would not be violated, to exercise discretion so as to maximize Orthodox authority and influence in any given situation.

This approach is underscored in his attitude toward the conversion of a gentile man who wanted to be able to marry a Jewish woman. The young woman in this case was only nineteen. She thus needed her father's permission to marry under civil law and had threatened to commit suicide or convert to Christianity if the young man was denied her. The father refused to grant such permission, however, unless the man converted to Judaism. The rabbi who had become involved in the matter, Jakob Hollander, told Hildesheimer that he was sure the young man would not be observant Jewishly after the conversion because his job necessitated his working on the Sabbath and Jewish holidays. Hollander was predisposed not to officiate at the young man's conversion.

There were, however, several other considerations in this case. First, the father had informed Hollander that if he refused to perform the conversion, he would take the gentile to a *mohel* who had already agreed to circumcise him. The father would then consider the young man to be Jewish and would betroth him to his daughter. Second, Hollander had heard that there was a liberal rabbi who would accept such a young man as a convert. Hollander feared that the man would go to this rabbi and thus mistakenly be identified, both in his own eyes and in those of the community, as a Jew. Here the Reform challenge to Orthodox religious authority within the community was made manifest and was seen as providing a possible reason for allowing Hollander to convert the young man to Judaism.[163] Hildesheimer agonized over what ruling to issue in this particular case. He replied to Hollander: "Your question is one of the most difficult of our times and, truly, it seems to depend upon *discretion*. It is [impossible] to render an absolute decision in this matter." He concluded by stating that Hollander should not feel obligated to convert the young man and left the final decision up to Hollander.[164] It would seem that Hildesheimer felt keenly the challenge Reform and nonobservance posed to the exercise of his religious authority. Yet he saw the response to be issued as a complex and subtle one which had to be based on a flexible recognition of the social and religious realities of the community. As a result, the Orthodox, in issuing rulings on such matters, had to be guided by discretion.

Although the principle of common sense often meant that a flexibility and openness to different solutions to given situations had to be recognized, it also indicated that, in certain instances, only one course of action could be followed. For example, Michael Cahn, a former pupil of Hildesheimer's who was the rabbi in Fulda, wrote to Hildesheimer and told him that he was having trouble securing funds for Russian Jewish refugees who were victims of the Russian pogroms of 1880–81. The reason for this difficulty was that the committee charged by a Berlin conference in 1882 with responsibility for the care of these people was unconcerned with the religious needs of the Russian Jews. Cahn suggested that a secret committee be established to care for their needs and that Hildesheimer and Samson Raphael Hirsch be on the committee. The information about the establishment of this committee would be circulated secretly in all Orthodox circles and a separate collection to aid the Russians could be instituted.[165]

Hildesheimer responded to Cahn's suggestions in a strongly worded letter on June 8, 1882. He labeled the plan "unsuitable, impractical, and dangerous." It would only serve to unleash "a storm of indignation" against the Orthodox and would diminish Orthodox prestige in the general community. Although Hildesheimer acknowledged that Cahn's idea was motivated by the highest concerns, he dubbed it a "piece of fantasy." It was essential, Hildesheimer told Cahn, to be realistic and to note the risks such an operation would pose to the Orthodox in the total community.[166]

Hildesheimer's ability to recognize the realities of a situation and to design or reject a program for effectuating Orthodox religious authority on the basis of such insight thus emerges as one of the most characteristic elements in his approach to the issue of religious authority. Hildesheimer, as we have seen, came to understand early in his career that Orthodox religious authority had to be exercised through influence, not command, if it was to be successful among the acculturated Jews of nineteenth-century central Europe. Changes in the social, political, and cultural structure of Jewish life during this era necessitated this new approach to the question of authority. An inability or unwillingness to adapt, as exemplified by the conduct of

Mattathias Levian in Halberstadt in 1847, would have resulted, in Hildesheimer's view, in less and less Orthodox influence and authority. Consequently, Hildesheimer appropriated modern cultural styles and arguments, which came naturally to him in light of his own education, as well as traditional ones, in his pursuit of religious authority.

After 1851, however, when he entered his duties in Hungary, Hildesheimer realized that Orthodox authority in general and modern Orthodox authority in particular could not be achieved in the entire community. The nonacculturated Orthodox Jews of Hungary rejected his manifestations of modernity—secular education, acceptance of choirs in the synagogue, modern dress, sermons in the vernacular, and the like—as heretical and branded him an enemy of Orthodox Judaism. Meanwhile, the Neologues regarded him as an obscurantist and condemned him and his commitment to modernity whenever possible. Hildesheimer accepted this situation and, in 1869, moved to Berlin, an arena that would prove more amenable to his brand of Orthodox Judaism.

His experience in Hungary and the existence of a Reform majority in the Jewish community of Germany from the very start predisposed him to recognize that Orthodox authority could not be attained in the total Jewish community of Germany. M. A. Shulvass provides the following analysis of German Jewry at the end of the century: "The bitter war between the Orthodox and the Liberals . . . was an inheritance of the past. It was now clear to Orthodox Jewry that it was consigned to a minority status among the Jews of Germany. Therefore, the major problem was to strengthen knowledge of Torah among Orthodox Jews, so that their Judaism would not be confined to the synagogue alone."[167] Shulvass's observation, though undoubtedly correct, shows that by the turn of the century the lines between Orthodox and liberal Judaism in Germany had been firmly drawn. The identities of the two communities were established, and there was no longer the need for the polemic which had marked earlier decades in the nineteenth century. Nevertheless, this should not alter our understanding of what was an ongoing and dynamic social process. For a group to maintain its cohesion and sense of identity, there remains a constant need to establish boundaries. As a result, Hildesheimer supported Orthodox efforts at secession and believed that modern Orthodoxy ought to accept the very real limits the modern situation placed on its adherents. The Orthodox, in Hildesheimer's opinion, needed to focus on consolidating and shaping their influence and authority among those Jews who affirmed a dual commitment to religious traditionalism and modern culture. This position, initially formed in Hungary, became fully developed in Germany during the last part of his career. In a sense, Hildesheimer's goals for achieving religious authority became less ambitious as they became more focused. Whereas the modern Jewish world was still taking shape in 1847, when Hildesheimer first served the community of Halberstadt, twenty-five years later, when he served the Jewish community of Berlin as a mature rabbi, the Jewish world was clearly defined and included a variety of constituencies. Hildesheimer came to accept that Orthodox authority could be influential only in the area of religion and therefore that he need only concern himself with those Jews who were "religious" on his terms.

The preceding examples show, however, that Hildesheimer remained very much aware of the total Jewish community. He eventually came to concentrate certain religious goals, such as his leadership of a separatist Orthodox congregation, exclusively within the modern Orthodox community. And though he maintained a unique consciousness of and concern for the wider, pluralistic Jewish and non-Jewish worlds, it was his recognition of those worlds that allowed him to distinguish between religious and nonreligious spheres. Having made such a distinction, Hildesheimer limited his efforts to exercising influential authority to the Orthodox realm.

Hildesheimer's career thus reveals a mixture of the pragmatic and the ideal, the traditional and the modern. Although he could not always avoid the ideological tensions such combinations could produce, this approach allowed him to create a viable Orthodoxy and a concomitant degree of religious authority among the Jews of nineteenth-century Germany. As a result, he established a paradigm for later generations of modern Orthodox Jews to follow in their search for religious authority. In this way, Esriel Hildesheimer's quest for religious authority holds up a mirror to the nature of Judaism's response to the modern world and contains a significance that extends beyond his time and place.

3

The Confrontations with Jewish Religious and Cultural Pluralism

J ewish life in medieval Germany was not monolithic. Tensions did exist in the religious and cultural life of the community. Yet in the eyes of Hildesheimer and the Orthodox, the premodern period of German-Jewish history was marked by a high degree of Jewish religious and cultural homogeneity. Most Jews, they believed, had held to the doctrine of *Torah Min HaShamayim* and assigned halakhah the central role in Jewish life during the centuries immediately before Emancipation. It is little wonder, then, that Hildesheimer perceived the heterodoxy that marked the Jewish community of Germany during the nineteenth century as unparalleled in Jewish history. Reflecting on the Jewish scene as a young man in 1847, Hildesheimer wrote: "The lawless who denied the Torah were dominant everywhere . . . and those who feared God cowered before such enemies and despisers of religion. . . . Such a time of distress had almost never been visited upon Israel previously."[1]

Under the leadership of Hirsch, Bamberger, and Hildesheimer, the Orthodox continued to affirm their belief in the divinity of *Torah Min HaShamayim* and to contend that the halakhah and faith in its divine legitimation were the most essential characteristics of the Jewish religion. Yet the Orthodox also had to confront the fact that most Jews in Germany during the nineteenth century neither made this assertion nor clung to this belief. Moreover, two trends in liberal Judaism (Reform and Positive-Historical) had arisen, claiming religious authenticity on the basis of theological doctrines that departed radically from the Orthodox. By the latter part of the century, secular movements such as Zionism had also begun to appear on the

Jewish scene. These developments could not be ignored, and, as we saw in the previous chapter, they played a significant role in shaping the stratagems Hildesheimer devised to effectuate Orthodox authority in the Jewish community. The reality of Jewish pluralism thus constituted a central element in the consciousness of Hildesheimer and the Orthodox during this era. Defining the nature of the relationship between Orthodox and heterodox Jewish groups became one of the crucial tasks of Hildesheimer's rabbinate.

The dynamics of this task were made more complex by two major considerations. On one hand, Hildesheimer and the Orthodox perceived themselves to be "the only legitimate bearer[s] of the Jewish tradition."[2] Cooperation with non-Orthodox bodies might imply recognition of their legitimacy, in the eyes of both Orthodox and non-Orthodox Jews.[3] This was a development Hildesheimer clearly wanted to avoid. On the other hand, the existence of these competing groups could not be denied. Moreover, on certain issues, the interests of the Orthodox might best be served by cooperating with the non-Orthodox. Guidance was thus sought as to how the Orthodox in Germany should address and relate themselves to these non-Orthodox persons and movements within the contemporary Jewish community. Esriel Hildesheimer endeavored to provide the leadership they were seeking.

As a student of both Rabbi Jacob Ettlinger and Hacham Isaac Bernays, Hildesheimer was greatly influenced by their attitudes concerning Jewish religious and cultural pluralism. Ettlinger and Bernays fought actively against the advances of Reform. Meir Hildesheimer, Esriel's great-grandson, has observed: "Rabbi Ettlinger did not enclose himself within the four ells of halakhah, but waged a stormy war against the Reform Movement and for this purpose founded the weekly journal, *Der Zionswaechter* [The Faithful Guardian of Zion]. The Hacham Bernays also fought aggressively against the Reformers. The example of these two . . . men taught him [Esriel Hildesheimer] that a rabbi in Israel is obligated to take an active part in improving the religious situation [of Jewry]."[4]

Following the examples set by his teachers, Hildesheimer felt compelled to engage in an active fight against religious reform. At the urging of his rabbis, Hildesheimer determined that he would earn a secular doctorate at a German university. Armed with this degree, and thus able to elevate "the estimation of our party" in the eyes of the public, Hildesheimer felt himself capable of doing battle with those groups that had deviated from normative Judaism.[5]

Exposed to and made conscious of Reform during his student days in Altona, Berlin, and Halle, Hildesheimer found the opportunity to combat Reform publicly as a champion of Orthodoxy in 1847 when he returned to Halberstadt to serve as secretary of the community. As described in an earlier chapter, Reform came to Halberstadt that year, and Ludwig Philippson, the editor of the *Allgemeine Zeitung des Judentums*, began to campaign on its behalf in the pages of his journal. When Philippson convened a meeting of all the Jewish communities in Saxony on October 22, 1847, Hildesheimer walked out of the conference and employed the Leipzig periodical *Der Orient* both to defend Orthodoxy and to attack Reform.[6] Echoing the sentiments of his teacher Ettlinger, who had stressed that "reproof and censure of wrongdoers is a moral obligation which a leader dare not shirk,"[7] Hildesheimer wrote that he had not desired to quarrel with the Reformers. "However," he continued, "the love of peace also has an end."[8] In addition, Hildesheimer wrote a pamphlet entitled "The Necessity of Protest against the Actions of the Reformers," which he circulated among all the delegates who had attended the Magdeburg Conference. Hildesheimer felt it his solemn duty to protect the Jewish community from the evils of religious reform. He described the feelings motivating his involvement in these disputes in a letter to Moses Mendelssohn of Frankfurt, an uncle of Samson Raphael Hirsch.[9] Writing on November 20, 1847, Hildesheimer stated: "When I began to fight with Philippson and his lawless peers . . . I was very bitter that no one else seemed to be upset over the situation, that no great man stood up in order to overturn these licentious persons who disrupted the vineyard of the Lord of Hosts. . . . Finally, when I saw that no one acted, I felt that this was no time to refrain from expressing my thoughts on account of embarrassment or humility."

In concluding this explanation to Mendelssohn, Hildesheimer added: "Not out of arrogance did I plunge in, but rather to raise the esteem of Torah and piety. And may this be my reward for all my labors."[10]

Hildesheimer was partially successful in his struggle with the Reformers in Saxony during 1847. His writings and his activities in these episodes reveal that Hildesheimer did not accept the legitimacy of religious pluralism with Judaism. He refused to concede the validity of non-Orthodox expressions of the Jewish religion.

As a result, Hildesheimer held totally negative attitudes toward both trends in German liberal Judaism, Reform and Positive-

Historical. His annoyance with and genuine anger at Reform can be glimpsed on almost every page of his writings. It is hardly surprising, then, that Hildesheimer wrote disparagingly of the Hochschule für die Wissenschaft des Judentums, the Reform rabbinical seminary established by Abraham Geiger in 1872. In a letter he sent to supporters throughout Germany calling on them to donate funds for the establishment of an Orthodox rabbinical seminary, he characterized Geiger's school as an institution devoted to the destruction of Judaism. He went so far as to apply the words of Psalm 137:7 to the institution, "Raze it, raze it to its very foundation."[11]

Hildesheimer's bitter opposition to the Hochschule and Reform was based, in part, on grounds of religious praxis. He decried the many violations of Jewish religious law exhibited by the Reformers and deemed them to be sufficient reason for defining Reform as an illegitimate religious movement and Reform rabbis as inauthentic and unqualified for the post of Jewish spiritual leader. These attitudes are borne out in a letter Hildesheimer wrote on January 15, 1879, to Moritz Baum of Bonn concerning Rabbi Emanuel Schreiber, a former student of Hildesheimer's in Eisenstadt. After receiving rabbinical ordination from Hildesheimer, Schreiber migrated to Berlin, where he attended the Hochschule and joined the Reform camp. Shortly thereafter, Schreiber accepted a position in Bonn. Baum had written to Hildesheimer to inquire whether Schreiber, particularly in light of his training under Hildesheimer, should be regarded as a rabbi. Hildesheimer replied by stating emphatically that a knowledge of Jewish sources and Jewish law alone was not enough to qualify one for the title of rabbi. To merit the title, a man must live according to Jewish law. Schreiber did not fulfill this last requirement. Hildesheimer concluded his letter to Baum by declaring, "I herewith rescind the rabbinical title which was bestowed years ago [by me upon Schreiber]."[12] Schreiber's failure to abide by Orthodox standards of religious practice meant that Hildesheimer could not legitimate his claim to the title of rabbi.[13]

Yet ultimately, Hildesheimer's reason for revoking Schreiber's rabbinical ordination was theological. Hildesheimer's teacher Rabbi Ettlinger had taught that the question of revelation was central to the differences dividing Reform from Orthodox Judaism. The fundamental principle of Judaism was that the Torah, both written and oral, had been revealed by the Almighty to the people Israel during their years in the desert. To deny this, Ettlinger believed, was to deny the essence of Judaism.[14] Hildesheimer concurred with this view and, consequently, could not recognize Reform Judaism as a legitimate form of religious Judaism. Similarly, the Hochschule could not be seen as a fit institution in which to study for the rabbinate because the religious views of its founder and head, Abraham Geiger, were antithetical to Orthodox notions of the nature of revelation. Geiger's *Urschrift und Uebersetzungen der Bibel,* published in 1857, was heretical, in Hildesheimer's opinion, inasmuch as it "denied the divine source of the Bible," thus undermining the traditional basis for Jewish faith.[15] Even if Geiger and the Reformers had been *orthoprax* in their observance of Judaism (which they were not), Hildesheimer, acting in accordance with traditional rabbinic usage,[16] would still not have recognized their legitimacy as rabbis and religious Jews because their theology negated the foundations upon which Judaism was established.

This point is underscored by Hildesheimer's actions in an episode that took place in 1867–68 while he was still the rabbi of Eisenstadt. Dr. Moritz Benedikt, a Viennese neurologist, wanted to marry a proselyte who had been converted to Judaism by a *Bet Din* consisting of Geiger, Rabbi Moses Landsberger of Darmstadt, and Rabbi Solomon Formstecher of Offenbach. Benedikt and his fiancée, Aloysia Lea Grimm, wanted to be married in Vienna. But because he hailed from Eisenstadt, civil law required that he be issued a certificate from the rabbi in his home community permitting him to be married in Vienna. Subsequently, Benedikt wrote to Hildesheimer requesting such a certificate. Hildesheimer, after learning all the facts in the case, replied to Benedikt that the matter was one of great import. He assured Benedikt that he valued his friendship very much and hoped that Benedikt would understand that in deciding whether to issue the certificate he had to follow the dictates of his conscience. Hildesheimer hoped that Benedikt would not take personal offense at his decision but stated that he could not issue Benedikt the certificate. To do so, Hildesheimer contended, would mean that he accepted the validity of the fiancée's conversion to Judaism and thus, by extension, the right of such a *Bet Din* to perform such an act. Though unfailingly polite and even warm in the tone of his letter to Benedikt, Hildesheimer was unbending in regard to what he saw as the religious principles involved in the case.[17]

Hildesheimer rejected the woman's conversion to Judaism on three specific grounds. First, he stated that her conversion document was invalid because it did not specify that she had been immersed in a ritual bath as required by Jewish law. Second, Hildesheimer claimed that as there was an ulterior motive for her converting to Judaism—she wanted to marry a Jewish man—"her acceptance is to be rejected."[18] Finally, and for this study this is the most important point, Hildesheimer contended that he could not accept the woman's conversion to Judaism because all three rabbis who sat on the *Bet Din* that had admitted her to Judaism were well-known "heretics," that is, persons who denied the fundamental principles of the Jewish faith. Hildesheimer's fierce opposition to Reform was thus based not only on the deviations Reform exhibited concerning Jewish religious practice but on the Reformers' departure from what he considered normative Jewish theology.

Hildesheimer's opinion of the Positive-Historical camp in central European Judaism and the Jewish Theological Seminary in Breslau headed by Zacharias Frankel was equally derisory. As Hildesheimer wrote: "How little is the principled difference between these reformers [the Breslau people] who do their work with silk gloves on their hands and the Reformer Geiger who strikes with a sledgehammer."[19] Although Hildesheimer drew a distinction between Geiger and Frankel in the realm of praxis, he believed that both men practiced and taught an inauthentic Judaism, which had to be tolerated because of contemporary conditions but could not be seen as genuine.

Hildesheimer's writings clearly express his position regarding Frankel and the Positive-Historical school. As early as 1861 Hildesheimer chided his friend Wolf Feilchenfeld for his association with circles close to the Jewish Theological Seminary in Breslau and, in the same letter, boasted: "I tell you that for a long time I have had the merit of dissuading youth from going to Breslau to study, for they can only be transformed there into hypocrites and worse."[20]

These remarks were occasioned by a letter in which Feilchenfeld had complained to Hildesheimer about a sharp attack issued by Gottlieb Fischer, in a series of two articles entitled "Ein Sendschreiben an alle Freunde unserer jüdischen Zukunft," against Frankel's *Darkhe HaMishnah*. The articles written in Hebrew and translated and published in German by Samson Raphael Hirsch, in *Jeschurun*, accused Frankel of heresy. Frankel's book, as Fischer interpreted it, cast doubts on the notion that the entire Oral Law emerged with Moses from Mount Sinai.[21] Feilchenfeld was very disturbed over the tone of the article, whereas Hildesheimer stated, "The article gives me satisfaction." Fischer, Hildesheimer reported, was a God-fearing Jew who deserved respect and thanks for what he did.[22]

Hildesheimer obviously held a different opinion of Frankel. Indeed, Hildesheimer admitted to Feilchenfeld that even before the publication of *Darkhe HaMishnah* he was "predisposed against him." This negative predisposition toward Frankel resulted from two separate incidents that had occurred approximately two decades earlier. In 1839, Rabbi Eleazar Rokeach, one of the most prominent Orthodox rabbis in Hungary, headed a *Bet Din* which investigated charges of religious misconduct against Rabbi Jonathan Alexandersohn of the community of Csaba. Tensions between Alexandersohn and a number of persons in the Csaba community had been rising in the past few years and Rokeach and his court, after hearing the evidence, concluded that Alexandersohn was guilty of attempting "to destroy the religion of our Holy Torah and the foundation of our faith." The Hatam Sofer concurred with their decision and Alexandersohn was forced to leave his post.[23]

Alexandersohn's response was to travel from place to place seeking support for his position and attempting to defend his honor against what he considered to be the unfair judgment of the court. One of his chief advocates in this struggle was Frankel. Frankel even sent a letter to Moses Sofer regarding Sofer's conduct in this entire episode. The letter containing the sharp attack on Sofer was also sent to the *Allgemeine Zeitung des Judentums*. Sofer himself never saw the published letter because it did not appear until November 21, 1839, almost seven weeks after Sofer's death in October of that year.[24] Sofer was, of course, seen as the foremost leader and outstanding champion of Orthodoxy in Hungary. To the young Hildesheimer and other Hungarian Orthodox Jews, Frankel's letter was a direct insult to Sofer and, through him, to Jewish Orthodoxy.

Frankel's actions two years later in an incident involving Hacham Isaac Bernays of Hamburg intensified Hildesheimer's suspicions and created feelings of genuine dislike in Hildesheimer against Frankel. In 1841, Bernays issued a strong attack against the Reform temple in Hamburg and its new reformed prayerbook. Frankel elected to comment on both the activities of the Hamburg Reformers and the criticisms issued against them by Bernays in an article in *Der Orient* in 1842. Although Frankel was likewise critical of several items in the new prayerbook adopted by the Reformers, he employed moderate and respectful language in expressing his dissent. He was brutal, however, in his criticism of Bernays, identifying him as "Mr." and not "Rabbi" Bernays. In Frankel's opinion, Bernays's attack was undignified. As Frankel wrote, "Mr. Bernays has taken an action which is not fitting for holy men and rabbis." Additionally, Frankel questioned Bernays's academic competence and claimed that Bernays erred in several criticisms he had offered against the Reformers. Consequently, "It is necessary to condemn him," Frankel wrote. He concluded by stating, "Mr. Bernays has sinned the greatest of all sins."[25]

As Bernays's student, Hildesheimer saw himself as walking in Bernays's footsteps. Frankel's attack on Bernays thus alienated, probably intentionally, Orthodox Jews in Germany such as Hildesheimer and clearly identified Frankel as being apart from their world. It is little wonder that Hildesheimer, in writing to Feilchenfeld in 1861, should have mentioned this episode as well as the one involving Frankel's attack on Sofer, as reasons why he disliked and distrusted Frankel.

Again, though, the point must be made that Hildesheimer's sharp attack on Frankel and the Breslau seminary extends beyond the personal pique he certainly felt. Rather, it stems from the fact that Hildesheimer, like Fischer, regarded Frankel's work on the development of the Mishnah, as articulated in *Darkhe HaMishnah*, as the work of a heretic. Indeed, Hildesheimer made this clear not only in the letter to Feilchenfeld but on at least two other occasions. In the first instance, Hildesheimer wrote a responsum in 1873, in which he declared that Frankel's book should not be treated with respect. He stated that were it not that God's name appeared in the work, "then perhaps it would be considered a commandment [*mitzvah*] to burn it." He asserted that *Darkhe HaMishnah* was the work of a *meshummad*, an apostate who literally seeks to destroy the Jewish religion and the Jewish people, "a more severe category than *apikoris*," a heretic who simply denies the fundamental principles of the Jewish faith for himself.[26]

Evidence of Hildesheimer's views can be seen in a letter he wrote to Wilhelm Karl von Rothschild on October 20, 1879: "I do not know whether you are aware that about three-quarters of a year ago some members of a community in Russia turned to Samson Raphael Hirsch, Dr. Lehmann, and myself with the question as to whether one can put one's mind to rest with the appointment of a graduate of the Breslau school [to the post of community rabbi]. . . . Our judgment, of course, was negative."[27] Hildesheimer's opposition to the Breslau seminary was intractable. It occupied such a prominent place in his consciousness that even on the occasion of his greatest joy, the opening of the Berlin Rabbinical Seminary in 1873, he was able to declare that his happiness was magnified because "the Children of Israel in Germany will no longer need to request rabbis from the seminary in Breslau."[28]

Similarly, in 1879, when a group of men in the community of Trier asked Hildesheimer whether it was permissible for the community to select a graduate of the Breslau seminary as its rabbi, Hildesheimer's reply was an emphatic no. Frankel's *Darkhe HaMishnah*, he declared, was a heretical work and, consequently, Frankel was unqualified to ordain anyone as a rabbi among the people Israel. Hildesheimer held that if a Breslau graduate was selected as the community's rabbi, observant Jews were obligated to secede from the community.[29] Hildesheimer delineated the reasons for his opposition to Frankel and the Breslau seminary in a correspondence he carried on with Theodor Kroner, a graduate of the Breslau seminary, who had applied for the post of community rabbi in Trier. Kroner, who considered himself to be a knowledgeable and observant Jew and rabbi, was naturally upset with Hildesheimer's recommendations to the community. Hildesheimer replied by assuring Kroner that his opposition to Kroner's candidacy was not meant as a personal attack on him. The letter against Kroner, Hildesheimer explained, was written "without jealousy and strove to be totally objective." Hildesheimer continued: "It is correct that I stated that no graduate of the Jewish Theological Seminary should be selected, and that one should secede from the community if he is picked. To my sorrow, my conscience does not permit me to come to another conclusion. . . . It grieves me greatly to have to write this."[30] As in the letter to Moritz Benedikt, Hildesheimer was unfailingly polite and exhibited no animus toward his religious opponent. But he was adamant and uncompromising on what he saw as a matter of religious principle.

Hildesheimer informed Kroner that graduates of the Breslau seminary could not be recognized as legitimate rabbis because the seminary—both its students and faculty—was not wholly committed "to the words of the Sages and their customs." Breslau graduates, Hildesheimer contended, did not prohibit the purchase of milk produced under gentile supervision. He admitted to Kroner, however, that this was a matter that was debatable even in Orthodox circles. Other issues were not debatable, he maintained. Thus, that Breslau graduates did not normally forbid the buying of gentile wine was, in Hildesheimer's opinion, a major violation of Jewish law. Indeed, he held that if one of his own ordinees would permit such a thing, he would immediately rescind his ordination. Breslau graduates were also guilty of another major and perhaps even more serious transgression of Jewish law. Most of them, Hildesheimer observed, allowed their wives to appear in public without a head covering. This was an extremely serious trespass of Jewish religious practice, and Hildesheimer insisted that no man could be considered a fit candidate for the rabbinate if he permitted such behavior. On these grounds of religious practice, then, Hildesheimer did not feel that he could accept the Breslau seminary and its graduates as suitable representatives of Judaism.[31]

Hildesheimer did not stop with these practical objections to the Positive-Historical school. Instead, he added that "there are important differences of [religious] opinion between us." Hildesheimer outlined these differences and professed that a graduate of the Breslau seminary could be deemed a qualified rabbi only if he fulfilled four conditions. First, the individual would have to proclaim publicly his belief in the doctrine of *Halakha l'Moshe mi'Sinai.* That is, he would have to declare that he believed that this talmudic phrase referred directly and literally to Moses' receipt of certain laws while he was on Mt. Sinai. This, he knew, would run counter to Frankel's research on the phrase. Frankel had declared that the phrase, when it appeared in the Talmud, simply referred to a law that was of such antiquity that it was as if it had been revealed to Moses at Sinai. This first condition thus meant that a Breslau graduate would, in effect, have to repudiate the scholarship of his own teacher, Zacharias Frankel, the man who had ordained him.[32] Second, Hildesheimer stipulated that the graduate would have to declare his belief in the holiness and divine origin of both the Written and Oral Law. Third, this individual would have to acknowledge publicly the erroneous conclusions of historical investigation about the development of the Oral Law as put forth by Frankel.[33] Finally, he would have to sever all ties with the Breslau seminary. Hildesheimer alleged that if all these demands were met, he might change his opinion and recognize the individual as a rabbi. But he gave no assurances that he would do so and stated that he felt these conditions were impossible to fulfill. He concluded by once again telling Kroner that he held no personal bias against him and that he hoped Kroner would understand that a matter of religious principle was at stake.[34]

Kroner did not give up after this first response from Hildesheimer and wrote to him again. The contents of his letter can be reconstructed from Hildesheimer's response. Kroner had written to assure Hildesheimer of his strictness in matters of religious observance and told Hildesheimer that he was even more stringent in this regard than were many graduates of the Berlin Rabbinical Seminary. He also informed Hildesheimer that he, as well as a majority of the students at Breslau, believed that the Oral Law was of divine origin and that it had not developed in history, as some historical critics claimed. Kroner thus portrayed himself as, and appears to have been, a very traditional graduate of the Breslau seminary.

Hildesheimer reassured Kroner that he accepted Kroner's testimony about himself. He was sure that Kroner was observant and that Kroner did affirm the literal notion of *Torah Min HaShamayim*, the fundamental axiom on which Judaism was based. Nonetheless, Hildesheimer noted that Kroner could not "deny that Professor Graetz has another view, and it is well known that he has always been an important force at the Jewish Theological Seminary. In fact, his strength and influence grow there daily even now."[35]

Hildesheimer had long regarded Graetz, with his historical approach to Judaism, as the worst of the heretics. Many years before his exchange with Kroner, Hildesheimer had commented disapprovingly on the propriety of Graetz's teaching in a rabbinical seminary in a letter to Feilchenfeld:

> Graetz teaches one class there [at the Breslau seminary] in Talmud. What a mockery under the guise of being Judaism. It is an unprecedented disgrace. Anyone who witnesses this needs to overcome a feeling of genuine grief. One sees innocent children being led there to the slaughter, one after another, and they are reduced to a lower level than that of common sinners in Israel. They are made into hypocrites, Jesuits, and heretics just like Graetz, who, as I know from a reliable source, waves the *lulav* in his hands on Succot as if he were a Hasidic rebbe.[36]

Hildesheimer's hatred of Graetz's religious views and Graetz's prominent place on the faculty of the Breslau seminary added yet another set of reasons to mark the seminary as totally unfit to train future rabbis. "So long as Graetz remains in the institution, we will never give our approval to students educated there," Hildesheimer wrote. Hildesheimer granted that it might be possible for a Breslau graduate (such as Kroner) to hold a belief in *Torah Min HaShamayim*, but he quoted the talmudic phrase "We do not depend upon a miracle" to indicate his doubts that, except in the rarest of cases, it would, in fact, happen.[37]

Hildesheimer did not let the matter rest even there. Returning to a practical level, he noted that many Breslau graduates served Reform congregations and communities and said that even traditionally oriented alumni of Breslau were inclined to "compromise several commandments and customs 'for the sake of peace.'" This, to Hildesheimer, was intolerable when matters of religious principle were involved. Yet he made clear once more that his ultimate objection to the Jewish Theological Seminary was based on ideology, not praxis. It is interesting in light of his objections to Frankel's religious views that Hildesheimer recognized Frankel as an outstanding scholar. Yet Kroner could not deny, Hildesheimer stated, that Frankel, like the more extreme Graetz, did believe in the principle of historical development in regard to Judaism. Graetz was, perhaps, more objectionable than Frankel, but both men, in Hildesheimer's view, were unacceptable from a religious standpoint. Certainly, neither was qualified to ordain rabbis in Israel. Thus Hildesheimer concluded his second letter to Kroner by observing: "How will it be possible for unity to exist between those graduates of the Jewish Theological Seminary who are inclined to [share our views] and us? To my sorrow, I can only answer you accordingly—in the present situation any unity is impossible."[38]

These letters to Kroner, taken in concert with his views on Frankel and Graetz, as well as Geiger and the Reformers, display an absolute consistency in Hildesheimer's attitude toward liberal Judaism. Both Reform and Positive-Historical Judaism, in Hildesheimer's view, deviated from normative Judaism. More serious, however, was the deviance they exhibited in religious belief. He recognized that Reform parted more radically from traditional Jewish practice than did the Positive-Historical school, but both were equally guilty of separating themselves from the traditional theological notions upon which Judaism rested. Although he strove to be courteous in his relations with non-Orthodox Jewish individuals on religious matters (e.g., Benedikt and Kroner), he would not yield an inch in condemning the religious illegitimacy each of their movements represented.

Hildesheimer held that even to cooperate with these non-Orthodox denominations on religious matters was unthinkable, for it might lead the unsuspecting into thinking that Orthodoxy sanctioned non-Orthodox varieties of Judaism. Thus in 1884, sixty-eight liberal rabbis issued a circular to defend the Jewish people from charges that Judaism countenanced a separate internal and external morality. The rabbis, in their petition, affirmed that Judaism commanded Jews to treat all persons, Jew or gentile, with love and justice so long as they fulfilled the prophetic injunction of Micah 5:8, "It hath been told thee, O man, what is good, And what the Lord doth require of thee; Only to do justly, and to love mercy, and to walk humbly with thy God." The Orthodox, led by Hildesheimer, refused to sign this statement. Their reasons were twofold. The first was that, from a religious point of view, the statement was incorrect. The principle of universal love, according to the Orthodox, was limited to those who observed the seven Noahide commandments, ethical duties which God prescribed for all humanity. The obligation to treat non-Jews "with love and justice" was thus derived from this element in Jewish tradition and not, as the Reformers mistakenly claimed, from the passage in Micah. The second reason that Hildesheimer felt the Orthodox could not sign the liberal circular was that to have done so would imply that non-Orthodox rabbis could legitimately speak for religious Judaism. Thus Hildesheimer declared, "Between the Torah-faithful and the more or less Reform rabbis a union is impossible."[39] For our purposes, the more important reason that Hildesheimer offered a substitute circular for the Orthodox rabbis to sign in this instance was that he saw the statement as one of religious policy and, therefore, did not want to associate with the liberals in any way. Fifty-nine Orthodox rabbis signed this alternative petition formulated by Hildesheimer.

Hildesheimer's refusal either to recognize or to cooperate with the non-Orthodox on matters of religious import is seen most clearly in an action he took almost at the end of his life. In 1884, the Verband der Rabbiner in Deutschland (Union of German Rabbis) was established, and in 1896 it was reconstituted as the Allgemeiner Rabbinerverband in Deutschland (General Union of Rabbis in Germany). The group was intended to be an umbrella organization that would embrace rabbis of all denominations. Hildesheimer, however, seceded from the General Union to form the Vereinigung traditionell-gesetzestreuer Rabbiner (Union of Traditional Torah-Faithful Rabbis), which was made up solely of Orthodox rabbis. Apparently Hildesheimer did not want to participate in any rabbinical organization that would have implied that the Orthodox conferred rabbinic legitimacy upon the non-Orthodox members of the German rabbinate.[40] Clearly, Hildesheimer was a religious sectarian on matters he deemed to be of an exclusively religious nature; he refused to acknowledge the validity of Jewish religious pluralism, counseling noncooperation with the non-Orthodox religious bodies on matters of religious import.

Religious voluntarism was not sanctioned in any of the provinces in Germany. All Jews were required by law to pay a tax to support their local community, regardless of personal religious beliefs. This practice paralleled the obligations that Christians in Germany had toward their own church. In the Jewish case, the Prussian Jew Law of 1847 raised each Jewish community to the status of a "public body" and required each Jew "to become a member of the community in his place of domicile."[41] The only way to escape this obligation was to convert to Christianity, an alternative unpalatable to most Jews.[42]

In 1873, however, the Prussian parliament promulgated a bill, Concerning Secession from the State Church, which granted every Christian the right to secede from the state church without thereby severing connection with Christianity. The passage of this law granted an excellent opportunity for modification of the Prussian Jew Law of 1847. As Salo Baron notes:

> Eduard Lasker, the Jewish leader of the then powerful National Liberal Party, suggested on March 19, 1873, that, in accordance with the general principle of equality of all citizens, the government also be asked to submit a bill on the right to secession from the Jewish community. When a conservative deputy . . . objected that the Jewish community would thereby lose a precious privilege safeguarding its unity, Lasker argued that this prerogative, based upon the denial of the liberty of conscience, was a *privilegium odiosum* and that the Jewish community itself should concur in its removal. The government promised to prepare a bill in due course.[43]

Lasker's proposal provoked a great controversy within the Jewish community. Non-Orthodox Jews and representatives of both the Hochschule and the Breslau seminary opposed it, claiming it would lead to the destruction of the Jewish community, while at the same time, political liberals who supported the ideal of freedom of conscience, and certain Orthodox Jews, notably Samson Raphael Hirsch, labored long and hard in an ironic alliance on its behalf.[44]

Hirsch appears to have been the major figure behind Lasker's proposal. He spoke personally with Lasker about the matter and enlisted his support in this cause.[45] In addition, taking advantage of the Christian *Kulturkampf* (which had led to the bill Concerning Secession from the State Church in 1873) and the general trend that favored religious freedom, Hirsch wrote a pamphlet in which he argued that compulsion could not bring shared religious duty into existence. Only a sense of shared religious purpose could do that. Hirsch concluded: "The divergence between the religious beliefs of Reform and Orthodoxy is so profound that when an individual publicly secedes he is only giving formal expression to convictions which had long since matured and become perfectly clear to himself. All the institutions and establishments in the care of a community are religious in nature, and they are . . . intimately bound up with the religious law."[46] Hirsch viewed Judaism solely in religious terms.[47] Consequently, it was both in keeping with his thought and in his interest to serve as a catalyst for this bill and to urge its passage. When the Lasker bill was passed on July 28, 1876, the lion's share of the credit for its success was attributed to Hirsch. The bill stated: "Every Jew is entitled, without severing his religious affiliation, to secede, on account of his religious scruples, from the particular community to which he belongs by virtue of a law, custom, or administrative regulation."[48]

Throughout this struggle, Hildesheimer both supported Hirsch and urged passage of this law. To the Prussian Chamber of Deputies in 1875 he wrote: "The gulf between the adherents of traditional Judaism and its religious opponents is at least as deep and wide as in any other religious faith; in fact, it is larger than in most and much greater than what is permitted by law." Like Hirsch, Hildesheimer argued that a Jew's decision to participate in the life of a Jewish community ought to be a matter of conscience, not compulsion, and he claimed that this entire matter was one "between man and God," not between an individual and the state.[49]

Hildesheimer's activities on behalf of Orthodox secession from the general Jewish community took other forms. In 1876 his former student Israel Goldschmidt was offered the position of community rabbi in Frankfurt. Hildesheimer wrote to him in February, encouraging him not to accept the position. There were several reasons for this decision, as will be discussed later in this chapter, but it is clear that a major one was that he did not want to weaken the *Austrittsgemeinde* (Orthodox secessionist community) in that city. Goldschmidt heeded his teacher's advice and turned down the proffered position.[50] Indeed, a year later Hildesheimer offered similar advice to his outstanding and beloved pupil Marcus David Horovitz, who had been invited to become the Orthodox rabbi of the general Jewish community in Frankfurt. Horovitz defied his teacher's counsel, but Hildesheimer's advice nonetheless indicates his wholehearted commitment to the concept of Orthodox secession, when necessary, from the larger Jewish community.[51]

Another illustration of Hildesheimer's views can be found in a letter he wrote to Lippman Mainz, a prominent banker and Orthodox member of the Frankfurt community. On the occasion of the twenty-fifth anniversary of the Israelitische Religionsgesellschaft (the Hirsch synagogue community in Frankfurt) in September 1876, Rabbi Hirsch announced his intention to secede from the general Frankfurt community and urged all members of his congregation to follow his example. A number of them did so, but a majority elected to remain within the general Jewish community as well as to continue to pay dues to the Religionsgesellschaft.[52] Mainz, who was among those who had chosen not to secede from the general Jewish community in Frankfurt, wrote a letter to Rabbi Elijah Munk, Hildesheimer's brother-in-law, telling him that he opposed secession and that he disagreed with Hirsch. Munk had informed Hildesheimer of this letter and Hildesheimer, unsolicited, decided to write to Mainz on October 22, 1876. He began by saying how disturbed he was at Mainz's position. After all, Mainz's family was renowned for its piety and Jewish learning. Therefore, wrote Hildesheimer: "I confess that your opposition [to Hirsch in this matter] is totally incomprehensible to me; and it is inexplicable to me that you, my friend, offer such opposition to the establishment of a holy congregation which is so exacting in all its details regarding observance, whether between a man and his fellow or between God and man." Religious viewpoints differ, he wrote, and these differences are not only fundamental, they find critical expression in the religious institutions of a community. Consequently, Hildesheimer contended, "there can be no such thing as a religiously neutral institution."[53] Hirsch was right to secede from the general Jewish community, and in Hildesheimer's view, Mainz was wrong to oppose Hirsch on this issue.

As this letter and Hildesheimer's other activities regarding both the passage of the secession law and non-Orthodox varieties of Judaism reveal, Hildesheimer believed that compromise involving religious issues was impossible. Like Hirsch, he denied the validity of religious pluralism in modern Judaism. He counseled noncooperation with and separation from non-Orthodox religious bodies, and he would not grant them legitimacy on either practical or theological grounds. On religious matters Hildesheimer was a "sectarian," for he certainly preferred Orthodox "isolation to compromise."[54] Yet to consider Hildesheimer purely as a religious sectarian would be to mistake his religious views for his total view of Judaism.

Isaac Unna has commented that, though Hildesheimer did advocate passage of the secession law and worked hard on its behalf, he "never considered secession the ideal; on the contrary, as far as possible, he maintained unity for the idea of 'klal,' the feeling of solidarity with all Israel."[55] Similarly, Isaiah Wolfsberg claims that Hildesheimer accepted the principle of secession only reluctantly and always tried to relate to all segments of the Jewish community on matters of common concern.[56] Hildesheimer reflected this conviction early in his life when, as a student in Berlin, he wrote the following to his fiancée, Henriette Hirsch, sister of the wealthy metal firm owner Joseph Hirsch: "The life of a religious Jew is never an autonomous one. [Judaism] is not a personal matter, closed or individual. In his thoughts, and also in his feelings of joy as well as pain, the Jew finds himself connected with the rest of his people."[57]

Hildesheimer had a strong notion of Klal Yisrael (the Community of Israel). His sense of Jewish peoplehood and unity is a trait he demonstrated throughout his life. While still in Hungary, Hildesheimer wrote in response to a query that "it is not only not forbidden" to strive for communal unity between Reform and Orthodox (so long as Orthodox principles were not compromised), but to do so was, in fact, "a noble deed [Werk]."[58] The correspondence between Rabbi Hirsch and Hildesheimer following the passage of the secession law in 1876 presents Hildesheimer's attitudes more fully. In a letter dated July 6, 1876, Hirsch assured Hildesheimer that Orthodox Jews would not exploit the secession law. Secession, Hirsch stated, would take place only in rare communities and then only for substantive religious issues. Orthodox Jews would not secede, Hirsch claimed, simply because they did not gain their way on a single issue.[59] Hirsch's letter would seem to indicate that Hildesheimer was not as enthusiastic as Hirsch about the prospect of Orthodox Jews forming secessionist communities all over Germany, for Hirsch was obviously concerned to alleviate Hildesheimer's misgivings on that score.

In addition, Hildesheimer was very distressed over the opposition to the law expressed by Seligman Baer Bamberger, the Würzburger *rav* and a great talmudist of German Jewry. Rabbi Moshe Mainz of Frankfurt, a prominent talmudist, opposed Hirsch's actions on halakhic grounds. As a result, Hirsch's supporters had approached Bamberger, expecting him to support their decision to secede. Bamberger consulted with Rabbi Mainz and was assured that the *Einheitsgemeinde* (general community) had agreed to Orthodox stipulations about the religious administration of the community. Bamberger refused to give his blessing to the Hirsch plan. He felt that secession from the general Jewish community by Orthodox Jews was legitimated only in the most extreme instances. He and Hirsch disputed publicly over the issue in an exchange of open letters. The conflict between the two men became heated, and when Bamberger died in 1878, Hirsch refused to attend the funeral.[60]

Initially, Hildesheimer was unaware of the communication between Hirsch's followers and Bamberger and could not understand why Bamberger had spoken out on the issue. Only later did Hildesheimer learn that some members of the Frankfurt Orthodox community had written Bamberger asking him whether they were justified in remaining in the larger community. Although Hildesheimer was sorry that Bamberger chose to reply, he could understand why he did so, for obviously this was a matter of great principle to Bamberger.[61] Nevertheless, the public airing of this dispute in the Orthodox world before the general community bothered Hildesheimer greatly. To Ludwig Stern, head of the Teachers' Seminary in Würzburg, he wrote: "This sad matter has distracted me from my work many hours, and it has caused me many sleepless nights in which I have shed many tears."[62]

Hildesheimer refused to comment publicly on this conflict for fear of alienating both sides. He felt no beneficial result could be derived from his public comment. Moreover, Hildesheimer claimed that Hirsch had "restored the traditional Judaism of our day to its place of prestige."[63] For this, all Jews owed him "eternal gratitude."[64] In addition to his respect, Hildesheimer clearly felt a bond of friendship with Hirsch. Finally, in analyzing this controversy, it is important to remember that both Hirsch and Hildesheimer spoke for a more sophisticated and urban class of acculturated German Orthodox Jews than did Bamberger, whose piety typified the much more traditional-minded *Landsjude* of the southern German countryside.[65] This meant that Hirsch and Hildesheimer, as representatives of a modern Orthodoxy, were much more aware of the dangers posed to their own Jewish communities by the advent of Reform and

DR. SAMS. RAPH. HIRSCH,
Rabbiner zu Frankfurt ⁰/ᴍ

Rabbi Samson Raphael Hirsch; detail from *Gallerie of Famous and Meritorious Men of Israel in the Present Century*, Germany, nineteenth-century (From the Collection of Hebrew Union College, Skirball Museum, Los Angeles, Lelo Carter, Photographer) nonobservance than was Bamberger, whose milieu in his home community was much more traditional and relatively homogeneous. Hirsch and Hildesheimer confronted the same social reality. Thus Hirsch and Hildesheimer may have shared a common vision of the best way to combat the modern evils of Reform and nonobservance which, in their opinion, presented an outright danger to the Orthodox Jewish community. Bamberger, in contrast, with his more traditional mind-set and social setting, did not perceive the problem in the same terms, thus partially accounting for his disagreement with them.

Curiously, Bamberger's traditionalism caused him to emphasize his commitment to a united Jewish people, whereas the traditionalism of the Hatam Sofer in Hungary had caused the Hungarian sage to be the first to promote secession of the Orthodox from the broader Jewish community. Sofer had regarded separation as a necessary means for preserving Orthodox Judaism. The modern situation had caused Sofer, despite his traditionalism, to be concerned about Judaism primarily as a religion. Like Hirsch, he implicitly defined Judaism "as an association of like-minded people." Bamberger, in contrast, refused to do so. For him, advocacy of secession in cases where it seemed unjustified would have been a tacit admission that the modern situation had reduced Judaism to the status of a religion alone—thus a rejection of the "medieval conception" that all Jews, even the nonobservant, were "living members of the organism of Klal Yisrael."[66]

Sofer hoped to keep the religion pure and uncontaminated by outside liberal influences. Bamberger either could not or would not acknowledge the influence of these other outside forces and thus spoke against secession. The final paradox is that, in Germany, Hildesheimer and Hirsch should have adopted Sofer's position on behalf of modern Orthodoxy, and simultaneously found themselves opposed to Bamberger, who represented more traditional Orthodoxy.

In any event, though Hildesheimer agreed in principle with Hirsch, he felt that Hirsch did not conduct himself in a proper manner regarding Bamberger. This, however, represents more than a simple dissent from the attitude of respect Hildesheimer felt Hirsch should have adopted toward a distinguished Orthodox colleague such as Bamberger. Rather, it stems from a basic attitudinal difference Hildesheimer had with Hirsch as to the nature of Judaism itself. For Hildesheimer did not view the Jewish people solely as a religious entity, as did Hirsch. He could not agree with Hirsch's statement, "All who turn from Torah have revolted against the Jewish people, and all who return to Torah become once again a part of the body which is Israel."[67] His notion of the peoplehood of Israel, though based on a religious foundation, went beyond it. Thus, although he agreed with Hirsch on the necessity of religious secession from a non-Orthodox Jewish community, he wrote to Hirsch: "I do dissent from several passages [in your open letter] directed against Bamberger which appear to me to be too strong. They make it even less likely for a bridge to be built from your congregation to those who are 'secessionists.' "[68]

The non-Orthodox Jews in Frankfurt were, in Hildesheimer's opinion, the secessionists. They, not Hirsch and his followers, had deviated from the traditional norms and standards of the community, thereby making the formation of the Hirsch community necessary. Nevertheless, they were clearly Jews and, consequently, Hildesheimer felt that Hirsch should have exerted every effort possible to bring them into his community, just as, in Hungary in 1866, such efforts would constitute "a noble deed." His decision not to side publicly with Hirsch in the dispute with Bamberger thus arose both from his conviction that no positive result would derive from such comment and because he had a greater sense of Jewish solidarity than did Hirsch. This sense did not permit Hildesheimer to define all Jews who were nonobservant as beyond the pale of the Jewish people.

This interpretation of Hildesheimer's attitude toward Jewish solidarity is underscored by his actions and correspondence concerning the appointment of his student Marcus David Horovitz to the post of *orthodoxer Gemeinderabbiner*, the Orthodox community rabbi, in Frankfurt in 1878. Hildesheimer had discouraged his former student Israel Goldschmidt from accepting this post in 1876. His principal reason for advising Goldschmidt against accepting the position was that Hirsch would regard Goldschmidt's coming as a personal insult. Hildesheimer wanted to avoid this, both because of the honor he felt was due Hirsch and because he feared that, if Goldschmidt did come, a fight comparable to the Emden-Eibeschütz controversy of the previous century might ensue.[69] Hildesheimer felt this would only lead to a "profanation of God's name," a spectacle he wanted to avoid.[70] It is significant, then, that Hildesheimer encouraged Goldschmidt to decline this offer not because of religious principle but because of the particular nature of the Frankfurt community and Rabbi Hirsch's presence there. In general, Hildesheimer did not object to his students' accepting the post of Orthodox community rabbi in other locales, and many of them did so.

When the community of Frankfurt turned to another of Hildesheimer's students, Marcus Horovitz, Hildesheimer's objections were similar to those he had put forth in the case of Goldschmidt. That is, Hildesheimer did not object to Horovitz's accepting the post because an Orthodox rabbi ought not to serve a general Jewish community. Rather, once again, Hildesheimer did not want to insult Hirsch. There were, in addition, several differences that distinguished the Horovitz from the Goldschmidt case. Chief among them was that, with the possible exception of Rabbi David Hoffmann, Horovitz was Hildesheimer's favorite pupil. Indeed, Horovitz's relations to Hildesheimer was comparable to Hildesheimer's relationship to Ettlinger. Horovitz had studied with Hildesheimer in his Eisenstadt yeshiva, and in his own volume of rabbinic responsa, the *Matte Levi*, Horovitz referred to his teacher Hildesheimer in the dedication as "a prince of Torah and pillar of piety . . . a man as strong as iron in his righteousness and like the very essence of heaven for the purity of his heart."[71] It is apparent that Hildesheimer reciprocated these feelings.

Horovitz, "whose soul was entwined with the soul of his teacher," in the words of Isaac Heinemann,[72] nevertheless, parted with him on the issue of secession in general and the acceptance of this post in particular. He had been serving as a rabbi in Gnesen when, in 1878, he decided to accept the post offered him by the Frankfurt community. For a time, relations between the two men were strained. Horovitz wrote to Hildesheimer informing him that he had spurned his advice and, apparently, interpreted Hildesheimer's advice not to leave his position in Gnesen as a "threat" (*Drohung*), not as a "caution" (*Warnung*). Hildesheimer was deeply hurt by this accusation. He responded to Horovitz: "Threats go against my entire nature. . . . [The insinuation] that I have not written this entire time on account of this 'threat' fills me with bitter tears. No, I do not deserve such a bitter judgment. . . . With the deepest sorrow I carry this incident with me, carry it alone."[73]

Horovitz, too, had a strong sense of Jewish solidarity and unity. Indeed, his decision to accept the post in Frankfurt can be seen, in some senses, as a logical outgrowth of the philosophy he had learned from Hildesheimer. Like Hildesheimer, and unlike Hirsch, Horovitz was an active member of B'nai B'rith. Whereas Hirsch wrote, "An Orthodox Jew must not consider joining a B'nai B'rith group for it

Rabbi Marcus Horovitz (Courtesy of Samuel H. Dresner, D.H.L.)

threatens traditional Judaism," Hildesheimer became an active participant in the Berlin lodge.[74] In short, though Horovitz and Hildesheimer disagreed over the issue of secession, many of Horovitz's attitudes toward Judaism were a direct result of Hildesheimer's influence. The only two members of the German Orthodox world to give Horovitz their immediate support and congratulations on his decision to accept the post were Jakob Barth, Esriel Hildesheimer's son-in-law, and David Zvi Hoffmann. Both of these men were on the faculty of the Rabbiner-Seminar and were close disciples of Hildesheimer.[75] This response testifies to the attitude toward Klal Yisrael that Hildesheimer transmitted to his students.

Therefore, it is not surprising that Hildesheimer finally acceded to Horovitz on this issue and, in 1879, gave Horovitz his approval. Earlier, in an obvious effort to appease Horovitz, Hildesheimer had written to him, "Believe me, I do not judge your intention one-sidedly."[76] Hildesheimer understood that there were two sides to the issue and allowed that there could be an honest difference of opinion between himself and Horovitz over it. Thus just a few years later, Hildesheimer came to Frankfurt to speak in the community's new Orthodox synagogue where Horovitz presided and thereby earned Hirsch's enmity.[77]

Hildesheimer's reconciliation with the defense of Horovitz, as well as his distinct attitude toward Jewish communal unity, can be seen in a pair of letters he wrote to Emanuel Schwarzschild in October 1879. Schwarzschild, a prominent banker in Frankfurt and one of Hirsch's leading supporters, also had a strong relationship with Hildesheimer. He had worked with Hildesheimer to found the Rabbiner-Seminar and continued to serve on its board of directors. Schwarzschild opposed Horovitz's entry into Frankfurt and demanded that Hildesheimer withdraw the consent he had ultimately given Horovitz to accept the post. Schwarzschild was concerned about the effect this action would have on Hildesheimer's relationship with Hirsch and exhorted Hildesheimer to reconsider his action.

Hildesheimer was upset over the letter and told Schwarzschild that "a devoted student, who is like a child to me, and whose whole future perhaps depends upon my opinion, asks me for the exact same yes or no." Hildesheimer then posed a question to Schwarzschild, "If your child came to you with a similar request, what would you do?" Hildesheimer knew that there were many considerations in this case. Yet it was also clear to Hildesheimer that Horovitz had made up his mind and, as is clear from the letter he wrote to

Schwarzschild, had a strong psychological need for Hildesheimer's approval. Likewise, Hildesheimer, as a "father," had a corresponding "need" to grant the approval and repair the breach with his beloved pupil. Thus Hildesheimer decided, "The future of an outstanding student and *zaddik* [righteous one], of whom among all the youth of this generation almost no one can be found, depends upon this position." Hildesheimer felt he could not refuse Horovitz his blessing. He regretted the ill-will that might arise between himself and Hirsch but explained that he was obligated to do "his duty" and grant Horovitz the permission he sought. Only in this way, Hildesheimer wrote, "can my conscience be clean."[78]

Schwarzschild was not satisfied with Hildesheimer's answer and wrote him a second time. He asked Hildesheimer to reconsider and contended that Hildesheimer should not publicly announce that he was giving Horovitz his permission because it would embarrass Hirsch. Selig Auerbach agreed with Schwarzschild, and both men claimed that, if Hildesheimer did not keep his opinion private (in the eventuality that he did not reverse it altogether), they would regard it as an insult. Hildesheimer replied by stating that he was hurt by Schwarzschild's letter and that he refused to consider their demands. Again, he expressed the hope that it would not affect their relationship, but he felt that he had no other option than to be totally honest and open in regard to the matter.[79]

In assessing the entire episode, it is clear that Hildesheimer's love and personal concern for Horovitz influenced his actions. Yet to view it solely as a personal response on Hildesheimer's part would be a mistake. For Hildesheimer shared, and had helped form, Horovitz's attitude toward the community of Israel. The shared opinions that marked the two men allowed Hildesheimer to hold a different view of secession from Hirsch and, in the end, to grant Horovitz his approval.

Isaac Unna has pointed out that Hildesheimer believed that "Jews of various nations were organs of the body of one nation."[80] His commitment to a sense of Jewish peoplehood can be seen in a letter he wrote to Judah Leib Rappoport on March 23, 1864. In the letter he spoke of his concern for the so-called Falashas, the Black Jews of Ethiopia, whom he feared were being lost to the Jewish people. Missionaries from England, Hildesheimer believed, were converting these Jews to Christianity, and Hildesheimer lamented the situation: "Woe is the spiritual situation of our brothers in the household of Israel who sit there [Ethiopia]. They wander like lost sheep without a shepherd. . . . Who does not tremble at hearing this? . . . Is there not one Torah and one Father in Heaven for all of us and is not the entire household of Israel responsible for one another?"[81] Hildesheimer proposed that Jewish teachers be sent immediately to these Jews to instruct them in the Jewish religion and to save them from the hands of the missionaries. In this way he hoped they would not be lost to the Jewish people.

This same notion of Jewish unity was manifest in a letter Hildesheimer wrote to the Ashkenazic rabbi of Cairo on November 10, 1892. The rabbi had written to Hildesheimer asking him to inform the government authorities in Egypt that the religious differences between Ashkenazic and Sephardic Jews warranted government recognition for the existence of two separate communities and, in light of that recognition, two separate chief rabbinates. Currently the government recognized only a single Jewish community and regarded the Sephardic rabbi as the chief rabbi of Cairo's Jews. Hildesheimer responded to the Ashkenazic rabbi by acknowledging that there were, of course, practical halakhic differences between the two communities, especially in the realm of *kashrut* (dietary laws). But he questioned whether these differences were so significant that they merited the recognition of two separate communities by the government authorities. Hildesheimer wrote, "Truly all Jews, whether Ashkenazim or Sephardim, are one people and they should not be divided into two."[82] Clearly Hildesheimer felt the ideal of Jewish unity very strongly. In both these instances involving Jews on the African continent, he displayed his commitment to the notion that Judaism constituted more than a religion that was confined to national boundaries. His arguments on behalf of the reinstitution of the *Bet Din* to adjudicate civil disputes for the Jews in Germany and western Europe support this same broad conception. As pointed out in the last chapter, his proposal concerning the *Bet Din* distinguished Hildesheimer from all the other modern Orthodox rabbis in Germany. Hildesheimer alone protested the Emancipation's dismantling of the political institutions of the medieval Jewish community.[83]

All these examples of Hildesheimer's dedication to the notion of Klal Yisrael merely illustrate that he did possess a sense of Jewish peoplehood; they do not elucidate Hildesheimer's attitude toward Jews whom he regarded as religious deviants. The Ethiopians of whom he spoke in 1864 were simply ignorant of, not rebels against,

Jewish law and tradition. By the same token, the Ashkenazim and Sephardim of Cairo were presumably both traditional. The question that remains, then, is how did Hildesheimer view those Jews who had, in fact, departed from and rebelled against what he regarded as normative Judaism? It is clear that Hildesheimer did not regard their religious views or institutions as religiously legitimate and would not acknowledge their authenticity in any way. But he did deal with them in other spheres, and he did feel that they were a part of the people Israel. How could he do so in light of his religious commitments?

Meir Hildesheimer, in writing about his grandfather Esriel, has noted that in regard to charity Hildesheimer felt "it was obligatory to participate in Jewish organizations with non-Orthodox Jews."[84] His willingness to cooperate with non-Orthodox Jews and institutions on certain matters of common concern can be seen in his involvement with the Alliance Israélite Universelle, a Paris-based Jewish charitable and educational organization. Hildesheimer addressed the Berlin chapter of the Alliance and participated in several of its activities. Non-Orthodox Jews, including graduates of the Breslau seminary, were active members of the group. The Paris head of the Alliance, Adolphe Crémieux, was not only non-Orthodox, but he had permitted his wife to have their children baptized. As a result, Samson Raphael Hirsch wrote: "I have absolutely no connection with the Alliance. . . . I fail to see how a man imbued with proper Jewish thought can attach himself to a group founded for the sake of a Jewish task when its founder and administration are completely removed from genuine religious Judaism. . . . Indeed it is very painful for me to see an honored name like Dr. Hildesheimer united with the Alliance and the men of the Breslau seminary."[85] Hirsch concluded by stating that this was not the way of the pious men of old who dwelt in Jerusalem and separated themselves absolutely from the rest of the community for the sake of preserving Judaism. As a total sectarian, Hirsch contended that the Jews in nineteenth-century Germany needed to follow their example.

Hildesheimer disagreed. He replied to Hirsch that an article written on behalf of the Alliance and its charitable activities by the famed central European rabbi and proto-Zionist Zvi Hirsch Kalischer persuaded him to join and lend the organization his support. Citing the charitable enterprises of the Alliance, Hildesheimer explained, "I feel myself obligated to promote the unity of various Jewish communities [through the work of this group]." Hildesheimer informed Hirsch that their common non-Orthodox opponents delighted in Orthodox detachment from groups such as this, for when the groups performed positive functions, these opponents were able to claim that the Orthodox were negative and isolationist. Crémieux was not, in Hildesheimer's opinion, a fit representative of Judaism, but Hildesheimer felt that Jews were still obligated to join the Alliance because of the positive functions it performed.[86]

Hildesheimer's stance on this matter can be contrasted with the position he adopted in response to another incident involving intermarriage and conversion to Christianity to reveal the distinction he made between religious and either charitable or secular organizations headed by non-Orthodox Jews. A Dr. Staadecker from Mannheim wrote to Hildesheimer to ask him what the relationship of the Orthodox to the general community in Mannheim ought to be. Staadecker reported that conversions to Christianity were common and that the head of the synagogue had a daughter who was baptized and married to a non-Jew. Hildesheimer responded in harsh tones to Staadecker on May 17, 1881, stating that these converts to Christianity upset him deeply and referring to them as "cowardly opportunists," who possessed weak ideas and mouthed the most banal platitudes. "Because we live in such bitter times," Hildesheimer continued, "all the more so is one [the Jew] commanded to hold one's head high." As for the attitude that should be adopted toward these apostates, Hildesheimer said, "It is a holy and pressing duty to bring such vile desertions into the open." Hildesheimer opined that there could be no role for an Orthodox Jew in such a community and told Staadecker that he and the other Orthodox should secede.[87] This letter was written at about the same point in his career that Hildesheimer urged Orthodox Jews to participate in the Alliance in spite of Crémieux's religious laxity. The dissimilar responses bear eloquent testimony to Hildesheimer's commitment to Jewish communal unity on charitable but not religious matters. Further, they reveal that Hildesheimer's conception of the Jewish community operated on two levels, the religious and the communal, and that divergence from the former did not exclude an individual from the latter.

Correspondence between Hirsch and Hildesheimer resulted in yet another episode that illustrates Hildesheimer's more moderate approach to the problem of Orthodox cooperation with the non-Orthodox Jewish world. As discussed earlier, in 1884 sixty-eight Liberal rabbis issued a circular denying the charges that Judaism promulgated an internal and external set of moral standards. Hildesheimer disagreed with the content of the memorandum and thus had offered another one for the Orthodox to sign in its stead. In this way, Orthodox rabbis would not be placed in the uncomfortable position of granting religious legitimacy to the liberals. At a certain point in these proceedings, Rabbi Rudolf Ungerleider, a non-Orthodox rabbi, came to Hildesheimer's home to discuss a proposed union between Orthodox and liberal rabbis on this issue. When Hirsch was informed of this meeting with Ungerleider, he charged that Hildesheimer had committed "an offense against the holiness and truth of our cause."[88] Hildesheimer dismissed Hirsch's complaint but informed Hirsch that he had inflicted a "very, very painful hurt" against him by making such an accusation. The whole matter, said Hildesheimer, was one of common sense. Although he had no intention of sanctioning such a union, he thought that refusal to see Ungerleider would have demonstrated a lack of common decency (Derekh Eretz).[89]

Hildesheimer had personal friendships with several non-Orthodox Jews with whom he worked on matters of shared concern. For example, Gottschalk Lewy, a liberal Jew who had very close ties to Graetz and the Breslau seminary, was one of his closest friends,[90] as was Samuel Kristeller, the head of the Deutsch-Israelitischer Gemeindebund and a nonobservant Jew. Hildesheimer reported that Kristeller refused to attend services on Yom Kippur on principle.[91] In any event, these friendships as well as the incident involving Ungerleider indicate that even when he was vitriolic in his denunciation of his opponents' religious views, he was careful to distinguish between the person and the person's opinion. In this respect, Hildesheimer's conduct reflects the influence of his teacher Ettlinger. Differing religious views did not prevent Hildesheimer from either establishing bonds of personal friendship or from working with those of different views on matters of Jewish communal interest.

Anti-Semitism was another such issue of common Jewish concern. Anti-Semitic sentiments in Germany grew throughout the last part of the nineteenth century, and Hildesheimer was extremely conscious of them.[92] Unlike Samson Raphael Hirsch, Hildesheimer chose not to exercise an independence from the general Jewish community in relation to this problem. As Sanford Ragins has reported, the Hirsch camp "welcomed the activities of the Christian defense organization, the Verein zur Abwehr des Antisemitismus." Yet Hirsch and his group "generally ignored" the workings of Jewish defense organizations, "except to attack them."[93] Ismar Schorsch agrees with this assessment of the Hirsch group's attitude of non-cooperation with non-Orthodox Jews even on matters of communal defense and notes, in comparison, the radically different position adopted by the Hildesheimer faction. Schorsch writes, "By October 1885 Hildesheimer, in contrast to Hirsch, had become convinced that the administrative projects of the *Gemeindebund* (which was composed primarily of non-Orthodox Jews) . . . were worthy of support." He likewise decided both to support and to participate in the Centralverein deutscher Staatsbürger jüdischen Glaubens, an organization composed of both religious and nonreligious Jews designed to defend German Jewish citizens from anti-Semitic attacks. Esriel's son Hirsch Hildesheimer declared, "The points that unite us are plentiful; those that separate us, few."[94] Hildesheimer's pragmatism caused him to feel that anti-Semitism was an issue that threatened the entire Jewish community, not just a segment of it. Moreover, he was convinced that the most effective way of combating it was for the Jewish community to be united, not fragmented, in its own defense. This attitude suggests the influence of pre-Emancipation thinking on Hildesheimer's approach to the problem of anti-Semitism. Emancipation had radically altered the religious, cultural, and political status of Jews by emphasizing these as extrinsic rather than intrinsic characteristics. Jewishness was reduced to a religious option which an individual Jew could either affirm or deny. In the face of anti-Semitism, however, Jewishness was a matter of fate, not choice. Thus for Hildesheimer anti-Semitism challenged the promise of Emancipation and in so doing had a unifying effect on the Jewish community. For Hirsch, however, the overriding concern for the religious purity of Judaism caused him to elevate the interests of religious Orthodoxy above the threat of anti-Semitism.

The differing attitudes of the Hirsch and Hildesheimer circles can be seen clearly in an exchange between Hildesheimer and Solomon Breuer, Hirsch's son-in-law and successor as rabbi of the Religionsgesellschaft in Frankfurt, in 1894. Breuer was very upset that Hildesheimer and other Orthodox rabbis such as Horovitz and Munk had signed a declaration issued "by a representative (i.e., Orthodox and Liberal) group of rabbis" protesting anti-Semitic attacks on the Talmud. The campaign against the Jews and their institutions (such as ritual slaughter) and literary works (especially the Talmud) was vicious. The Talmud actually became the subject of parliamentary inquiry.[95] Hildesheimer perceived the situation to be a grave one for the Jews and, consequently, felt justified in participating with non-

Orthodox Jews on such projects. Breuer, however, was only angry that Hildesheimer had cooperated with the *poshim,* the sinners. Breuer felt that Hildesheimer's signing the petition implied tacit recognition of the legitimacy of liberal rabbis and could not restrain his annoyance with Hildesheimer for signing. Indeed, the *Allgemeine Zeitung des Judentums* called the proclamation "an important, historical-cultural witness for the religious unity of Judaism," thus feeding into Breuer's accusations.[96] Hildesheimer responded by charging Breuer with myopia. Hildesheimer insisted that Breuer had to recognize the common fate of all Jews on this matter and that he must not let his religious views blind him to the dangers, lies, and wickedness of anti-Semitism, which, Hildesheimer claimed, bound all Jews together. Hildesheimer rejected Breuer's reprimand outright. He wrote, "I am of the opposite opinion [from you], as . . . one is obligated to act in concert with them [the liberals] as far as the conscience permits."[97]

Hildesheimer found the liberals equally unrealistic in their views toward anti-Semitism, although for different reasons. In December 1890, Hildesheimer commented bitterly on the development of anti-Jewish feeling in Germany and the shortsightedness of the Reformers in believing that Emancipation would bring the Jews of Germany total freedom and equality. Of the Reformers and their efforts to alter Jewish tradition, he wrote: "The chief thing in their opinion was equality with the inhabitants of the land, and the path of Judaism and its existence was thought by them to be a drop in the bucket. And what did God do? He brought anti-Semitism upon us, a hatred which seizes and destroys Jews in every land, but especially in Germany. . . . For, to our enemies and oppressors, it is sufficient not only if a Jew is born, but even if one is born who has a Jewish parent or grandparent."[98]

Although Hildesheimer offered a theological explanation for the phenomenon of anti-Semitism in which the Reformers were the culprits, he still recognized that the scourge of anti-Semitism was widespread and that all Jews, religious and nonreligious, felt its effects. Therefore, joint activity between the various elements of Jewry was not only desirable but necessary.

A circular Hildesheimer wrote in 1881 provides eloquent testimony to his belief that on certain issues Jewish communal interests transcended particular religious viewpoints. Moreover, in these instances, Orthodox Jews were commanded to join in and promote these joint communal activities. Moritz Lazarus, a professor at

Berlin and an outstanding leader of Reform, had delivered two speeches in which he developed a program of defense against and answer to anti-Semitism. To say that Hildesheimer disagreed with the religious positions that Lazarus advocated regarding Judaism would be an understatement. On another occasion, Hildesheimer noted that Lazarus, as the author of a Reform prayerbook, "placed the Christian ethic above the Jewish." Indeed, Hildesheimer felt he could recognize virtually nothing Jewish in the book. In Hildesheimer's opinion, Lazarus's religious views were only to be condemned.[99] Nevertheless, in the circular Hildesheimer addressed to rabbis in some sixty communities, he asked them to aid the efforts of the committee that was circulating Lazarus's speeches against anti-Semitism. Hildesheimer understood that some of these Orthodox rabbis had a natural reluctance to publicize the work of Lazarus and thereby bestow upon him a modicum of credibility as a Jewish spokesman. But Hildesheimer stressed the gravity of the situation and told the rabbis that this was a matter about which "my conscience informs and obligates me."[100] He therefore urged them to support the work of Lazarus and the committee.

The last part of the nineteenth century was, in Hildesheimer's opinion, "an era of anti-Semitism."[101] Hildesheimer was convinced that the era of Enlightenment was ended, and he was certain that rational refutation of anti-Semitic charges was not sufficient to defuse the potential explosion that could be unleashed against European Jewry. Thus, on May 5, 1881, in writing to the board of the synagogue-community in Marienwerder, which was at that time the center of anti-Semitic agitation, Hildesheimer stated that August Röhling's book *Talmud Jew* was an unmitigated anti-Semitic libel. Furthermore, Hildesheimer commented that Franz Delitzsch, "Christian professor and foremost authority in this area," had shown all of Röhling's book to be a lie. Hildesheimer noted that Rabbi Joseph Nobel had also written a refutation of Röhling's book. He concluded pessimistically, however, that he knew that such material would continue to be published and that though efforts to combat these lies had to continue unabated, there was little chance such efforts would be wholly successful.[102]

The seriousness of the situation caused Hildesheimer to work with and congratulate Reform Jews for their efforts to combat anti-Semitism. In May 1881, for example, Hildesheimer wrote a letter to Hermann Cohen, the famous German philosopher and exponent of liberal Judaism, thanking him for defending Judaism in court against attacks of the notorious anti-Semite Ferdinand Fenner. Hildesheimer said that he wrote "to offer [Cohen] an expression of our deepest thanks in which surely many thousands of our coreligionists join us." Hildesheimer noted that Cohen's defense of Judaism would "remain unforgotten as a monument to [your] uncompromising honesty and strength of character." He added that Cohen's views were academically founded and correct. His letter, officially issued by the *"Rector und Docenten des Berliner Rabbiner Seminars,"*[103] bespeaks Hildesheimer's ability to acknowledge a non-Orthodox Jew as a legitimate spokesman for the Jewish people on certain matters.

Moshe Samet, in writing about the characteristics of Jewish Neo-Orthodoxy, states that the modern Orthodox, in contradistinction to the traditional Orthodox, affirmed the modern notion of freedom of conscience.[104] Hildesheimer's activities in the fight against anti-Semitism would seem to affirm Samet's insight. On August 2, 1878, Hildesheimer wrote to the Chancellery in Berlin and noted that public elections were scheduled for the seventeenth of the month, a Saturday. Hildesheimer pointed out that this involved a clear constraint upon conscience for the Jew who was religiously observant, forcing the Jew to choose whether to exercise his civic duty or obey his religious principles. Hildesheimer concluded by expressing the hope that the interests "of freedom of religious conscience" would be deemed sufficient for making the demand that election day not be set on Saturday.[105]

Although Hildesheimer—and Hirsch—may well have affirmed, as Samet claims, notions of religious freedom, it is clear that such arguments stemmed from prudential concerns. Because the Orthodox Jews shared the minority status assigned all Jews in Germany, and in view of the liberal-secularist majority in the Jewish community itself, it was in their own best interests to espouse this principle. Otherwise their own causes—the preservation of institutions for the observance of *kashrut* and the maintenance of Orthodox rabbis and synagogues in particular locales—might have been lost. Indeed, Hildesheimer's efforts to prevent the Reformers in Halberstadt from exercising their right of religious freedom in 1847 would seem to indicate that his espousal of the cause of religious freedom in the 1870s and 1880s was an act of convenience or, at the very least, a position he came to adopt fully later in life.

The ability to employ the concept of religious freedom in their quest for realizing Orthodox goals is best revealed in the joint efforts of Hirsch and Hildesheimer to fight against attempts to outlaw *shehitah* (the ritual slaughtering of animals for kosher meat). Lobbying to prohibit *shehitah* in Germany began in 1882. Proponents of this effort were ostensibly motivated by a humanitarian concern for the welfare of the animals slaughtered in this Jewish process. One of the major arguments put forth by opponents of *shehitah* was that "the animal retains consciousness—and sensitivity to pain—even after being cut." This is the background against which the Hildesheimer episode must be understood.[106] Thus, as Sanford Ragins has observed, "the campaign to outlaw ritual slaughter" replaced criticisms of the Talmud as the "favorite target of anti-semites." Ragins writes: "Anti-semites, first in the 1880s and then with greater intensity in the 1890s, pressed efforts to convince legislators and the public that *shehitah* was inhumane and an example of inveterate cruelty to the weak."[107]

In February 1886, Der Verband der Tierschutzvereine in Deutschland (Society for the Protection of Animals in Germany) petitioned the legislature to pass a law forbidding *shehitah*. The Orthodox, of course, were not taken by surprise when this measure was introduced and had been preparing to combat it for several years. In 1885, Herz Ehrmann, Orthodox rabbi of a separatist community in Trier, published a book, *Tierschutz and Menschenschutz* (Protection of animals and protection of man), devoted to this question. The work contained the opinions of fifty prominent non-Jewish authorities on the subject of *shehitah* and defended the humane basis of Jewish ritual slaughter.[108] In addition, the Orthodox enlisted the support of Ludwig Windthorst, a Catholic deputy of the Center party. Windthorst had spoken out against the efforts of anti-Semites to exclude Jews from government positions in 1880. As a result, he had earned the enmity of conservative elements in the German body politic. An anonymous pamphlet published in 1881 stated: "It is our duty to combat liberals of the Center party led by Ludwig Windthorst . . . who has for some reason determined that anti-Jewish activities are not compatible with the political interests of Catholics. . . . We are defending the Christian national spirit and not the interests of the politicians in the Reichstag."[109] In the struggle against *shehitah*, Windthorst remained the Jews' most important parliamentary ally.

Hildesheimer was aware of the importance of Windthorst's support and felt it was crucial to heed his advice, as far as halakhically permissible, in the struggle to defeat the opponents of *shehitah*. In talks with Windthorst, Hildesheimer became convinced that the Orthodox had to present the most effective case possible before the

German parliament in their petition against the Society for the Protection of Animals. Windthorst was apparently cognizant of some of the legal regulations surrounding the ritual slaughter of animals. He felt that if the Orthodox indicated that a blow to the head of the animal after the slaughter was impermissible, it would prejudice their case before the Reichstag.[110] Jewish law admitted of two interpretations on this issue.[111] In an article published in *Die Jüdische Presse*, Hildesheimer argued that, though Jewish law prohibited such a blow before the slaughtering, it was not opposed to such a blow being delivered after the *shehitah* had been performed.[112] He thus chose to advance that interpretation of Jewish law which he felt would be most advantageous to the Orthodox position in this struggle. This is not to suggest that Hildesheimer's interpretation did not have ample support and precedent in the Jewish legal tradition. In a letter to Hirsch, who opposed the administering of such a blow as contrary to halakhah, Hildesheimer contended that his view of the law in this matter was the dominant view of Jewish legal authorities.[113] Hildesheimer's decision to opt for this rather than Hirsch's interpretation of Jewish law certainly aided Windthorst in his struggle with the anti-Semites. There was clearly an affinity between Hildesheimer's decision to promote this view of Jewish law and the practical demands of the situation.

Hildesheimer differed with Hirsch on two other counts concerning how best to fight anti-Semitism. Hirsch opposed any effort at cooperation with the non-Orthodox rabbinical authorities. Thus when a liberal rabbi in Vienna, among others, issued a report to the German Reichstag defending the practice of *shehitah*, Hirsch wanted to inform the parliament that such a man was not to be trusted. Hildesheimer wrote and urged Hirsch not to take this stand publicly because he felt it would only weaken the Orthodox case before the German government.[114] In addition, Hildesheimer did not agree with Hirsch that Ehrmann's book should be distributed to all members of the German parliament. Hildesheimer had originally conceived this idea and had ordered four hundred copies of the book for distribution. In a letter to Hirsch on June 4, 1886, however, he said he had changed his mind. The work, Hildesheimer felt, contained several passages which he believed would hurt the Orthodox cause and prove to be counterproductive.[115]

Hirsch and Hildesheimer did agree that the most effective means to secure an Orthodox triumph on this issue was to argue that the law posed a potential curtailment to religious freedom in Germany.

As Hirsch wrote, "Every religious confession is endangered" by this potential law.[116] Moreover, Hirsch contended that such an argument would gain the support of liberals and centrists in the parliament. "Therefore," Hirsch wrote to Hildesheimer on June 8, 1886, "we turn to the Reichstag for a defense of our religious freedom."[117] Hildesheimer concurred. The petition to forbid *shehitah* failed, resulting in "a full, complete success" for the Orthodox.[118] Despite their differences, Hirsch and Hildesheimer obviously understood the realities of nineteenth-century German politics well enough to wage a successful battle against the anti-Semites.

The successful conclusion of this first campaign against the anti-Semitic attempts to ban *shehitah* did not prevent the anti-Semites from making additional attacks in this area. Nor did it mark the end of differences between Hirsch and Hildesheimer concerning the best way to combat these factions. Later in the year Hirsch, in anticipation of a new effort to ban Jewish ritual slaughter, circulated a petition among the Orthodox rabbinate of Germany. Hildesheimer, writing to Hirsch on November 25, 1886, opposed Hirsch's petition and claimed that it would have adverse effects on the German Jewish community. First, he felt that its wording was too apodictic and would harden extremists in the anti-*shehitah* camp. Second, he believed that the petition was premature and would precipitate anti-Semitic attacks on the Jewish community. He thus opposed Hirsch at this time.[119] Seven years later, in 1893, Hildesheimer adopted a similarly prudential position when the Society for the Protection of Animals renewed its campaign against *shehitah*. A supporter of Hildesheimer informed him that he planned to bring the matter before the court on religious affairs because it marked an attempt to curtail and limit the religious freedom of Jews in Germany. Although Hildesheimer had supported this approach seven years earlier, conditions had so deteriorated in Germany that he considered such an action "very risky." He stated, "One must be cautious and see whether it [taking the matter before a gentile court] might cause anti-Semitism."[120]

For Hildesheimer, one final Jewish interest transcended sectarian boundaries. Hildesheimer had long toiled on behalf of the Jewish settlement in the Land of Israel and had raised significant funds to support it throughout his career. As early as 1858 he and his brother-in-law Joseph Hirsch had established the Society for the Support of Eretz Yisrael, which supplied housing to Jews living in the Old City of Jerusalem.[121] Furthermore, in the very first issue of *Die Jüdische*

Presse in 1870, Hildesheimer announced the formation of a society, Verein für Palästinensische Angelegenheiten, to aid the poor in Eretz Yisrael. The centrality of Israel in Hildesheimer's thought is evidenced in a letter to his friend Akiba Lehren in 1872: "When I was in Eisenstadt, except for my teaching in the yeshiva, I made concern for matters of Eretz Yisrael my highest priority."[122]

Hildesheimer's love for Zion sprang from deep religious roots, and his commitment to Eretz Yisrael should be regarded primarily as religious-philanthropic, not secular-nationalistic.[123] Thus in direct response to Abraham Geiger, who, in January 1870, had commented that "Europe is our Jerusalem," Hildesheimer wrote, in June of that year in *Die Jüdische Presse*, that "Europe is not our Jerusalem."[124] Instead, Hildesheimer maintained that "Israel is our homeland [*Heimatland*]."[125] Nevertheless, Hildesheimer said that love of Zion and support for colonization in Eretz Yisrael in no way conflicted with the duties and love a Jew owed his native land.[126] Hildesheimer was able to adopt such a stance and make such a claim in part because he did not view the Land of Israel in secular-nationalistic terms. He viewed Eretz Yisrael in religious terms only. Esriel Hildesheimer was not a modern Zionist.[127]

His strong religious commitment to Zion is borne out in a letter Hildesheimer wrote to M. Schrenzel of Lemberg in July 1881. Schrenzel had authored a pamphlet "The Solution of the Jewish Question" in response to the pogroms that were then ravaging Russian Jewry and the growing spirit of anti-Semitism that was threatening the security of Germany's Jews. Schrenzel, a secular Jew much like Theodore Herzl, had proposed the creation of a Jewish state in the vicinity of the United States as a land of refuge for the Jews. Palestine, in his opinion, was unsuitable for colonization. Schrenzel was aware of Hildesheimer's concern over the rising tide of anti-Semitism then sweeping Europe and asked Hildesheimer for support in realizing this project.[128]

Hildesheimer replied that he could not in good conscience support Schrenzel's proposed colony. His reasons were twofold. First, Hildesheimer noted that the colony would be peopled by non-Orthodox Jews, who, he was sure, would be lost to Judaism "in two, at the most three, generations" in the irreligious atmosphere of America.[129] Thus, even though Hildesheimer observed that "the situation [confronting eastern European Jews] was indescribable and the misery exceeds all bounds,"[130] religious scruples caused him to oppose the emigration of these persons to America. Second, his strong attachment to the "Land of Our Fathers" led Hildesheimer to favor Palestine, not America, as the proper site for Jewish colonization. Indeed, Hildesheimer's strong attachment to Zion led him to recommend—at a Berlin meeting of Jewish representatives gathered from all over the world to deal with the problem of Russian Jewish refugees fleeing from the 1881 pogroms—that the stream of refugees be directed toward Eretz Yisrael, not the United States. Hildesheimer was supported in this position by only one other delegate.[131] Yet when he addressed the same issue again in 1885, Hildesheimer stated, "America or Palestine—on *religious grounds* I plead for Palestine,"[132] therein reflecting his commitment to a religious conception of Judaism which included the Land of Israel as an integral part.

In 1872, Heinrich Graetz, whose religious views Hildesheimer detested, and two companions, one of whom, Gottschalk Lewy, was a friend of Hildesheimer's, went to Israel and toured the entire land. Upon their return, the three men issued a report describing the depressed economic and social conditions of the Jewish settlement.[133] Particularly disturbing to Hildesheimer was their report concerning the number of orphans who were entirely neglected, both spiritually and physically, by the existing Jewish communities in the land. In addition, the report contended that Christian missionaries were luring neglected youngsters into the Christian fold by offering them physical sustenance in Christian homes and educational opportunities in Christian schools. Thus Hildesheimer's concern over the report issued by Graetz and his friends was heightened by his worry over the souls of these children and his strong attachment to the Land of Israel. Hildesheimer's involvement with the land as well as his feelings for the community of the people Israel led him to regard the sad state of affairs in the Jewish settlement in Palestine as a "profanation of God's Name."

In light of Hildesheimer's strong feelings for both the land and the people of Israel, it can be understood how deeply disturbed he was by Graetz's report and why he wholeheartedly supported Graetz's suggestion that an orphanage be established to ensure proper care for these youngsters. In a memorandum circulated in December 1872, Hildesheimer called for the immediate establishment of such an orphanage in Palestine. Hildesheimer distrusted the means employed by the Palestinian rabbis for the distribution of charitable funds[134] and consequently advocated placing the administration of the orphanage in the hands of a committee located in Europe. This committee would appoint a local committee in Zion to administer the daily affairs of the proposed orphanage. Marcus Lehmann, editor of *Der Israelit,* suggested that the committee be headed by Hildesheimer, Akiba Lehren, his close friend and one of the founders of the Verwaltung der heiligen Stadt (Administration of the Holy City), and Rabbi Seligman Baer Bamberger.[135] Hildesheimer's final suggestion, in accordance with Graetz's recommendation, was that the education of these youths be based on the "Holy Torah," but secular subjects be added to the curriculum to ensure that they would be able to lead independent and productive lives.[136]

Hildesheimer's proposal had its opponents. The rabbis in Eretz Yisrael were adamant in their critique of Hildesheimer's proposed orphanage, both because it threatened their autonomous control of the dispersion of charitable funds and because of the proposed inclusion of secular studies in the curriculum of the school. Hildesheimer replied to this latter criticism by noting that the world was changing and that "the need for this [secular education] grows every day."[137] Here, as we shall see more fully in the next chapter, Hildesheimer's educational philosophy clashed directly with the approach toward learning advocated by the rabbis of the old Jewish settlement in Eretz Yisrael. As for the former point—that Hildesheimer's plan threatened the financial autonomy of the rabbis living in Palestine—Hildesheimer frankly doubted whether the rabbis could be trusted to distribute the funds fairly and equitably.

For purposes of this discussion concerning Hildesheimer's response to pluralism in the Jewish community, the key point is that opposition to Hildesheimer's plan arose in Europe because "the heretic Heinrich Graetz" had first suggested it and not because of the project's merits or demerits. Thus Bamberger and Lehren would not support Hildesheimer's proposed orphanage. Hildesheimer subsequently told Lehmann that he would not serve with Bamberger and Lehren on any committee that would discuss his plan.[138] Hirsch likewise wrote to Hildesheimer:

> I feel myself obliged to inform you that . . . the idea to establish an orphanage in Israel both to rescue the orphans from the hands of the missionaries and to raise the level of culture is the idea of Graetz. Already this proposal has resulted in an exchange of letters between the committee in Amsterdam and men of reputation in Jerusalem. As you can see from looking at it, Graetz's entire assertion [about the situation in Jerusalem] is fundamentally a lie. . . . Thus, I cannot refrain from telling you, my honored friend, that if the sages and heads

of the Holy City state that a claim is an absolute lie in such a total manner, then I do not feel free to cast even the slightest doubt upon their faithfulness, especially not based upon the word of a man like Graetz, who arrogantly permits himself to diminish the honor of sages of Israel through his patently false lies. A man like this is not fit to be trusted by us.[139]

Hildesheimer responded both to Hirsch and to other rabbis in Europe who were critical of supporting any plan proposed by Graetz by reconfirming his opinion that Graetz was a "religious heretic." No one, Hildesheimer stated, had fought Graetz and his heresies as adamantly as he.[140] Moreover, Hildesheimer was critical of Graetz for speaking out publicly against the negative aspects of life which he had observed in Israel but ignoring the positive aspects of Jewish life there.[141] It is clear that Hildesheimer was here trying to appease his Orthodox colleagues and make his case for the necessity of the orphanage as convincing as possible. Nevertheless, Hildesheimer wrote: "Graetz and his party say repeatedly, 'Do not believe us.' Send people yourselves. Pick them yourselves. Only be fair and you will see."[142]

Hildesheimer had no doubts that the report issued by Graetz and his traveling companions was factually correct. In a letter he wrote to Rabbi Lehren on December 30, 1872, Hildesheimer stated that, although he had fought with Lewy, Graetz's fellow traveler, many times over religious issues, in his opinion Lewy was "a man who never lied, not even the slightest bit."[143] Lewy's testimony, taken with Graetz's eagerness for the Orthodox to send a group of independent observers to confirm the reports of his party and other accounts Hildesheimer had received about the missionary schools in Jerusalem, convinced Hildesheimer that Graetz's report was accurate and that it ought to be relied on to coordinate the active response of the European rabbinate. Therefore, Hildesheimer wrote to Hirsch: "A grave situation has arisen in opposition to my program among circles who do not wish to distinguish between the heresies of Graetz and his reports regarding established facts in our times; and there are great dangers bound up with this approach."[144]

Hildesheimer felt it was essential to distinguish between a man's religious views and other aspects of his person. Even though a man such as Graetz might hold despicable religious beliefs injurious to the continuity of Judaism, Hildesheimer did not hold that one should therefore totally isolate oneself from such a Jew or refuse to act in concert with him on positive projects designed to aid the Jewish people. Hildesheimer contended that to act thus, and thereby abstain from vital work that would enhance the lives and the image of Jews and the Jewish people throughout the world, was tantamount to "throwing the baby out with the bath water."[145] As Hildesheimer phrased it, "The truth is the truth even if it be on the side of our opponents."[146]

Hildesheimer's proposed orphanage never achieved fruition, and ultimately he abandoned his efforts to establish it. Nevertheless, this and other episodes and attitudes indicate that Hildesheimer's position regarding the non-Orthodox Jewish world was distinct from Hirsch's and that it rested largely on his strong sense of the physical unity of the Jewish people.

Esriel Hildesheimer displayed a complex but consistent attitude toward the issue of Jewish religious and cultural pluralism in the post-Emancipation European world. As an Orthodox Jew, Hildesheimer would not countenance any interpretation of Judaism that was not based on the principle of *Torah Min HaShamayim*. But Hildesheimer's religious attitudes and educational background also caused him to adopt a strong sense of what can most properly be labeled kinship with the entire community of Israel. That is, his religious attitudes predisposed him to work, whenever possible, with non-Orthodox Jews on matters of shared communal concern.

Jacob Katz has summarized the changed world of central European Jewry: "Jews entered European society but did not merge with it."[147] Hildesheimer confronted the reality of Jewish religious and cultural pluralism in the contemporary age by telescoping a vision of Orthodoxy that permitted him to remain true to his own religious principles while simultaneously participating with the non-Orthodox Jewish world on matters he felt did not conflict with those principles. This stance of selective and limited cooperation with the non-Orthodox Jewish world provides one of the paradigms contemporary Jewish Orthodoxy has adopted toward the reality of Jewish religious and cultural pluralism. It thus provides an insight into one segment of modern Orthodox Judaism's reaction to the contemporary world. The literature does not indicate, however, whether Hildesheimer personally resolved the tensions inherent in his position. In this sense, one may view Hildesheimer as paradigmatic of the modern Orthodox Jew of whom Samuel Heilman speaks in his article "Constructing Orthodoxy." This Jew, Heilman states, oscillates constantly between the tug of traditional and modern values, and this fight is waged, Heilman contends, at the price of a great deal of psychic stress. Such tension, whether or not directly acknowledged by Esriel Hildesheimer, was at the heart of his dilemma in confronting the post-Emancipation Western world. Hildesheimer's genius resided primarily in a flexibility that permitted him to assess each and every situation according to its particular circumstances. This ability allowed him to develop policies for confronting and leading diverse Jewish constituencies who defined their Jewishness in a variety of ways.

4

The Tasks of Education

Esriel Hildesheimer's approach to education cannot be understood apart from the concept of *Bildung*, a notion that dominated the world of nineteenth-century German culture and pedagogy. As George L. Mosse has observed, "The word *Bildung* combines the meaning carried by the English word 'education' with notions of character formation and moral education." It suggested the accomplishments of the privileged and the aspirations of the middle class with a lofty philosophical view of human potential. *Bildung* was thus a natural outgrowth of the Enlightenment, with its stress on the individual and reason, as well as romanticism. Its function was "to lead the individual from superstition to enlightenment."[1]

Hildesheimer's commitment to this ideal is evidenced in his choice of citation for the frontispiece of the first annual report issued for his Eisenstadt yeshiva. The frontispiece featured an aphorism of Johann von Herder: "Places of learning are the spiritual guardians of the land."[2] Herder was one of the greatest proponents of *Bildung* ideology and believed, as Mosse has described it, "Man must grow like a plant . . . toward the unfolding of his personality until he becomes an harmonious, autonomous individual exemplifying both the continuing quest for knowledge and the moral imperative."[3]

For "modern Jews" seeking to integrate Jewish tradition into the larger German culture, *Bildung* provided a rationale and context for their acculturation:

> [Herder] had already envisioned the concept of *Bildung* as a means of overcoming the inequality between men. He wanted to level the dif-

115

ferences between the bourgeoisie and the aristocracy by confronting the nobility with an ideal which would deflate its pretensions. The instrument used to abolish the inequality between bourgeois and aristocrat might also work to transcend the differences between the Jewish and the German middle classes. The centrality of the ideal of *Bildung* in German-Jewish consciousness must be understood from the very beginning . . . [as] fundamental to the search for a new Jewish identity after emancipation.[4]

Hildesheimer exemplified this post-Emancipation German-Jewish consciousness. In his own upbringing and schooling and in the philosophy of education that guided his decisions about how to train others to serve the Jewish community, Hildesheimer exhibited a twin commitment to the "quest for knowledge" and the "moral imperative." In other words, he not only reflected a commitment to the preservation of Jewish tradition, he perpetuated the ideal of *Bildung* as well. Simultaneously, his rabbinic leadership and his educational institutions provided pragmatic means toward achieving this distinctive synthesis of Judaism with the modern world.

Hildesheimer devoted his life's work to the survival of Orthodox Judaism in the modern world. To his way of thinking, survival was dependent on the forging of educational policies and the establishment of Jewish educational institutions which would suit the changed character of the nineteenth-century central European Jewish world.[5] Hildesheimer felt that the need for secular studies, in addition to traditional Jewish knowledge, grew daily. If Orthodox Jews wanted to persist and flourish, they had to create educational institutions that would reflect this contemporary need.[6] While still in Hungary, Hildesheimer commented that "the only possibility for a future directed against absolute destruction and the deadening paralysis of indifference" lay in the building of a rabbinical seminary, as well as elementary and high schools, where a modernist educational policy of *Torah im Derekh Eretz* would be implemented.[7] In Hildesheimer's words, such institutions "were the one bulwark offered against the spread of ignorance in relation to Torah and its commandments [in the present as well as in the future]."[8] Several years later, when he had moved to Berlin, he again wrote that the "one remedy" for the situation confronting contemporary Orthodox Jewry was "to educate our children in accordance with the philosophy of *Torah im Derekh Eretz.*"[9]

The tasks of education constituted the core of Hildesheimer's activities and interests throughout his lifetime. The building of educational institutions, the creation of appropriate curricula for these institutions, the administration and teaching required to run them, the engagement in academic research, and the forging of an educational philosophy all stand as specific areas to which he devoted his energies. Indeed, Hildesheimer's fame and the major part of his legacy to the Jewish world rest upon his achievements in each of these spheres of education.

The roots of Hildesheimer's attitudes toward the relationship between Jewish and secular culture can be traced back to his own childhood education in Halberstadt. Hildesheimer was enrolled as a student in Hasharat Zvi, the first Orthodox elementary school in Germany to include secular subjects in the elementary school curriculum.[10] The curriculum at Hasharat Zvi reflected an educational philosophy that departed radically from that deemed advisable by an earlier generation. For example, Rabbi Pinchas Horowitz, the teacher of Esriel's father, had felt that secular learning constituted "a neglect of the study of Torah." He and other traditionalists took to heart the words of the talmudic maxim "Go out and discover an hour which is neither day nor night, and in that hour apprehend Greek wisdom [i.e., secular knowledge]" (*Menahot* 99b). Hildesheimer was thus exposed from a very early age to a system of education which deviated from the classical medieval European Jewish yeshiva education with its exclusive emphasis on Jewish textual studies.[11]

Hasharat Zvi differed in two other highly significant respects from the traditional Jewish elementary school of the European Middle Ages. First, the language of instruction was German, not Yiddish. Such an innovation indicates a positive attitude toward German culture on the administration's part and a desire that the graduates be able to participate fully in the intellectual and political life of the nation in which they lived. Moreover, this positive attitude toward contemporary Germany and sensitivity to current cultural trends are evidenced in the school's second major departure from the past. In 1827, Esriel's second year in the school, the administration decided to admit girls into the institution. Thus, from his earliest years, Esriel was a part of a system of Jewish education that saw no unbridgeable gap between secular and religious learning, between a devotion to Judaism and a commitment to German culture and citizenship, or between an affirmation of tradition and educational innovations (e.g., the education of women in formal educational settings)[12] which could be countenanced by halakha.[13]

All these views were reinforced by his years of study with Rabbi Jacob Ettlinger in the Altona yeshiva and through Hildesheimer's lifelong relationship with Ettlinger. Ettlinger, too, stood apart from his Orthodox contemporaries; he believed that a mastery of the vernacular was essential for Orthodox rabbis, and his educational program emphasized the importance of fluency in modern languages. German, not Yiddish, was the language of instruction in his yeshiva, in contrast with the custom in the central European yeshivot of the day. Furthermore, Ettlinger preached, wrote articles, and even prepared prayers in German and Danish—all of which marked him as a crucial figure "in the emergence of Modern Orthodoxy in Germany." Judith Bleich reports that Ettlinger's German sermons represent a departure from the traditional genre of halakhic discourse delivered by the medieval European rabbi and, instead, typify the moral and religious exhortations of the nineteenth-century German Jewish preacher.[14]

Ettlinger's attitude toward secular education, his divergence from the approach of traditionalists such as the Hatam Sofer, is manifest in a private religious elementary school which he opened in Altona in January 1839. At the time, Altona was in the kingdom of Denmark, and the study of Danish constituted a core part of the general studies curriculum. Though Ettlinger insisted that all teachers in the Jewish studies section of the school be Orthodox Jews, he employed non-Jews to teach secular subjects. Approximately nine to thirteen hours a week were devoted to Jewish studies—about 30 percent of the instructional time. Ettlinger, in Bleich's words, "was fully aware of the necessity of offering students a secular education . . . and stressed the need to train students in good citizenship, social conduct, and deportment."[15]

Ettlinger also favored offering women the opportunity for formal religious instruction, and he permitted girls to be educated in his school. Though he separated the girls from the boys in the classroom, Bleich recounts that Ettlinger provided the girls with opportunities to be educated in both secular and Judaic subjects. The education of women "was seen by Ettlinger . . . as a necessary component of the communal educational system." Although "formal religious education of women was certainly an innovation in Orthodox circles," Ettlinger justified it by an appeal to tradition.[16] Hildesheimer's early impressions at Hasharat Zvi were therefore confirmed by the attitudes transferred to him by his teacher Ettlinger.

In addition, it is significant that Ettlinger considered the establishment of a modern Orthodox rabbinical seminary to be one of the greatest desiderata of modern Orthodoxy. Ettlinger felt that, if such a school was not erected, the cause of Orthodox Judaism in the modern world might be lost. There is no doubt that this attitude penetrated deeply into Hildesheimer's outlook, for in 1872, when Hildesheimer was compelled to justify the ideal of a modern Orthodox rabbinical seminary to hostile and conservative Orthodox critics, he pointed to Ettlinger's proposed seminary.[17]

Yet, though Ettlinger affirmed the worth of secular study and scholarship, he felt that "to the Jew Torah study must always occupy the central position in terms of his intellectual endeavors." Indeed, secular studies were of secondary import, he wrote, and should be pursued "only to the degree and measure which is [necessary for the] strengthening of Torah."[18] This view that secular studies served to enhance both the study of Torah and the position of Orthodoxy in the modern world meant that Ettlinger departed subtly from the *Torah im Derekh Eretz* philosophy of Rabbi Samson Raphael Hirsch, as will be discussed below. Ettlinger differed from Hirsch in that, though he regarded secular scholarship as vital, he always considered it as a handmaiden to Torah.[19] Ettlinger's attitude greatly influenced Hildesheimer's own philosophy of *Torah im Derekh Eretz*, which is one of the theoretical, if not practical, contrasts between himself and Hirsch in the realm of education.

Finally, Bleich provides a summary of Ettlinger's view of education which proves to be equally insightful for understanding Hildesheimer's strong commitment to innovative education:

> Ettlinger . . . [was] imbued with the conviction that the survival of Judaism was directly dependent on the success of the education and training of its youth. The cause of Orthodoxy . . . could not be served by quiescence. *Orthodoxy must move beyond rearguard action to constructive efforts.* Communications and writings publicizing Orthodox views were useful and necessary, but education was an even more essential area of communal concern. To survive and succeed, Orthodoxy must fashion educational institutions which would prove viable in modern society.[20]

Hildesheimer's personal convictions are apparent in a letter he wrote to his fiancée, Henriette Hirsch, while he was still a graduate student. At the time, Hildesheimer was pursuing his doctorate (another indication of Ettlinger's influence), and he complained that nine-tenths of the Jewish students he encountered at the university were either heretics or indifferent to religion. He expressed his views on religion and education: "Religion demands from its adherents a solid character . . . and gives one the strength to withstand any tempest. . . . Only that which is connected with religion, more or less, receives my full stamp of approval. *This explains my constant, unremitting engagement in academics because for me it stands in the service of religion.*"[21] This youthful outlook on the value of secular education and the role he assigned it in his philosophy of *Torah im Derekh Eretz* echo the views of Ettlinger and foreshadow the mature Hildesheimer's thoughts on secular studies. For though Hildesheimer was a defender and an enthusiastic proponent of the necessity of secular learning throughout his life, he did not acknowledge the parity of secular and religious studies. Given the place of *Bildung* in shaping his own educational experiences and outlook, it is paradoxical that he too regarded secular studies as a "handmaiden" to religion.[22]

Hildesheimer's views regarding the relationship between religious and secular studies can be found in his correspondence with Meir Hirsch in 1847. Hirsch, a former classmate from the Altona yeshiva, wrote to ask Hildesheimer's opinion on whether secular learning was permissible and to inquire as to Hildesheimer's view of the proper relationship between secular and religious studies. Hildesheimer replied that secular studies were not only permissible, they were a "necessity" in light of contemporary conditions. Indeed, without secular knowledge, the Orthodox Jew would be unable to explicate Judaism in a suitable manner to the masses of Jewry and, in addition, would be incapable of earning a living in a society in which most jobs demanded secular knowledge and skills. But Hildesheimer was equally resolute in asserting that a correct sense of priorities had to be established by the religious Jew in assessing the relative importance of each of these areas of knowledge. Hildesheimer wrote, "That which is of primary significance [the *ikar*] should not be reduced to a status of that which is of secondary significance [the *tafel*, i.e., secular learning]; nor should that which is of secondary significance be elevated to a rank of that which is of primary significance [i.e., religious learning]."[23] In theory, then, although Hildesheimer was an enthusiastic advocate of secular studies, he does not appear to have felt they were worthy of study in their own right. Rather, they served a useful purpose, aiding one either in the study of Torah or in earning a living.

Similarly, in the first report Hildesheimer issued about his Eisenstadt yeshiva in 1858, he justified the inclusion of secular subjects such as mathematics, Latin, Greek, geography, and history in the school's curriculum by claiming that their study would aid in the mastery of traditional Jewish religious subjects. A knowledge of mathematics, for example, would help the students with their comprehension of certain sections in the Talmud. He defended the study of Latin and Greek on the grounds that a familiarity with these languages would aid the student in mastering certain terms in both Talmud and Midrash.[24] Hildesheimer also wrote in his third report on the yeshiva in 1869 that a "knowledge of language and mathematics is essential for being an educated man," thus reflecting his commitment to and affirmation of secular culture and *Bildung*. In light of Hildesheimer's view that secular studies were subordinate to religion in his philosophy of *Torah im Derekh Eretz*, it is equally significant that he included no philosophy courses in the curriculum of the Eisenstadt school. Hildesheimer undoubtedly feared that exposure to such secular modes of thought could lead his students into the path of heresy.[25] Secular studies were ostensibly pursued in the Eisenstadt yeshiva because of the contribution they could make to the cause of Orthodox Judaism. For Hildesheimer, as for his teacher Ettlinger, the affirmation of secular modes of thought and culture was not meant to imply that such learning enjoyed a position of parity with traditional religious learning. Secular studies were not to be undertaken when they might conflict with religious values; they were to be pursued if they aided "the cause of Torah" and were to be neglected if they did not.

Samson Raphael Hirsch held to a different philosophy of *Torah im Derekh Eretz*. In his commentary on Genesis 3:24, Hirsch defines *Derekh Eretz* as "the way of culture, the way of social refinement . . . the first tutor and educator to morals, manners, and order." This all-embracing sense of *Derekh Eretz*, very much akin to *Bildung*, appears to have come down through the generations of the Hirsch family, for the term *Derekh Eretz* is found in the writings of his immediate ancestors. His grandfather Rabbi Menahem Mendel Frankfurter employed the term, and in 1805 his father, Raphael Aryeh, established a "Beth Midrash for Jewish Boys" dedicated to the teaching of "Torah, morals and wisdom, and good behavior, and

Derekh Eretz." The school was continued and developed by the Hakham Bernays after 1822. Hence, for Hirsch, *Derekh Eretz* represented the vibrant social fabric of Jewish life in all of its moral, cultural, and intellectual breadth. Israel could no more exist without this social fabric than it could exist without Torah. Thus Hirsch elevated *Derekh Eretz* to a religious level, and for him, *Torah im Derekh Eretz* represented the essence of Judaism.[26]

Mordechai Breuer has pointed out that the relationship between Torah and *Derekh Eretz* in the educational philosophy of Hirsch are as form and matter to each other. In words that seem to reflect a Platonic ideal, Breuer quotes Yehiel Yaakov Weinberg's encapsulation of Hirsch's doctrine: "*Derekh Eretz* is none other than the matter which is molded into form by the activity of Torah." The two are interdependent. As "Judaism and culture . . . achieve complete identity," there is to Hirsch no such thing as "secular or 'extraneous' wisdom and studies." All true wisdom and knowledge, both that which is labeled Torah and that which is labeled "ostensibly secular," have as their source the one God. And because the two are defined as a single identity, parts of a unified whole, a "marriage" (*Vermählung*) takes place between Torah and *Derekh Eretz*, from a Hirschian perspective. This, in Breuer's view, allowed Hirsch to assert that there was "no compromise of principle with the spirit of the time" in his *Torah im Derekh Eretz* philosophy.[27] Hirsch endowed *Derekh Eretz* with religious significance. His approach to the concept was a "philosophical-humanistic" one. Hildesheimer, by contrast, took a "practical, pragmatic" stance toward *Derekh Eretz* and never appears to have conferred on it a comparable sacred status.[28]

The complexity of Hildesheimer's attitude toward secular knowledge, as well as the ultimately pragmatic stance he adopted in regard to it, can be seen in his position on the education of girls. On one hand, Hildesheimer had been exposed to coeducation in his elementary school classroom in Halberstadt; later, his teacher Ettlinger advocated the education of women. Thus, on one level, Hildesheimer did not perceive the education of women as a radical departure, a break from a traditional to a modern practice. On the other hand, Hildesheimer was careful to justify his support for the education of girls on the basis of a mishnaic passage found in Sotah 3:4 (Ben Azzai says, "A man is obligated to teach his daughter Torah"). He obviously understood that the education of women was a controversial issue in Orthodox circles and, consequently, wanted to justify it by an appeal to the tradition.[29]

More significantly, Hildesheimer pointed out the pragmatic advantages to be gained by Jewish men if women were educated. For example, in a pamphlet he wrote in 1871, *A Few Words Regarding the Religious Instruction of Girls*, Hildesheimer argued that educating girls in Judaica would have a positive impact on Jewish family life and would enable these girls, upon their entry into adulthood, to aid in the Jewish education of their sons. It was a necessity, Hildesheimer claimed, to educate these girls in Bible and Hebrew, for "if it is true that knowledge is power, then the Jewish knowledge of our wives and young ladies will contribute to an invincible Jewish power—to a power in the home, in Jewish family life, and to a priceless influence in the area of the education of our sons." Thus Hildesheimer established a curriculum in his Berlin congregation in which young women were taught the Pentateuch, Prophets, Hebrew, liturgy, history, the grace after meals, the ethics of the fathers, and Maimonides' Thirteen Principles of Faith. Unlike the boys, however, they were not taught Talmud, Midrash, or codes.[30]

Seventeen years later, in a letter to his pupil Josef Rosenfeld, Hildesheimer again stressed that instruction of girls in Bible was permitted by both the Talmud and codes. Moreover, Hildesheimer recommended such education both on traditional religious grounds and because "the education of a child, and naturally of a girl as well, rests in the first place upon an ethical consciousness and on the promotion of a sense of morality, which, however, can only be achieved by a knowledge of the original [biblical] text." Hildesheimer also encouraged this instruction from a religious point of view and stated, "I am acquainted with many cases where such instruction was so eminently successful that the girls were able to instruct their sons in biblical knowledge."[31] In the critical area of the Jewish education of women, we thus see that Hildesheimer, in spite of his strong support for what must be regarded as an innovation, argued for this reform on utilitarian grounds, which he justified by an appeal to the strengthening of tradition. On the practical level, in assessing Hildesheimer's attitude concerning *Torah im Derekh Eretz*, there is little to distinguish his approach to secular learning from that of either his more liberal colleagues or, for that matter, Samson Raphael Hirsch. On the theoretical level, however, since he did not accord Torah and *Derekh Eretz* parity, the distinction is real and apparent.[32]

Fully to apprehend Hildesheimer's attitude toward *Torah im Derekh Eretz*, it is instructive to analyze his struggles for implementation of this philosophy in the curriculum of the proposed orphanage in the Land of Israel. This was the project that grew out of Heinrich Graetz's report on the pitiful conditions under which many Jewish orphans in Israel were forced to live. Hildesheimer felt the only solution to this dilemma was to establish a Jewish orphanage and training school where these youths could be cared for physically and learn a trade. Moreover, though Hildesheimer felt that the education of these children should be based on the "Holy Torah," he also felt it was essential that they receive instruction in certain secular subjects and trades. Only in this way could the youngsters later lead independent lives. For the girls this meant instruction in household duties, as "household management is their principal task in life."[33]

Hildesheimer's vision of the effects such an education could have on Jewish life in Zion is found in an article he wrote in *Die Jüdische Presse:*

> A radiant picture of Jerusalem stands as an ideal before my eyes . . . an upright, loyal young generation of which one may be justly proud, brought up in Palestine, imbued with deep and real religious feeling, and equipped with *indispensable secular knowledge.* By their peace-loving and blameless conduct they are to uphold the honor of Jerusalem. The average individual shall have a sound knowledge of Bible and Talmud, and the majority, according to their capacity and inclination, should penetrate deep into Jewish Scriptures; they should earn their living by their own toil—by craftsmanship or trade which is properly learned and honestly exercised.[34]

Yet such support of secular learning on the Jewish soil of the Land of Israel provoked hostile attacks against Hildesheimer on the part of Jewish religious leaders living there. These leaders proclaimed that even if the founders of Hildesheimer's proposed school "were learned, righteous, strong in faith, and knowledgeable in Torah; even if they say the school was founded for the sake of heaven in order to increase faith . . . they should not be heeded."[35] Particularly disturbing to these religious leaders was Hildesheimer's proposal that "only the most suited be educated exclusively in Torah. The others should be directed toward agriculture, industry, and trade."[36] The Jerusalem rabbinate viewed this as a direct profanation of the Holy Land and 325 rabbis (all Ashkenazim) signed a petition to oppose Hildesheimer's proposed school. They felt that the old educational system, in which secular subjects were banned from the curriculum, ought to be retained, and in a pamphlet issued on the Fourth of Kislev 5633 (1872), these rabbis declared that anyone who taught secular subjects in the Land of Israel would be subject to a ban of *cherem* (excommunication). Furthermore, Rabbi Meir Urbach and his court sent a special letter to Hildesheimer telling him of their shock and outrage concerning the proposed orphanage, in which "not Torah alone, but also secular subjects would be taught," and which would produce "technicians."[37]

Hildesheimer refused to be cowed by these attacks. Although criticism of him and his proposals mounted, he continued to insist that the one remedy for the situation then obtaining in the Land of Israel was "to educate the children according to a philosophy of *Torah im Derekh Eretz.*"[38] The modernization of education in Israel had to proceed at as rapid a rate as was possible for, Hildesheimer observed, "knowledge is power." Failure to grasp this fact would consign Jewish Orthodoxy, in Palestine as in Europe, to a position of weakness.[39] Only individuals who were economically self-sufficient could claim real strength, in Hildesheimer's opinion; and these individuals could never attain such a position without a knowledge of secular subjects, as well as industrial and agricultural training. Thus he persisted in support for this educational policy and, in 1882, when writing about the controversial stance he had taken, Hildesheimer wondered, "Who has more enemies than I, standing against me with sword and spear? But as a German saying has it, 'Many enemies. Much honor.' "[40]

Hildesheimer's commitment to secular studies and his refusal to back down in the face of these assaults on his person and his educational philosophy emerge in correspondence he had with Rabbi Akiba Lehren of Amsterdam in 1873. Rabbi Lehren, who was one of the most active supporters of the Jewish settlement in Eretz Yisrael during the nineteenth century, asked Hildesheimer to withdraw his support for the proposed school in Jerusalem. Lehren acknowledged that secular learning was essential for the Jews of Europe, but this was the case only because it permitted the Orthodox to attain a position of honor and respect in the eyes of the gentile world. Further, it allowed the Orthodox to combat the Reformers on their own terms. In other words, for Lehren, secular study was legitimated only by practical considerations. In the Land of Israel, therefore, where such study would diminish the time that could be devoted to the study of Torah, it would be a profanation.[41]

Hildesheimer disagreed vehemently with Lehren. "It is as clear as the sun," Hildesheimer wrote, "that Jewish souls are being lost every day." It was thus crucial, in Hildesheimer's opinion, to construct schools in which secular subjects would be part of the curriculum. Isolation from the dominant cultural trends of the nineteenth century was impossible, according to Hildesheimer; and though he did not advocate the establishment of an educational system based on the model of the German *Gymnasium*, he did claim that enough secular subjects had to be taught to allow the students "to be in the world and become economically self-sufficient." Not all students were "as gifted as Abbaye and Rava." Therefore, to teach them Torah exclusively was, in Hildesheimer's opinion, a mistake.[42]

Hildesheimer's commitment to an educational philosophy of *Torah im Derekh Eretz* was absolute. He did not see it, as did Rabbi Lehren, simply as a concession to the European environment. He expanded its application to Eretz Yisrael as well. Nevertheless, there does not appear to be a philosophical difference between the two men. For nothing Hildesheimer stated in his debate with Lehren alters the view expounded earlier that Hildesheimer did not assign secular study the same level of priority he did to religious study in his philosophy of education. Even in this struggle, Hildesheimer was ultimately the pragmatist. Hildesheimer did not defend the need for secular study for its own sake. Rather, he claimed that "the *need* for such learning grows daily, even in the Orient." Hildesheimer's stance regarding secular study was as practical, in theory, as Lehren's. Secular study, in his opinion, would result in practical gains for the Jewish people in general and Orthodoxy in particular. The one distinction between the two was that for Lehren the gains were limited to Europe, whereas for Hildesheimer these gains were expanded to include the promise of economic self-sufficiency for the Orthodox Jews of the Holy Land. This should underscore the point that Hildesheimer seems never to have legitimated the study of secular subjects as worthy in their own right. Indeed, in writing to Lehren, he highlighted the primacy of Torah at the end of the letter when he wrote, "All my efforts are meant only to magnify and expand the glory of Torah."[43]

In realistic terms, of course, this theoretical distinction meant little. For Hildesheimer's pragmatic defense of secular education meant that the institutions he created were as geared to the necessity for secular learning as were the institutions created by the Reformers or Samson Raphael Hirsch. Thus Hildesheimer permitted Jewish schoolchildren in Germany to exercise on the Sabbath lest they be treated with contempt by the German gentile school authorities. In so doing, Hildesheimer obviously acquiesced to the social reality of a world in which Jewish children attended school on the Sabbath. Although Hildesheimer was certainly not happy about that, he realized that he was powerless to prevent attendance and did all in his power to lessen the offenses a Jewish schoolchild might commit by attending school on the Sabbath.[44] Also, Hildesheimer established a *Musaf* (additional) prayer service with a full reading on Saturday afternoon in his own congregation in Berlin, Adass Jisroel, for youngsters who had to attend school on Saturday morning. Hildesheimer clearly accepted the social reality of his day and, in large measure, justified the need for secular study on the grounds that such learning could not be prevented and was, in fact, a necessity of the times.

A particular incident reflects Hildesheimer's personal commitment to *Bildung* and the implication that contemporary secular studies and modern pedagogical advancements could be elevated so as to possess positions of significant status within Jewish law. In an article later published as a responsum, Hildesheimer discussed the question of whether deaf-mutes were eligible to serve as witnesses in Jewish legal proceedings and other ritual matters. After citing the opinions of legal authorities on both sides of this issue, Hildesheimer included a testimonial letter from Rabbi Joel Deutsch, head of the Institute for the Deaf-Mute in Vienna. Deutsch claimed that the students trained in his school were fully capable intellectually, and he sent Hildesheimer two articles written by a graduate of the institute, Bernhard Brill, to underscore his point. After praising the articles and scholarly capabilities of their author, Deutsch wrote, "I doubt there are many non-impaired people who are able to express their ideas in a sharper or clearer manner than Bernhard."[45]

Hildesheimer agreed with Deutsch and said that these articles certainly disproved the arguments of Maharam Schick, the Hungarian halakhic authority, who dismissed deaf-mutes as intellectually incapable and therefore incompetent to serve as witnesses in Jewish legal proceedings or ritual matters. It was this point of intellectual competence that Hildesheimer considered to be of prime concern in determining the matter. In rabbinic times, when no pedagogic devices existed for the instruction of these persons, the rabbis naturally ruled that they were ineligible to serve as witnesses. But the law that forbade the deaf-mute from serving as a witness in Jewish legal proceedings did not foresee the modern pedagogic techniques which had been developed to educate such handicapped persons.

Hildesheimer contended that the rabbinic text was not intended literally to exclude persons who were born deaf-mutes. Any individual who demonstrated intellectual abilities comparable to those of Bernhard Brill should not be considered, in Hildesheimer's opinion, ineligible to serve as a witness according to Jewish law. Moreover, in its broadest sense, the halakha made provision for such scientific advancements, and consequently, the disabled individual who satisfactorily completed the training offered in institutions such as the Viennese Institute for the Deaf-Mute was to be considered a Jew with full legal powers and responsibilities.[46] Hildesheimer stands here as a modernist, who clearly affirmed the value and worth of modern education and its techniques, unlike his slightly senior colleague Schick (1807–79), who adamantly opposed granting even the slightest role to modern education and educational techniques in a Jewish legal matter such as this.

Hildesheimer's philosophy of *Torah im Derekh Eretz* was to serve as the intellectual foundation upon which his educational institutions rested. On one hand, there is no question that, on the theoretical plane, secular studies did not enjoy the same status he ascribed to religious knowledge and study. Hildesheimer's attitude toward secular learning, from this perspective, must fundamentally be described as traditionalist. On the other hand, his attitude had little practical impact on the educational positions he adopted. His advocacy of the education of women, for example, marks him as a "modern" willing to break with the medieval tradition of Jewish education in a significant way. Furthermore, his view of the contemporary world and the demands it placed on Judaism made him regard secular knowledge and learning as absolutely necessary. He promoted its inclusion in the curriculum of his own and other Jewish educational institutions and, in every instance, was unyielding whenever opposition was voiced to such educational programs.

Undoubtedly, his stances on these matters reflect his pragmatism and his sense of the exigencies of his time. But they also reveal his own educational immersion in and exposure to the world of nineteenth-century German culture, one preeminently informed by the value of *Bildung*. His educational efforts, to whose description we now turn, represent the concrete expression of these attitudes, values, and concerns.

In 1851, the leaders of the Eisenstadt community instructed their new rabbi, Esriel Hildesheimer, to devote his major efforts to the field of education, "an area currently neglected."[47] Hildesheimer gladly complied with this request and stated that concern with educational matters was his "highest priority."[48] Although Hildesheimer attended to all facets and levels of Jewish education, he decided to focus his attention on a reform in the educational training of rabbis. This meant that Hildesheimer decided to depart from the traditional model of rabbinic education and to cultivate leadership by educating rabbis in secular as well as religious subjects.

Immediately upon his arrival in Eisenstadt, Hildesheimer established a yeshiva which was probably the first in history to include both secular and religious subjects in its curriculum. Moreover, Hildesheimer decided that all courses in his yeshiva would be taught in the vernacular, and not in Yiddish, as was customary in other *yeshivot* of his day. Both of these innovations roused the ire of his Hungarian Orthodox rabbinical colleagues. They viewed the changes as major deviations from traditional Judaism; some, indeed, considered the changes as signs of heresy on Hildesheimer's part and condemned him for them.[49] Hildesheimer did not yield to the critics. As he wrote, "It is only in the reorganization of the yeshiva . . . that there still exists the one guarantee for the future, the one bulwark against the spread of ignorance in relation to Torah and *Mitzvot*. . . . [The yeshiva alone] provides the hope for a better future."[50] It is crucial that even in these early years in Hungary, Hildesheimer did not see a "reorganization" of the yeshiva as sufficient to accomplish his goal of producing capable rabbinic leaders for contemporary Orthodoxy. Rather, he felt that the ultimate solution to this problem was the establishment of a first-rate modern Orthodox rabbinical seminary. Several incidents attest to this view.

In the first place, Hildesheimer refused to join with the other Orthodox rabbis in Hungary in their intractable opposition to the creation of a modern rabbinical seminary. For, in Hildesheimer's opinion, the creation of such an institution was Orthodoxy's major hope for the future.

That Hildesheimer viewed his own Eisenstadt school as potentially being such a school is indicated by the first report he published describing the yeshiva, its accomplishments, its curriculum, and its goals. Appearing in 1858, the report was entitled *Erster Bericht-Lehranstalt für Rabbinats-Kandidaten zu Eisenstadt*. The report contended that the school was dedicated to "our Orthodox faith, our holy Tradition, which must be the spirit of this and every age."[51] The opening page quoted the passage from Pirkei Avot,

"Raise up many disciples and make a hedge around the Torah," as an indication of the school's goals. In apposition to this traditional text, Hildesheimer cited the words of the great German poet Johann von Herder: "Places of learning are the spiritual guardians of the land." This symbolic juxtaposition of passages, one a classic rabbinic text, the other a modern avowal of the philosophy of *Bildung*, reveals the broader goals of Hildesheimer's institution. Through the use of these two quotes in Hebrew and in German, Hildesheimer expressed his commitment to the educational philosophy of *Torah im Derekh Eretz*. The bulk of the report was issued in German, not Hebrew, thus highlighting further the departure of his yeshiva from the more traditional ways of the previous centuries.

This alone does not indicate that Hildesheimer regarded his yeshiva as the embryo out of which a full-scale seminary might eventually emerge. An analysis of the requirements for admission to the school and its curriculum, however, leaves little room for doubt as to Hildesheimer's plans. To qualify for admission, students were expected to be familiar with German, geography, and general history. In addition, every student was to have some grounding in mathematics and Latin. Overall, Hildesheimer insisted that students needed to be grounded in the humanities before they could qualify for ordination as rabbis in the contemporary world.[52]

This precondition—that students be competent in the humanities to qualify for admission to the rabbinical school—was observed more in theory than in practice. In the same year that Hildesheimer issued his first report (1858), he was attacked by Leopold Löw, a follower of the Positive-Historical school, in the pages of the liberal journal *Ben Chananjah*. Löw focused his attack on the poor backgrounds in secular subjects possessed by candidates for the Eisenstadt yeshiva and the low level of secular instruction there. Of course, as a supporter of Frankel and the Jewish Theological Seminary in Breslau, Löw was interested both in discrediting Hildesheimer and in pointing out that Hildesheimer's school did not merit the title "seminary." He hoped thereby to lower the prestige of both Hildesheimer and his school in the eyes of the acculturated central European Jews to whom Hildesheimer's report was obviously addressed. In reply to Löw, Hildesheimer acknowledged that most of his students did possess weak backgrounds in secular subjects and that many of the thirty-nine students who made up the student body in 1858 were not fully qualified to be admitted as candidates for rabbinical ordination.[53] But Hildesheimer also stated that one of the goals of the yeshiva was to bring students up to the level where they could master these subjects. Consequently, the Eisenstadt yeshiva established a preparatory program to educate otherwise capable students who lacked sufficient secular educational backgrounds to be able to attend the school.[54]

It should be mentioned, as Löw did not, that in creating such a program in secular studies for these students, Hildesheimer was simply borrowing a practice initiated by Frankel in Breslau in 1851. In that year Frankel saw that there were not enough qualified candidates to meet the entrance standards of the Breslau seminary and, therefore, established a preparatory program to correct their deficiencies.[55] Hildesheimer's compensating measures should not be regarded as signs that he failed to adhere to the theoretical standards he created for admission to the rabbinical school. Rather, they indicate that, in 1858, though elements of central European Jewry desired rabbis equipped with a modern secular education, the community had not yet become sufficiently acculturated to produce enough qualified candidates for the rabbinical training that either a Frankel or a Hildesheimer envisioned. Further, the establishment of the preparatory program by Hildesheimer shows that he did desire that his students be as well qualified in secular education and upbringing as were graduates of the Breslau seminary, thus testifying to his commitment to the creation of a modern seminary on the foundations he was building in Eisenstadt.

The curriculum of the school most firmly embodied Hildesheimer's commitment to a modern rabbinical seminary. Although the bulk of instruction was devoted to Talmud and traditional rabbinic codes of Jewish law, mathematics and Latin were also required because Hildesheimer felt that certain sections of rabbinic texts could not be properly understood without a prior knowledge of these subjects. In addition, Hildesheimer focused on traditional rabbinic commentaries on the Bible and made such instruction a regular part of the rabbinic course of study. Homiletics became a standard course, and students were required to study Hebrew grammar with Gesenius and to read Josephus in Latin translation to gain a mastery of ancient Jewish history. German grammar, general history, geography, and Bible rounded out the curriculum. All of these last subjects were, of course, not a part of the curriculum of the traditional yeshiva. Thus, already by 1858, Hildesheimer's yeshiva appeared more closely akin—in its curriculum, its admissions requirements, and the philosophy of its founder—to a modern seminary than it did to a traditional yeshiva.[56]

The Eisenstadt yeshiva obviously fulfilled a need for Orthodox

Jewry in central Europe and throughout the world. By 1868, when Hildesheimer issued his second report on the school, enrollment had grown to 115 students, of whom 95 were enrolled as regular and 20 as preparatory students. They came from all over Europe, and one even hailed from New York. By that time the formal course of study was set for three to four years, and Hildesheimer had added Greek to the curriculum.[57] Formal academic papers by members of the faculty were appended to the report. In this way Hildesheimer once more determined that his rabbinical school conform to the model of a modern seminary, for it was the custom of seminaries such as Breslau to publish the researches of their faculty in seminary-sponsored publications.[58]

Obviously proud of the growth and stability of his yeshiva, Hildesheimer issued another report in 1869, his last year in Eisenstadt. In his introductory remarks, Hildesheimer observed that the moment was a crucial one in the cultural history of those Jews in Hungary and central Europe who were still faithful to the tradition. Even they, Hildesheimer contended, regarded a knowledge of languages and mathematics as essential if one were to be considered an "educated person." Although Hildesheimer maintained that the principal object of study in the school would always remain "Torah," he held that the secular instruction that supplemented this study was of enough import to assign the bulk of teaching duties in this area to himself.[59] An exact measure of the relative weight Hildesheimer assigned to *"Derekh Eretz"* as opposed to *"Torah"* can be derived from a glance at the students' schedules and curriculum.

Students in the Eisenstadt yeshiva generally attended classes for fifty-one to fifty-three hours per week. Thirty-five hours were devoted to Jewish learning while the remainder were spent on secular studies. The actual breakdown of the students' schedules was as follows: thirty hours a week, Talmud and codes; two to three hours, prophets and writings; two to three hours, Hebrew grammar; three hours, German; two to three hours, Latin (Cicero and Virgil); two hours, Hungarian; one hour, Greek (Homer); five hours, mathematics; one hour, geography; one hour, history; one hour, natural science.[60] Hildesheimer taught thirty-five to forty hours a week and instructed the most advanced students in Talmud and codes, as well as all students in many of the secular subjects. He encouraged the use of Hebrew as a spoken language within the yeshiva, and a Hebrew-speaking students' club was formed. This commitment to Hebrew, as well as his insistence that students master its grammar, reflects a nineteenth-century sensibility and represents yet another departure on the part of Hildesheimer and his yeshiva from the traditional European yeshiva model. Moreover, Hildesheimer believed that knowledge of Hungarian was becoming "more essential daily." His decision to include Hungarian and German in the formal curriculum of the school reflects both his commitment to spreading Orthodoxy among "enlightened" segments of the community and his immersion in and sensitivity to the dominant social and cultural trends of his day. That approximately two-thirds of the instructional time in the yeshiva was devoted to a mastery of traditional rabbinic literature also attests to the priority he assigned to religious as opposed to secular learning. In addition, there is no indication, aside from the emphasis that Hildesheimer placed on the mastery of Latin and Greek as an aid to the study of Talmud, that instruction in Talmud was conducted in accordance with modern standards of scholarship. Rather, it can be assumed that Hildesheimer, in teaching Talmud and codes to the students, did so in the traditional manner in which he himself had been instructed at the yeshiva of Jacob Ettlinger.[61] In this area there was notable continuity between past and present.

Hildesheimer was gratified by the success his yeshiva was enjoying, and his combination of religious and secular subjects apparently appealed to a significant segment of Jews in Europe during the nineteenth century. The enrollment at the Eisenstadt yeshiva in 1869 was 134. Of these students, 120 were regular and 14 were preparatory.[62] The secular educational status of European Jewry had obviously risen in the eleven years that had passed since the issuance of his first report in 1858. The school was now the second largest in Hungary, following the Sofer family yeshiva in Pressburg. Hildesheimer's students easily found employment as rabbis throughout Europe. In assessing his accomplishments, Hildesheimer was able to say that his yeshiva succeeded in producing students who were able "to fight the war on behalf of Torah and her commandments"[63] and enjoyed the respect of both "their congregants and their opponents."[64]

In spite of these successes, Hildesheimer remained the target of bitter attacks by his Orthodox colleagues, which made the criticisms of Leopold Löw appear mild by comparison. These Orthodox rabbis could not tolerate the reforms Hildesheimer introduced into the curriculum of the yeshiva and, precisely because Hildesheimer was Orthodox, regarded him as more dangerous than a "Reformer."

The views of Rabbi Eliezer Zusman Sofer are typical of the attitudes of these men. Rabbi Sofer wrote to Hildesheimer: "[Your seminary] is opposed by hundreds of scholars, and among them are the great leaders of Israel. . . . Secular learning is a foreign fire and almost all who encounter it do not return. . . . Therefore, the course of study [you prescribe] is a danger to youth." Speaking directly of the Eisenstadt yeshiva, Sofer continued: "We hear what your youth do there, walking around with maidens and sullying themselves with words of desire. Is it possible to remain in *kedushah* [sanctity] in this way?" Sofer concluded by expressing the hope that Hildesheimer would close his yeshiva and agitate no further for a seminary. Although such attacks were not unusual, Hildesheimer did reply to Sofer and, through him, to other critics of himself and his students. To begin with, Hildesheimer pointed out that "there is no *Bet Din Gadol* [high court] in our day. Thus no large scale authoritative decrees can be issued." In effect, Hildesheimer was pointing out to Sofer that which the Reformers and liberals often said to the Orthodox—that the authoritative structure of a Jewish past (it does not matter whether mythical or factual) no longer existed. Yet, unlike the Reformers, Hildesheimer did not then go on to argue that no such authority existed whatsoever. Rather, Hildesheimer said that there was an authority—Jewish law as codified in the Shulhan Aruch. Such law did not forbid, in Hildesheimer's opinion, the instruction he offered in his Eisenstadt school, nor did it proscribe the curriculum that might be offered in a full-scale modern rabbinical seminary. Moreover, Hildesheimer denied that his students were nonobservant and considered such defamations of their character "a deceit, a lie, and a slander." Hildesheimer continued: "About me, you are able to say what you want. You may call me 'sectarian,' a 'sinner,' or whatever you will. But an insult to my students I will not forgive."[65]

Sofer and Hildesheimer's other Orthodox colleagues in Hungary could not, in light of their commitment to the Hatam Sofer's policy of total resistance to the enticements of the contemporary world,[66] countenance or refrain from condemning Hildesheimer's reforms, but Hildesheimer remained firm in his refusal to yield to their censure. Hildesheimer pointed out that many of these critics condemned him for his refusal to accept students who had no background in secular studies into his yeshiva. "You rabbis," Hildesheimer wrote to Sofer, "rage against me" because of the failure to admit such students. "We are unable to change the whole world." Herein lies the major distinction between Hildesheimer and his Hungarian colleagues. Both groups, obviously, wanted to preserve traditional Judaism in the modern world. Both were committed to Jewish law in its totality, as they understood it. But their stratagems for achieving this goal, as Hildesheimer observed, were as different "as East is from West." Hildesheimer believed that attempts to erect a bulwark against the encroachments of the modern world were futile. Consequently, his educational policies were radically different from theirs. Thus in concluding the letter to Sofer, Hildesheimer stated:

> God has granted me the merit of having many excellent students . . . and because of this communities throughout the world contact me to send them rabbis who are educated in *Torah im Derekh Eretz*. Indeed, I am able to fulfill less than a quarter of those requests. . . . Thus, I find myself obligated to enlarge my school with all the powers at my disposal. . . . And, in spite of this, my lord Sofer and his friends think that all of this is a great sin and that I seduce and lead astray the young men of the Children of Israel.[67]

Hildesheimer's years in Hungary enabled him to solidify his educational policies and experiment with curriculum. His eighteen years as head of the Eisenstadt yeshiva refined his leadership skills and whetted his appetite for the chance to realize his dream of a modern rabbinical assembly. It was not long after this exchange of letters with Sofer that his chance appeared.

When members of Congregation Adass Jisroel and the Beth Hamidrasch Verein in Berlin approached Esriel Hildesheimer in 1867 to ask him to come to Berlin, he made it clear to them that the tasks of education, not the duties of the congregational rabbinate, were his first priority. He wrote, "I am and will be a teacher; thus my whole nature propels me. . . . Therefore, I will dedicate the greater part of my time [should I come to Berlin] to this holy vocation."[68] Moreover, Hildesheimer made it plain that he would not leave Eisenstadt unless the prospects for creating a seminary in Berlin were excellent.[69]

Arriving in Berlin in 1869, Hildesheimer focused his educational efforts on two fronts. First, he established a religious school for the children of Adass Jisroel. Boys and girls studied the prayerbook and the Pentateuch together, though boys alone studied one of the early

Adass Jisroel, exterior of synagogue, Berlin. This building also housed the Rabbiner-Seminar. The architecture is typical of formal German structures, including government buildings, of the time. (From the Collection of Hebrew Union College, Skirball Museum, Los Angeles, Lelo Carter, Photographer)

Adass Jisroel, interior of synagogue, toward the Ark (From the Collection of Hebrew Union College, Skirball Museum, Los Angeles, Lelo Carter, Photographer)

prophets. In addition, boys were taught either Isaiah, Psalms, or Job, while the girls received instruction either in Pirkei Avot or Proverbs. All students learned grammatical Hebrew, but the boys also received instruction in practical aspects of Jewish law. Bar mitzvah candidates were taught to read from the Torah and to conduct services in preparation for the bar mitzvah. The more advanced among them, who Hildesheimer hoped would one day become rabbis, studied Talmud and *Shulhan Aruch* with Hildesheimer himself seven hours a week. Hildesheimer offered these more advanced students courses in postbiblical Jewish literature.[70] Hildesheimer's active role in the establishment of this part-time school and the hours he spent teaching in it reveal once more his commitment to education as the key to assuring the Jewish future.

Nevertheless, Hildesheimer's major involvement remained the creation of a modern seminary. When Hildesheimer came to Berlin in the autumn of 1869, he immediately began the task of reorganizing the curriculum of the Beth Hamidrasch. Hildesheimer contended that academic subjects had to be added to the traditional curriculum of the school so that rabbis could be produced who were properly trained to fulfill their roles in the contemporary world. Consequently, he proposed that the curriculum be broadened from its exclusive concentration on Talmud and codes to include lessons in Bible, Mishnah, Hebrew grammar, Jewish legal decisors, Jewish history, Musar literature, pedagogical techniques, homiletics, and medieval Jewish philosophy. There were to be three levels of instruction, depending on the knowledge and abilities of the students. Hildesheimer regarded all these proposed changes, however, simply as an intermediate step in the transformation of the Beth Hamidrasch from its role as a place of traditional rabbinic learning to the status of a modern seminary. The board of the Beth Hamidrasch did not share Hildesheimer's vision. It was prepared to allow Hildesheimer to create a rabbinical department but was committed neither financially nor ideologically to the prospect of establishing a full-time seminary. As a result, Hildesheimer felt he could no longer center his attention on the Beth Hamidrasch as the focus for the development of a modern Orthodox rabbinical seminary. He began to look elsewhere for the realization of his dream.[71]

In May 1872, Hildesheimer addressed a letter to ten prominent and wealthy Orthodox Jews in Germany soliciting their support for the creation in Germany of a modern Orthodox seminary which would train candidates "for the high post of rabbi." Although it is unclear if all ten persons responded to Hildesheimer's appeal, the contents of the letter reveal Hildesheimer's concerns regarding the establishment of the seminary and the position he felt it would occupy in the life of German and ultimately all of European Jewry. At the outset, Hildesheimer noted that there were already two institutions in Berlin devoted to Jewish learning on an advanced level. The first, the Veitel-Heine-Ephraim'sche Stiftung, offered studies aimed at an ecumenical audience of Jews and Christians. Hildesheimer said little about the quality of the institution but opined that it could do little to regenerate genuine Jewish religious life in Germany and, obviously, it could not perform the function of training rabbis for German Jewry. Far more significant, and dangerous, was the second institution, the Hochschule für die Wissenschaft des Judentums, which had opened in 1872 for the purpose of training young men for the rabbinate. This school, headed by Abraham Geiger, could only lead its students to heresy. Geiger had shown himself to be a heretic by publishing his *Urschrift* on the Bible. And Hermann Steinthal, the German philologist and philosopher, who, along with Geiger, constituted "the soul of the institution," was equally heretical, in Hildesheimer's opinion. Hildesheimer stated that Steinthal's publications demonstrated that he was an atheist, an absolute denier of God's existence. Having men such as Geiger and Steinthal at the head of the Hochschule was worse than having no institution for the education of rabbis. Further, the decision to appoint David Kassel, an observant Jew, to the faculty demonstrated the danger such men posed to German Jewry at large. Kassel's appointment could only mislead the public into believing that authentic rabbis could be produced at the liberal institution. Therefore, Kassel's appointment was to be regarded as a prime example of chicanery on the part of Geiger and Steinthal. Hildesheimer was obviously attempting to persuade his potential supporters of the absolute need for an Orthodox rabbinical seminary. By criticizing and dismissing Kassel's appointment to the Hochschule faculty, he was eager to counter any potential claim that a traditional rabbi could be produced at the Hochschule. Ultimately, he wished to emphasize that there was a major institutional void in the life of the German Orthodox Jewish community.

Hildesheimer went on to speak of the significance Berlin as the imperial capital occupied in the cultural and social life of German Jewry. Its influence extended far beyond its confines, and its Jewish population was the largest in Hohenzollern Germany. Indeed, Hildesheimer claimed that the absence of proper Orthodox rabbinical leadership in Berlin had been a chief reason for his decision to leave Eisenstadt in favor of the capital. It is obvious that Hildesheimer, in addressing these prominent Jews who lived in scattered parts of Germany, was trying to persuade them of the wisdom of choosing Berlin as the site for his proposed seminary. In addition, though he did not mention it explicitly, it may be that Hildesheimer wanted to counter political claims that some contributors to his seminary may have made about the Jewish Theological Seminary in Breslau. Some of the persons to whom he was writing may have considered Frankel and his seminary sufficiently conservative to negate the rationale for creating a new Orthodox seminary in Berlin.

Having thus attacked the Hochschule theologically and disposed of the challenge of Breslau on practical grounds, Hildesheimer wrote of the necessity for properly qualified, university-trained Orthodox rabbis who could answer the challenge of Reform. Yet where would these rabbis come from? Lest there be any mistake, Hildesheimer carefully pointed out that the Orthodox-controlled teacher training institutes in Würzburg and Düsseldorf were not capable of educating such leaders. Although they could be praised for the task they did perform, it was clear that their standards were not those of an advanced seminary. Hildesheimer's letter, up to this point, clarified the need for creating an Orthodox rabbinical seminary and the need to locate the seminary in Berlin.

Hildesheimer was now ready to address the heart of the matter. He stated that throughout his years in Eisenstadt the need to secure funds in support of the yeshiva had been a constant and pressing concern. Nonetheless, Hildesheimer claimed that he never forgot, nor should the contributors, the larger purpose for which the money was sought—the cause of Orthodox Judaism in the contemporary world. Thus, in asking these persons to make considerable contributions to the potential Orthodox rabbinical seminary in Berlin, Hildesheimer wrote: "Behold, I dedicate this fund to the holiest of all causes. For the seminary must be acknowledged as a necessity; and for even an hour's delay in establishing it, we must give a strict accounting, given the sharp attacks from all sides on our holy religion."

Hildesheimer continued by defining precisely his goals for the proposed seminary. First, he stated that the seminary must be Orthodox and that the Orthodox Jewish community must be responsible for supporting it financially. Clearly, Hildesheimer viewed his proposed institution as a denominational one. Second, Hildesheimer insisted that the seminary be located in Berlin for the reasons cited above. Further, in light of the demands of the day, Hildesheimer contended: "There is an absolute necessity that our institution be able to meet the competition. Consequently, it is necessary that our faculty be able to answer the demands of the time, i.e., that they be fit to give academic lectures."

Indeed, the problem of securing the proper faculty was, in Hildesheimer's opinion, the most pressing. For the men who filled these positions not only had to be outstanding scholars, but, in contradistinction to the professors at the Hochschule, they had to be men of outstanding religious piety as well. Fortunately, Hildesheimer wrote that he had located such men. In fact, his initial appointments to the Rabbiner-Seminar faculty in 1873 and 1874—David Hoffmann, Abraham Berliner, and Jakob Barth—indicate that he was successful in securing men of exceptional academic repute and impeccable Jewish Orthodoxy. Hildesheimer's last goal for the proposed seminary was that it aim to serve the Orthodox Jewish community by preparing rabbis to serve Germany, Europe, and the rest of the world.

With this last goal stated, Hildesheimer again asked the recipients of his letter to give generously in support of this project. He wrote that the establishment of the seminary was of "infinite importance" to the life of German Jewry. Only the seminary, he concluded, "will strengthen and increase the power of Orthodox Judaism internally and raise its esteem externally. . . . From the day Israel was exiled from its land, no matter has been more important than this."[72]

The immediate result of Hildesheimer's letter was the formation of a central committee to raise funds for the proposed seminary. It consisted of two rabbis and five lay people from various parts of Germany: Oberrath J. Altmann of Karlsruhe, Rabbi Selig Auerbach of Halberstadt, Chief Rabbi Salomon Cohen of Schwerin, A. H. Heymann (a banker) and Gustav Hirsch of Berlin, Sally Lewisohn of Hamburg, and Emanuel Schwarzschild (another banker) of Frankfurt. In addition to this central committee, local committees throughout Germany and Europe were formed. They were successful in quickly raising money for the proposed seminary from contributors both inside and outside Germany, and land on which to erect the seminary was soon purchased. The government gave its authorization to the project and, on October 22, 1873, less than eighteen months after Hildesheimer penned his initial letter, the seminary was opened.[73]

True to his proposal that the seminary be an Orthodox institution, Hildesheimer named the school the Rabbiner-Seminar für das Orthodoxe Judentum. Within ten years, the school dropped all reference to Orthodox Judaism from its name and called itself instead Das Rabbiner-Seminar zu Berlin. Obviously, events from 1873 to 1883 caused Hildesheimer to feel that it was no longer necessary for the seminary to identify itself explicitly as an Orthodox institution, since the struggle between the liberals and the Orthodox had diminished from a state of open conflict to one of a realistic acceptance of "peaceful coexistence."[74] Or perhaps Hildesheimer decided to change the name of his institution and delete the denominational label from the school's title as a way of implicitly asserting that his school represented not merely a single branch of Judaism but was *the* legitimate bearer of Jewish tradition on German soil. Indeed, the decision to avoid denominational labels parallels decisions made at both the Hochschule and the Breslau seminary, neither of which included any denominational term in its name, thereby implying that each spoke for the whole of religious Judaism.

In any event, Hildesheimer clearly desired his seminary to appeal to individuals beyond the confines of the Orthodox community. Jacob Rosenheim (1870–1965) of Frankfurt, who grew up in Samson Raphael Hirsch's school and remained devoted to Hirsch's ideals throughout his life, has a passage in his memoirs that supports such a view of Hildesheimer. He reports that Hirsch questioned Hildesheimer's methods for financing the seminary. Hirsch was specifically critical of the broad circle of supporters upon whom the seminary was financially dependent, many of whom were far removed from Adass Jisroel and Orthodoxy. Indeed, the seminary's benefactors included liberal as well as Orthodox Jews, and Hirsch considered these to be dangerous associations.[75]

When Hildesheimer's seminary opened in 1873, it had for its motto "In all your ways acknowledge Him, and He will direct your paths" (Proverbs 3:6). Twenty students enrolled the first year, with only seven being designated full-time matriculants working toward a degree. All seven of these students came from Germany. The other thirteen, nonmatriculants who had to complete a *Gymnasium* education before being admitted as full-time degree candidates in the Rabbiner-Seminar, mostly hailed from outside Germany.[76]

Hildesheimer saw the opening of the seminary as the crowning moment of his life. *Der Israelit* described the day's events in the following words:

On the first day of Marheshvan, 5633, the gates of the seminary for the education of Orthodox rabbis, which was established through the efforts of Rabbi Esriel Hildesheimer of Congregation Adass Jisroel in Berlin, opened. Many persons and honored guests came from near and far to this seat of higher education on its day of dedication. Governmental officials also came to see the honor given Torah, and the Minister for Cultural Affairs himself sent a letter apologizing that he could not appear at the festivities, but he explained that he had been sick for the past several days and could not leave his house.

There are no words in our language to describe the glory of this great day. With all our heart we bless the great Rabbi and Gaon mentioned above, for soon may our eyes and the eyes of the entire household of Israel behold the fruits which will spring from this great labor; and may it not be necessary for the Children of Israel in Germany to wander any longer in the forest of Breslau to seek their rabbis. May God grant that the rabbis who emerge from the new rabbinical school in Berlin be imbued with Torah and piety and that faith and understanding will walk together like twins in their hearts and in their deeds. May this be God's will and let us say amen.[77]

The seminary was not without its critics. Just a few days before the opening of the seminary, Samson Raphael Hirsch employed the pages of *Der Israelit* to attack Hildesheimer and the Rabbiner-Seminar for the decision to study *Wissenschaft des Judentums* within its walls. Hirsch feared that the Rabbiner-Seminar would simply replicate the program of the Breslau seminary and that sufficient attention would not be paid to the study of traditional rabbinic texts.[78] In response to these charges, Hildesheimer emphasized in his remarks at the opening of the seminary that the study of *Wissenschaft des Judentums*, which was to be a hallmark of the Berlin school, could and would be harnessed in the service of traditional Judaism.[79] Hildesheimer's address at the inauguration of the Rabbiner-Seminar should thus be seen as both a statement of his own educational philosophy and a response to Hirsch and other potential Orthodox critics. Hildesheimer stated: "It is impossible that the quest for knowledge in one area of learning will not build a bridge to other areas of knowledge."

Anxious to assert the primacy which the study of religious texts would assume in the curriculum of the seminary, Hildesheimer continued: "Jewish learning is 'our life and the length of our days,' as we pray every day in the evening prayers. And it is inconceivable that this ideal will not sink anchor in other waters of the spiritual world. We are proud, very proud, about this sanctification of God's

Name. . . . Our time here will be devoted as much as possible to Talmud and *Poskim* [Jewish legal decisors]." Hildesheimer also pointed to the importance of *Wissenschaft des Judentums* and defended its inclusion in the curriculum of the Rabbiner-Seminar:

> Yet, our other studies will not be neglected and we will engage in these different areas with the same love, as all our study will be for the sake of heaven. The second half of this century has brought several changes: the new Science of Judaism has paved the road for these changes, and areas that have been known for a long time, i.e., Bible commentary, demand investigation from a new point of view and require the usage of valuable linguistic materials. . . . In our desire to engage in these areas as our own, we will attempt to work in them with absolute academic seriousness and for the sake of, and only the sake of, the truth.

Finally, speaking of the significant void in German-Jewish life the seminary was designed to fill, Hildesheimer again underscored his commitment to producing rabbis trained in *Wissenschaft des Judentums*:

> The raising of funds for the establishment of the seminary in less than a year and a half testifies like a hundred witnesses to the pressing need for an institution founded on the basis of Orthodox Judaism whose goal will be to qualify its graduates as rabbis, based upon a fundamental and all-embracing knowledge of the Bible, Talmud, and all the works spawned by them. Secondarily, [our goal] is to present them with knowledge in all branches of *Wissenschaft des Judentums*, inasmuch as such a knowledge is a demand of our times.[80]

Rabbi Salomon Cohen, one of the chief supporters of the fledgling school, also spoke at the opening ceremonies and echoed Hildesheimer's vision of the rabbis who would be educated at the Rabbiner-Seminar. Cohen said that there was a critical need for future rabbis to be trained both in traditional rabbinic texts and in *Wissenschaft des Judentums*. Only rabbis learned in both secular and religious subjects, who knew how to apply contemporary scholarly techniques to the study of Jewish texts, could successfully protect the Jewish people and their religion from the onslaught of communal disintegration and unbelief. Cohen went on to compare these future graduates of the Rabbiner-Seminar to the members of the Sanhedrin who ruled Israel in ancient days. Cohen maintained that those early leaders of Judaism were able to preserve the unity of the Jewish people and the integrity of the religion because they were educated in both secular and religious fields of knowledge. Clearly, according to Cohen's analogy, the Rabbiner-Seminar was simply following in the path originally forged by the Sanhedrin and its members. The work of the Rabbiner-Seminar was thus justified by a simultaneous appeal to contemporary realities and the traditions of the past.[81]

Such a defense was necessary, for although Hirsch and his followers were enthusiastic proponents of secular culture, Hirsch felt that *Wissenschaft des Judentums* was antithetical to the spirit of genuine Judaism and, as practiced by most Jewish academics in contemporary Germany, would lead to heresy. Authentic Judaism, in Hirsch's opinion, held that the law—both written and oral—was "closed with Moses at Mount Sinai." Hirsch thus rejected the claims of historical development in Jewish law, custom, and practice put forth by the practitioners of *Wissenschaft des Judentums*. For this reason, Hirsch maintained that such studies were of no utility for religious Jews.[82]

Hirsch ultimately failed to give his approval to the Hildesheimer rabbinical school because he feared that the Rabbiner-Seminar, with its commitment to *Wissenschaft des Judentums*, did not differ sufficiently from the Breslau school to merit the title "Orthodox."[83] Similarly, Seligman Baer Bamberger, the Würzburger *rav*, is reported by Hildesheimer to have said, "I hate Hildesheimer's seminary more than Geiger's."[84] Presumably Bamberger considered Hildesheimer guilty of destroying the traditional nature of rabbinical education through the inclusion of academic subjects in the curriculum of his rabbinical school. In issuing such a charge and in making the comparison he did between Hildesheimer and Geiger, Bamberger was echoing the charges leveled against Hildesheimer years before in Hungary by other Orthodox critics. Those other central European Orthodox rabbis found Hildesheimer's reforms in the Eisenstadt yeshiva especially pernicious because they were introduced by an Orthodox, not a Reform, rabbi. Such changes made it difficult to draw clear boundaries between Orthodoxy and Reform.

Closely related to these attacks was another charge issued against the Berlin seminary and its students by Hirsch and Rabbi Isaac Halevy (1847–1914), the famed Polish scholar and author of *Dorot Harishonim*. In the same article in which Hirsch complained of the practice of *Wissenschaft des Judentums* at the Rabbiner-Seminar, he also voiced a concern that the emphasis on academic studies would prevent the students from devoting a proper amount of time to the study of traditional rabbinic texts and codes. Halevy took Hirsch's argument a step further; he claimed that this concern was not a fear but already a reality. The students of Hildesheimer's seminary were, he wrote, "ignoramuses, and none of them are experts in the Talmud, or for that matter, even in the Bible." The only solution for this problem, as Halevy saw it, was for the students to travel to the East and study there for several years in a yeshiva headed by some great scholar upon completion of their studies in Berlin. Otherwise, they would never possess the rabbinic knowledge necessary to merit the title "rabbi." Moreover, like Hirsch and others, Halevy laid the blame for this sad state of affairs at the Hildesheimer seminary on the school's unyielding commitment to *Wissenschaft des Judentums*. Halevy wrote, "Our society [of scholars] is not like the Berlin group, to whom it is unimportant whether a person writes either for or against Torah."[85] Regardless of the ostensible Orthodox commitment evidenced by the members of the Rabbiner-Seminar faculty, their absolute professed attachment to *Wissenschaft des Judentums* rendered them, in Halevy's opinion, incapable of training students in traditional rabbinic texts and of inculcating within them proper Jewish piety.

Rabbi Jacob Rosenheim, a student and follower of Hirsch and a leader of German and world Orthodoxy in his own right in later years, condemned the original faculty of the Rabbiner-Seminar for living in a world that was based on *"Wissenschaft* alone."[86] It seemed to him that the seminary did not produce students who possessed a "burning faith" because the faculty focused on scholarship and not on implanting a proper religious outlook (*hashkafah*) in the hearts of the students.[87] Rosenheim claimed that there was no one on the faculty who would prepare students for the rabbinate "worthy of the name, whose faith would not be blemished by a 'tear in the heart' and doubts."[88]

Of course, Hildesheimer and his circle responded to these charges and attempted to defend themselves against the efforts to label them "deviants" from Orthodoxy. On one hand, they did acknowledge that the German rabbinate was not as learned in Jewish law and rabbinic literature as the East European rabbinate. Indeed, David Hoffmann, Hildesheimer's beloved pupil and his successor as the head of the Rabbiner-Seminar, observed that the talmudic knowledge of the German rabbinate was limited. The German students simply did not possess the requisite background to attain a deep talmudic expertise.[89] On the other hand, a list of their academic accomplishments illustrates that they were extremely learned in other areas. A look at the *Bericht über die ersten fünfundzwanzig Jahre seines Bestehens* (1873–98) of Das Rabbiner-Seminar zu Berlin contains a list of the seminary's graduates and their publications.[90] Their work covers an impressive range of topics, but all of their research reveals their *wissenschaftlich* orientation. They wrote on topics as diverse as French politics under Pope Leo IX, the philosophies of Kant and Eberhard, the writings of Flavius Josephus, Jewish elements in the Koran, and the punctuation of the Mishnah.[91] The subjects are illustrative of the academic orientation of the Hildesheimer graduates. The commitment to *Wissenschaft des Judentums* is self-evident. It is thus irrelevant to judge the seminary students by the standards of an East European yeshiva. They served a different cultural world than did the East European rabbinate. Orthodox German rabbis had more in common culturally with their German liberal peers than they did with their East European counterparts. Their orientation was different from that of an East European *rav*.[92]

Hildesheimer's insistence on the inclusion of *Wissenschaft des Judentums* in the curriculum of the seminary is reflected in every facet of the institution: its admission standards, its faculty, and its curriculum. Hildesheimer demanded that all fully matriculated students at the Rabbiner-Seminar be graduates of the German *Gymnasium* or its equivalent. "We are able," he recorded, "to open the gates of the seminary only to those who are graduates of a *Gymnasium*."[93] On numerous occasions, Hildesheimer penned circulars in the East European Jewish press advising young aspirants not to come to Berlin to receive their rabbinic education unless they had first completed a secular education. Typical of these notices is one found in *HaLevanon*, an East European Hebrew periodical, in 1876. Hildesheimer wrote:

> I have raised my voice several times already to warn yeshiva students in faraway countries—especially Russia, Poland, and Galicia—. . . who come with a recommendation in their hand [from an East European rabbi] and say to me, "Please accept me in one of the departments in the Rabbiner-Seminar." . . . It breaks my heart every time that I must reject these students who come only with talmudic knowledge, and lack the secular diploma [*Gymnasium-Faecher*] necessary to be qualified for entry to the upper level.[94]

Thus the first annual report of the seminary stated that graduation from a *Gymnasium* was a prerequisite for admission to the

Rabbiner-Seminar.[95] The Breslau seminary and the Hochschule maintained the same admission standards, and Hildesheimer deemed it essential that the Rabbiner-Seminar should "meet the competition." Both of these institutions were committed to producing rabbis infused with *Wissenschaft des Judentums* and were convinced that a *Gymnasium* education was required to engage in proper *wissenschaftlich* studies.[96] Although Hildesheimer was severely criticized by the East European rabbinate for this policy,[97] he would not yield his position. To do so, he claimed, would lower the standards of the Rabbiner-Seminar and would mean that students who entered its portals would not be capable of pursuing studies in *Wissenschaft des Judentums.* By demanding that students entering the Rabbiner-Seminar be graduates of the *Gymnasium*, Hildesheimer was assured that the level of instruction in his institution could be on an academic par with that of Breslau and the Hochschule. Though sensitive to the pleas and demands of an East European rabbinic ethos, Hildesheimer's primary referent clearly remained the cultural ambience of Germany. For a time, Hildesheimer did establish a preparatory school for students who came to Berlin with inadequate backgrounds in secular studies, but he was able to discontinue it by 1882 because by then the educational life of European Jewry had improved to the point that a sufficient number of students with the requisite educational attainments were applying to the school.[98]

Nevertheless, Hildesheimer continued to defend the standards of Jewish Orthodoxy instituted by and practiced in his rabbinical school. He wrote, "I know our 'Orthodoxy' does not meet the standards established by Samson Raphael Hirsch's son, Isaac Hirsch." Furthermore, "the question arises as to whether Rabbi Hirsch sees our institution as an Orthodox one." Hildesheimer claimed that such charges were both unfair and unfounded. In Hildesheimer's judgment, the opposition of Hirsch and other Orthodox critics reflected a position of "harsh inflexibility."[99] He responded to this criticism by authorizing his son Hirsch Hildesheimer to write a letter defending the seminary and its Orthodoxy to Emanuel Schwarzschild.

"Everything I have written is only the opinion of my father who transmitted it to me exactly," wrote Hirsch Hildesheimer at the outset of his letter. "The future of Orthodox Judaism in Germany depends upon the Rabbiner-Seminar." Moreover, the task of applying *Wissenschaft* to the study of Judaism was, Hildesheimer felt, not contrary to Orthodoxy. Rather, he contended that it had to be employed if the Berlin seminary was to fulfill its mission. Hildesheimer noted that Samson Raphael Hirsch had attacked two members of the Rabbiner-Seminar faculty, Jakob Barth and David Hoffmann, for academic works they had published. Barth, the famed Semitist who taught Bible at the Rabbiner-Seminar, was criticized for his claim—in keeping with the findings of contemporary scholarship—that there was a second Isaiah. Jacob Rosenheim considered this view irresponsible in addition to being heretical. He wrote that Barth had "accepted the theory of the biblical critics that there were two prophets named Isaiah . . . without paying attention to the fact that through this [teaching] all the faith of his youthful students in the truth of the Tradition . . . would of necessity be undermined."[100] Hoffmann was attacked for his work on Mar Samuel, the third-century Tanna who lived in Babylonia. Hirsch complained that Hoffmann's work on this famed rabbi displayed a historical bias akin to that of Zacharias Frankel and others at the Jewish Theological Seminary in Breslau. Indeed, Hoffmann's study of the Babylonian rabbi and his teachings reflected the view, in Hirsch's opinion, that Jewish law was the result of historical developments and sociological pressures of a contemporary age, and not the product of a revelation by God to Moses and the Jewish people at Sinai.[101] Hirsch censured Hoffmann for publishing such a work in his position as professor of rabbinics and biblical exegesis at the Rabbiner-Seminar. Both Barth's and Hoffmann's studies were examples of "heresy" and indicated the danger posed by the use of *Wissenschaft des Judentums* in the training of Orthodox rabbis.

In response to these charges against members of the Rabbiner-Seminar faculty, Hirsch Hildesheimer wrote, "It is apparent that Rabbi Hirsch has a different approach to general culture than does my father. Rabbi Hirsch desires and is able to label a book as loyal to Orthodoxy only when *he* deems it worthy of the appellation." Hildesheimer argued, however, that there could be an honest difference of opinion between observant Jews and said that he, unlike Hirsch, "would never attempt to force others to accept his opinions." Although he respected Hirsch, Hildesheimer certainly did not intend his professors to be subject to Hirsch's censorship. In addition, Hildesheimer refused to wait for Hirsch's "stamp of approval" on books written by his faculty members before allowing their publication. Hildesheimer acknowledged that he was deeply wounded by Hirsch's failure to approve the Rabbiner-Seminar, but he would not yield to Hirsch on the issue of *Wissenschaft.*[102]

Lest the differences between these two camps of German Orthodoxy be overstated, it needs to be pointed out that Hildesheimer and Hirsch both emphasized *Rechtglaubigkeit*, correct faith or belief, as a basis of Orthodox Judaism. Indeed, Hildesheimer himself admitted that their disagreement over *Wissenschaft des Judentums* was more one of tactics than of actual substance.[103] Yet if this is so, how did Hildesheimer and his circle avoid the theological strictures that so troubled Hirsch on this matter? How did Hildesheimer and his colleagues, Jakob Barth and David Hoffmann, understand and justify their approach to this discipline so that the demands of faith could still be met? Or, to pose yet another query, did they accommodate their faith to the requirements of scholarship, or their scholarship to their faith?

In 1884, Barth published "Beiträge zur Eklärung des Jesaia," in the *Jahresberichte des Rabbiner-Seminar zu Berlin.* The substance of this material was the same as the lectures he delivered to his students. Thus these are the teachings for which Samson Raphael Hirsch had criticized him. In his introduction to the work, Barth noted that at times he used his academic research to justify the approach of earlier traditional Jewish commentators to Isaiah, while at other times he explained that Isaiah had to be understood within the historical context of his time. He then added, in defense of his Orthodoxy, that the words of Isaiah were words of revelation, "the divine and true source." Barth agreed with modern critics who claimed that the prophecies in Isaiah 40–66 did not arise during Isaiah's time and that it was doubtful that he had uttered them. He concurred with them that the prophecies in these chapters referred to events that had already taken place and not to events yet to occur. Still, he defended these views by citing the Sages of the Talmud who never assumed that Isaiah himself had uttered these prophecies. Rather, in Baba Bathra 15a, the Sages say that the passages were added by Hezekiah and his party. In this way the critics' claims were not diminished nor was Barth's Orthodoxy suspect. The critics' claims could be entertained precisely because there was, in Barth's opinion, rabbinic warrant for them. Academic research, in this instance, did not conflict with Orthodox belief.[104]

In the field of biblical studies, Hoffmann, the other academic target of Hirsch's criticisms, offered two enduring contributions which reflect the nature of his approach to this subject. The first of these is his commentaries on the Books of Genesis, Leviticus, and Deuteronomy; the second is his famous work arguing against Karl Heinrich Graf and Julius Wellhausen and their methods. The work, entitled *Die wichtigsten Instanzen gegen die Graf-Wellhausensche Hypothese,* was published in two volumes in 1903 and 1916. A sampling of his writings will permit a clear understanding of the relationship between scholarship and faith in Hoffmann's biblical works.

In his introduction to the volume on Leviticus, Hoffmann establishes the parameters which faith erects for scholarship: "I willingly agree that, in consequence of the foundation of my belief, I am unable to arrive at the conclusion that the Pentateuch was written by anyone other than Moses; and in order to avoid raising doubts on this score, I have clearly outlined the principles on which my commentary is based in my General Introduction." Hoffmann then went on: "The first principle is this: We believe that the whole Bible is true, holy, and of divine origin. That every word of the Torah was inscribed by divine command is expressed in the principle *Torah min HaShamayim.* . . . We must not presume to set ourselves up as critics of the author of a biblical text or doubt the truth of his statements or question the correctness of his teaching."[105]

Moreover, Hoffmann maintained that the Hebrew Bible could not be understood in and of itself but only in conjunction with the Oral Law:

> The Jewish expositor of the Pentateuch has to bear in mind a special factor that must influence his interpretation and, to a certain extent, dictate the rules for his exegesis. This factor is our belief in the divinity of the Jewish tradition. Authentic Judaism regards the Oral Law as well as the Written Law as being of divine origin.
> . . . The Jewish commentator must [therefore] constantly be on guard against interpreting the passage in such a way as to appear to be in conflict with traditional Halakhah. Just as the Torah as a divine revelation must not contradict itself, in the same way it must not contradict the Oral Law which is of divine origin.[106]

Finally, Hoffmann insisted on the integrity of the Massoretic text. Although he was familiar with other versions and translations of the biblical text, he also understood what was at stake when scholars offered emendations of it. If this were permitted, Hoffmann observed, "Instead of the divine Bible, we would then be reading a human book."[107] There is nothing in this introductory statement of his principles which Rabbi Hirsch or, presumably, any other Orthodox scholar would find objectionable.

Rabbi David Hoffmann (Courtesy of the Leo Baeck Institute, New York)

Before drawing any conclusions from this description of Hoffmann's approach to biblical texts, it will be instructive to turn to his major essay attacking the Graf-Wellhausen hypothesis. In this classic attempt to refute the content of their arguments, Hoffmann did not engage in wild polemics. Rather, he argued calmly and rationally against the specific points of this theory, with the result that Hoffmann did not deal with the notion of the Documentary Hypothesis itself. Although he certainly would not have confirmed it, he chose to refute it by pointing out the logical inconsistencies within the Wellhausen theory. Hoffmann seems content to have implied that the theory of multiple biblical sources was false, insofar as he skillfully and, in his view, successfully destroyed the particulars of the Graf-Wellhausen argument.

Wellhausen had argued that the Priestly Code was the latest source in the Pentateuch. It was preceded by H—the Holiness Code— which, in turn, was preceded by D, the Deuteronomic source. Wellhausen's position was that by the time of Leviticus the Deuteronomic reform instituted by Josiah was so ingrained that the Priestly Code was not at all concerned with the problem of centralization of the cult. Therefore, there were no instances of anything cultic except the centralized cult.[108] Hoffmann, however, in his chapter on the Passover sacrifice in the Priestly Code, found several logical inconsistencies in Wellhausen's evidence. Hoffmann took issue with the late dating of the Priestly Code, questioning why Exodus 12:7, considered to be part of the Priestly Code, commanded the Israelites to "take of the blood, and put it on the two side-posts and on the lintel, upon the houses wherein they shall eat it." Clearly such a text refutes the role of a centralized cult, and Wellhausen's notion that the Priestly Code presupposes the centralization of the cult. Obviously, then, Wellhausen must be wrong.[109]

The correctness of the arguments aside, it is clear that Hoffmann's interpretation allows him to posit here, against Wellhausen, that the two documents, D and P, were at least contemporaneous and preexilic. It appears that Hoffmann felt that, if he could topple Wellhausen's dating of P, the whole Documentary Hypothesis would fall. Indeed, Meyer Waxman, in his volume on the science of Judaism in western Europe (*Hochmat Yisrael B'Maarav Airopa*) states: "And with the downfall of this principal foundation—that the Priestly Code was written after the Babylonian Exile—the entire theory is destroyed [*hi nehersa kula*]."[110] Of course, this seems absurdly simplistic, for though Hoffmann may have dealt Wellhausen's dating of

P a severe, if not fatal, blow, he can hardly be said to have addressed, much less destroyed, the notion of the Documentary Hypothesis itself.

In analyzing Hoffmann's approach to biblical studies, it seems that he principally employed this scholarship to defend the dogmas of his Orthodox Jewish faith. His familiarity with Wellhausen and other scholars, as well as his citations from cognate literatures, all point to his complete academic mastery of this field of research. Nevertheless, these examples culled from Hoffmann's work support the statement of Alexander Altmann, himself a graduate of the Rabbiner-Seminar, that at least as far as Hoffmann's biblical scholarship is concerned,

> Here not certainty was sought but certitude. And the certitude of faith was not in danger. Historicism was not allowed to touch the citadel of belief. "Wissenschaft des Judentums," to be sure, had prominent representatives in German-Jewish Orthodoxy. Men like David Hoffmann . . . were adornments of Jewish learning. But their historical studies did not bring them into conflict with their faith. . . . Biblical criticism could evoke only contempt or indignant rejection. Hoffmann's learned and skillful rebuttal of Wellhausen was more in the nature of apologetics than of modern scholarship, no matter how justified were his strictures in details.[111]

What, however, was the nature of Hoffmann's scholarship in his other major field of academic study, rabbinics, which Hirsch had labeled "heretical"? In examining this area of Hoffmann's academic work, it is clear that some of the same patterns evident in his biblical studies are present here, too. In nearly all of his works, the same, seemingly obligatory statements about the nature of authentic Jewish faith are found. In his rabbinic investigations, in contrast to his biblical studies, however, Hoffmann appears to be more of the contemporary academic. Throughout his works he cites the scholarship of Rappoport, Frankel, Geiger, and Graetz, sometimes approvingly, sometimes disapprovingly—but never, it seems, tendentiously. In this way, Hoffmann becomes one among several academic scholars involved in a community of research. In addition, Hoffmann often employs an approach to the field of rabbinic history which marks him as a practitioner of *Religions-Wissenschaft* in the broadest cultural sense, an approach that allowed him to consider the ways in which the surrounding culture of the ancient Near East may have influenced rabbinic civilization, something he would never have considered doing in his biblical studies. For example, in his *Mar Samuel*, Hoffmann points out that the rabbis were identified as *Hachamim*, "*Weise.*" Then, in a footnote, he states, "One also designated the Savants of other peoples with the selfsame title."[112] It was remarks such as this, along with his citation of "heretics" such as Graetz and Frankel, which undoubtedly aroused the ire of Orthodox colleagues like Hirsch and caused them to view at least this work of Hoffmann's as *kefirah*, heresy.

Hoffmann's writings on the evolution of the literary structures, forms, terminology, and modes of interpretation in both midrash and Mishnah would seemingly be even more dangerous to the foundations of Orthodox Jewish faith. Yet there is no question that Hoffmann did investigate these texts in a manner that makes it difficult to distinguish him from Frankel, Geiger, or other scholars of rabbinic literature. This does not mean that Hoffmann agreed with them either on particular points or specific theories. But Hoffmann was clearly involved in discourse with these men. Like Frankel's *Darkhe HaMishnah*, Hoffmann's *First Mishna* reveals that he saw development and variety in the different strata of mishnaic literature. His notion that there was a "First Mishna" before the destruction of the Second Temple and that there were disagreements among the later tannaim as to its form; his efforts to reconstruct and discover that form; his willingness to investigate the disparate strata which undergirded that form; as well as his work on the halakhic midrashim, all combine to reveal the seminal nature of his studies in the academic area of rabbinics. Proactive as opposed to reactive, his scholarship in this area is clearly distinct from his efforts in the discipline of Bible.

Still the question remains: How did Hoffmann manage to incorporate such studies within the framework of Orthodox faith? What were the "intellectual arrangements" that allowed such probings into rabbinic texts but would not permit them into biblical ones? The answer can be found in his introduction to *The First Mishna and the Controversies of the Tannaim*, in which Hoffmann writes:

Mikra [Bible] is the word of God in content as well as in expression. Its origin can be timed . . . exactly. It has been given a definite, immutable formulation immediately . . . after it originated, and has been preserved thus to our days. The Mishna on the other hand . . . is for the best part of divine origin as far as its content is concerned, but the form has only been fixed at a relatively later time. From Moses until the Tannaim the form of the Mishna was fluid, and each transmitting teacher handed down the received teaching in the formulation that appeared fittest to him (*Iggeret Sherira Gaon*).

Thus in the study of the Holy Scriptures on the one hand, we consider the authenticity and integrity to be absolute, and we can recognize as true only such results as do not question that premise. With the Mishna, on the other hand, any criticism (unless it contradicts a halakhah fixed in the Talmud) as well as any research as to the age of the Mishna and the time of its expression in the extant form is not only considered permissible to us, but even required for the scientific examination of the tradition.[113]

Just as the tradition, in Barth's view, justified his approach to the Book of Isaiah, so too did the tradition, in Hoffmann's opinion, legitimate academic studies of rabbinic history and literature. According to his reading of it, the tradition itself acknowledged that the form of the Oral Law had evolved over a long period of time. Hence a study of its evolution, so long as such study did not contradict any established *halakhot*, was no threat to the belief that the Oral Law, like the Written, was divine. Orthodox leaders such as Samson Raphael Hirsch and Jacob Rosenheim were of another opinion. Nevertheless, it is indisputable that Hoffmann and his colleagues at the Rabbiner-Seminar were able to understand their engagement in *Wissenschaft des Judentums* in such a way that it did not conflict with the verities of Orthodox Jewish belief.

The curriculum of the school exemplified Hildesheimer's commitment to *Wissenschaft des Judentums*. The course of study was set at six years, two of which were spent in the lower division and four in the upper. If a student came with an unusually strong background in rabbinics, he was permitted to omit the first two years. A parallel institutional structure which divided the school into upper and lower sections was found at both the Hochschule and the Breslau seminary. The standard course of study at the Hochschule was set at five years, while at Breslau the course was set at seven years.[114] Students at the Rabbiner-Seminar, like those at the Hochschule, were expected to attend a university, generally Berlin, to earn a doctorate. During the third and fourth years of study at the Hildesheimer seminary the course load of the students was reduced to allow them to work on their doctoral dissertations at the university.[115] Hildesheimer's commitment to *Wissenschaft* and to the education of rabbis who would be "armed with science" is apparent.

The course of study in the seminary was heavily weighted toward traditional rabbinic texts. During the students' first two semesters they focused on Talmud and *Orah Hayim,* devoting approximately two-thirds of their time to the study of these classical rabbinic texts. Particular attention was paid to those parts relevant to contemporary German Jewish life. Two additional hours were spent on the study of the Pentateuch, two more on Hebrew grammar and exegesis, and one on midrash and homiletics. In the second year two additional hours were devoted to the study of Jewish history. Five hours per week went to Talmud in the third and fourth years of study, while an additional two to five hours (depending on the individual student's schedule) were spent on responsa. In the third year two hours per week were spent on a study of Exodus, two were devoted to Jewish history, and two to the geography of Palestine. The fourth year provided two hours on the Prophets and two on Jewish history and literature. Students in the fifth and sixth years were required to spend five hours per week on Talmud, three on responsa, two on the Pentateuch, two on the Prophets, and two on Jewish history and literature. Other elective courses on topics ranging from Maimonides' *Guide for the Perplexed* to historical sources in the Talmud and Midrash were also offered to round out the students' education. Students were required to attend a series of lectures (for which no credit was given) as an introduction to *Wissenschaft.* This introductory series, combined with the time each student spent at a university attaining his doctorate, permitted the seminary to provide each student with what is called "a Judaic-scientific education."[116]

A fuller picture of the nature of the curriculum can be drawn by looking at the teaching assignments of each of the instructors during the first two years of the Rabbiner-Seminar's existence. Hildesheimer himself taught two courses in Talmud during the school's first semester. A six-credit course in *Yevamot,* which focused on the laws of personal status, and a smaller course on *Shabbat* in the Jerusalem Talmud comprised the content of the fall curriculum. In the spring Hildesheimer continued his course in *Yevamot* and added a three-credit course in *Ketubot,* which examined the talmudic sources for the Jewish laws of marriage. The selection of these particular texts, dealing as they did with matters of contemporary import to the German rabbinate, reflect Hildesheimer's concerns for the practical application of his students' talmudic knowledge. In addition, Hildesheimer taught a course on Judah Halevi's *Kuzari* with a comparison to selected portions of Maimonides' *Moreh Nevuchim*. He also taught a course entitled "Jewish History from the Babylonian Exile to the First Maccabean Princes." Finally, Hildesheimer's course load was rounded out by an offering called "Source Criticism: An Investigation of the Newer Biblical Critics." Hildesheimer was keenly aware of and paid careful attention to the new science of biblical criticism and the challenges it posed to belief in the Mosaic authorship of the Bible.[117]

David Hoffmann taught a course in Talmud (*Shabbat*) each semester for the less advanced rabbinic students. He also offered instruction in the *Orah Hayim, Hilchot Shabbat* (laws of the Sabbath), Leviticus, and Levitical sources of Jewish holidays. Abraham Berliner, the famed historian of Italian Jewry, taught a Jewish literature course entitled "From the Close of the Talmud to the End of the Geonim" and two other courses on responsa collections from the Gaonic period.[118]

During the next academic year, Hildesheimer continued the history course he had begun the previous year. The title of the course in the second year was "From the First Maccabean Princes to the Death of Herod." He continued to give instruction in Talmud. David Hoffmann expanded his teaching duties and not only offered Talmud courses in Menahot, Megillah, and Sukkah but also gave instruction in *Hilchot Mikvaot* (laws of the ritual bath), *Hilchot Trefot* (dietary laws), and Deuteronomy. Berliner taught a course entitled "History of Jewish Literature from the Period of the Piyut-Poetry" and others called "The *Massorah*," "Poetic Parts of Onkelos," and "Rabbinic Commentaries—Exodus 1–10 with Ibn Ezra." Finally, Jakob Barth, who joined the faculty during the 1874–75 school year, taught courses in Bible and Hebrew grammar. As the school evolved over the next few years, other courses such as homiletics, "The Use of Historical Sources," "Historical Sources in Talmud and Midrash," and various courses in medieval Jewish philosophy were added to round out the curriculum.[119]

In addition to these formal classes, students were expected to pass examinations in Talmud and codes to qualify for rabbinic ordination. Specifically, students had to demonstrate the ability to study Talmud with Rashi and traditional commentaries, as well as the ability to write responsa on Jewish legal issues taken from *Even HaEzer, Yoreh Deah,* or the *Orah Hayim.* Interestingly, the *Hoshen Mishpat,* that part of the *Shulhan Aruch* which deals with Jewish civil law, was ignored both in the curriculum of the Berlin seminary and in the ordination examinations. For all intents and purposes, Jewish civil law was obsolete in the modern German environment, despite its central role in classical tradition. Thus the rabbinic curriculum of the Rabbiner-Seminar reflected the reality of a world in which Jewish civil autonomy had disappeared.[120] Students who performed exceptionally well on the examinations and demonstrated excellent mastery of the rabbinic materials were given the traditional rabbinic diploma of *"Yoreh, Yoreh, Yadin, Yadin"* (literally, "May he teach? He may teach. May he judge? He may judge"). Figuratively, this title grants the holder the right to rule on whether certain foods and ritual practices are permitted or forbidden, as well as the authority to adjudicate civil disputes. Few students, however, actually received such ordination from Hildesheimer and the seminary. Instead, most received a German diploma which authorized the bearer to serve as a rabbi and religious teacher. These students were not permitted to render Jewish legal decisions, and the diploma stipulated that they were to depend on others in such matters. Finally, a codicil was appended to the diploma which directed the bearer to be faithful to Orthodoxy and stripped him of his title if he was not.[121] Such measures reflect the nature of the nineteenth-century German-Jewish world and illustrate once more that Hildesheimer realized that his students, despite their combined secular and religious knowledge, were not the equals of East European rabbis in traditional rabbinic learning. But it was not his purpose to create a medieval *rav*. Rather, a graduate of the Hildesheimer seminary, like his liberal counterpart at Breslau or the Hochschule, was trained as a *Rabbiner*—someone capable of disseminating Orthodoxy and defending it in a challenging world.

All these developments have caused Alexander Altmann to comment that the German rabbi was a "unique cultural type."[122] For despite the differences that separated the three major theological institutions of German Jewry, their common commitment to *Wissenschaft des Judentums* and to university training meant that, in many ways, graduates of the three schools bore a greater resemblance to each other than any one of them did to the East European Orthodox rabbis. The accuracy of Altmann's observation can be seen in a glance at the curricula of the Breslau seminary and the Hochschule.

In both Breslau and the Hochschule, major attention was paid to the study of Talmud and codes.[123] Indeed, the courses in Talmud and codes offered at the Breslau seminary were virtually identical in content to those at the Rabbiner-Seminar. Frankel paid special attention to Jewish laws of marriage and divorce, and Israel Lewy taught the same class for the students at the Hochschule.[124] Students at the Breslau seminary were also expected to master the following areas of study: Holy Scriptures and their exegesis; Hebrew language and grammar; historical and methodological introduction to Mishna and Talmud; history of the Jews together with a history of Jewish literature; religious philosophy and ethics according to Jewish sources; midrash; ritual practice; pedagogy; and homiletics. Students in the Breslau seminary, like their counterparts at the Rabbiner-Seminar, were expected to take courses for their doctorate at a university, generally Breslau.[125] In this way students would become imbued with Western culture and a belief in the centrality of *Wissenschaft des Judentums*, which in turn would lead to a proper understanding of the "essence" of Judaism. As Zacharias Frankel wrote, "Without the academic study of Judaism, Judaism could not exist [in the present day]."[126]

At the Hochschule, Abraham Geiger taught a required course entitled "Introduction to *Wissenschaft des Judentums.*" This course, which was parallel to the one offered at the Rabbiner-Seminar, was even assigned course credit. In addition, students were required to take courses in the following areas: introduction to the Bible; biblical exegesis (traditional rabbinic); history of biblical exposition among the Jews through the present day; statement of religious ideas in biblical writings; Hebrew and Aramaic in postbiblical writings; Talmud; history of halakhah and aggadah; history of those groups that did not acknowledge the authority of the Talmud; Jewish history and history of Jewish literature; history of Jewish religious teachings and philosophies—the meaning and problems of Judaism in the present age; comparative religious history; and homiletics. In any given semester the study of Talmud constituted approximately 50 percent of the student's course load. Similar to the Rabbiner-Seminar and the Breslau seminary, students were expected to be concurrently enrolled for their doctorates at a university.[127] Ordination at the Hochschule demanded a special examination in codes and, as a result, some of the students there possessed a knowledge of Jewish law equal to that of students at the other two seminaries. Indeed, the distinguishing characteristic of the curriculum of the Hochschule was its disproportionate (compared to the other two seminaries) emphasis on the Bible, although this simply reflects the different theological orientation of its administration and must be seen more as a difference in degree than kind. The Hochschule devoted special courses to the study of those groups in Judaism which had denied the binding authority of the halakha—another illustration of its distinct theological stance.[128]

The commonalities between the courses of instruction at all three seminaries is apparent. The commitment to *Wissenschaft des Judentums* was central to all of them. Yet all devoted the bulk of their curriculum to the study of rabbinic codes and texts. In addition, each one emphasized the study of Jewish history, Jewish literature, Bible, homiletics, Hebrew grammar, and biblical exegesis. Similarly, each one encouraged its students to engage in scholarship and took great pride in the academic accomplishments of its graduates.[129] All of these factors contributed to the creation of the distinctive German rabbi to whom Altmann has referred.

Esriel Hildesheimer was proud of the high standards of scholarship maintained at the Berlin seminary. He claimed in 1881, seven years after the opening of the school, "No institute on earth displays more openness and honesty, more seriousness and less ulterior motives in pursuing religious along with secular study than does ours; and none . . . in such a short time . . . has made such a name for itself in the academic world."[130] Ismar Schorsch has written that the historical and academic study of the Jewish past was pursued "no less assiduously [at the Rabbiner-Seminar] than at Breslau or the *Hochschule*." Indeed, the examination of these three institutions led Schorsch to observe:

> In nineteenth-century Germany the study of Jewish history functioned as both authority and medium. . . . In the Middle Ages these two functions were fulfilled by different disciplines: a rich and flexible legal tradition generally served as sole authority for changes within the Jewish community, while philosophy offered the common idiom in which Judaism could be expounded for Jew and non-Jew alike. In the wake of emancipation . . . history assumed the role of both. It became the functional equivalent of halakhah and philosophy in the medieval world.[131]

On the surface and in view of what has been reported here, Schorsch's comment would appear to be correct. The commonalities that marked the rabbinic training in each of these schools are real and must be emphasized. Nevertheless, equally real differences distinguished the approach to *Wissenschaft des Judentums* taken by

Hildesheimer and his circle from that advocated by its practitioners at the Hochschule and the Breslau seminary. In effect, Hildesheimer and his group said that the academic study of Judaism was permissible as long as it did not negate certain doxologies, that is, the divinity of the Oral Law and the Mosaic authorship of the Bible. Returning to Schorsch's analogy, then, it is difficult to maintain that history functioned as both medium and authority for Hildesheimer and those at the Rabbiner-Seminar. *Wissenschaft des Judentums* did assume the role Schorsch assigns to philosophy in the Middle Ages. For Hildesheimer and his circle it was the medium whereby Judaism could be "expounded for Jew and non-Jew alike" in the nineteenth century. Halakhah, however, remained authoritative. Although the communal structure that supported it had collapsed, thus necessitating certain practical changes in its implementation in the modern world, halakhah still retained its position of authority for Hildesheimer and his party. Hildesheimer and his circle's unique achievement was that they employed the predominant academic and cultural mode of expression of their day, *Wissenschaft des Judentums*, which in the eyes of many of his peers was heretical, to defend traditional beliefs.

It thus appears that Hildesheimer's critics from both left and right were in part correct in the claims they lodged against Hildesheimer and his use of *Wissenschaft des Judentums*. Hildesheimer did place boundaries around the extent to which academic investigation could proceed. To his liberal critics this tainted Hildesheimer's employment of *Wissenschaft des Judentums*, whereas his critics from the right, such as Hirsch, felt that Hildesheimer did not properly understand the implications of applying academic inquiry to Judaism. The results of such investigations would have disastrous consequences for traditional Jewish conceptions of revelation and the immutability of the Oral Law. Insofar as history could demonstrate that Judaism and Jewish law were not impervious to, but had developed in time, it could logically lead to the conclusions of a Graetz or a Frankel or a Geiger. Precisely because Hirsch was able to grasp these intellectual implications, he was able to embrace *Wissenschaft* and German culture while yet rejecting the notion of *Wissenschaft* as applied to Judaism.

Hildesheimer, however, was able to ignore these attacks on his use of *Wissenschaft des Judentums* for two reasons. The first is that Hildesheimer was less philosophically oriented than Hirsch. As one commentator has put it, Hildesheimer, in spite of his intellectual abilities and attainments, was essentially a man of action. He was an institution builder.[132] Unlike Hirsch, he was generally more concerned with the new practical significance of his actions and relatively less concerned with creating a philosophy of Judaism. In fact, it is astounding to find an almost total absence of any sophisticated theological vision in Hildesheimer's writings. He took a more pragmatic, sociological approach to issues than did Hirsch. On one level, this permitted Hildesheimer much greater flexibility. Thus, in this instance, Hildesheimer felt that the prestige of Orthodoxy in contemporary Europe was dependent upon its ability to engage in *Wissenschaft des Judentums* and, consequently, he advocated it. On another level, this allowed him, unlike Hirsch, to ignore the potential dangers *Wissenschaft* posed to Orthodox Jewish faith.

A second reason, more fideistic in nature, arises in considering why Hildesheimer ignored his critics from both right and left on this issue. Hildesheimer left few explanations in his writings, but a clue can be found in a comment made by David Hoffmann in his *Commentary on Leviticus*. Hoffmann affirms his belief that the Pentateuch was revealed by God to Moses and then continues, "It is solely in an attempt to base these 'dogmatic assumptions' on scholarly grounds that I have constantly sought to apply only arguments whose justification would be recognized from other standpoints as well."[133] Hildesheimer also claimed that there was no conflict between scholarship properly followed and faith.[134] Assured of the truth of the tradition, Hildesheimer and Hoffmann appear to have been asserting that faith provided conclusions which reason could then prove necessary.

In any event, Hildesheimer's particular philosophy of *Torah im Derekh Eretz,* as embodied in the curriculum of the Rabbinerseminar, seems to have been a success. The school grew from twenty full-time students in 1873 to sixty in 1899.[135] As early as 1888 Hildesheimer commented that his students were so sought after by Orthodox congregations throughout Europe that he could not fulfill all the requests for rabbis that came to him.[136] Although Seligman Baer Bamberger had opposed the creation of the seminary, his son Moses Bamberger asked Hildesheimer in 1881 if he would establish a preparatory institute for the Rabbiner-Seminar in Würzburg.[137] Hildesheimer turned down the proposal, but that it was made bespeaks the esteemed position the Rabbiner-Seminar had come to occupy in the life of German Orthodoxy less than a decade after its founding. A letter written by Isaac Elchanan Spektor and a fragment from an autobiography of Chaim Tchernowitz illustrate the vital role played by the Berlin seminary in the world of late nineteenth-century European Orthodox Jewry. Tchernowitz, who came to be a world-renowned scholar of rabbinics and the author of the famous *Toldot HaHalakhah* and *Toldot HaPoskim,* writes of how he yearned for secular knowledge as a youth growing up in Russia. He then states, "I did not enter into the community of the *Maskilim,* the majority of whom were totally ignorant in Jewish matters." Rather, "I began to think seriously about my future. And although I had fallen into the snare of Enlightenment, in spite of all this, I was not able entirely to part from the domain of the traditional House of Study and the world of the traditional rabbinate. My aim was a synthesis of Torah and science, and my goal was to be accepted as a student in Dr. Hildesheimer's Rabbinical Seminary in Berlin. In that way I would become a modern rabbi.[138]

Hildesheimer's seminary evidently achieved unusual prestige and fame among the Orthodox youth of eastern Europe who yearned for secular knowledge. The comments of Isaac Elchanan Spektor, the leading Orthodox rabbi in Russia and eastern Europe, underscore the respect Hildesheimer came to enjoy as a result of his educational attainments:

> The evil of Reform grew so in Germany that the memory of Talmud and Judaism was almost completely forgotten there. . . . However, how wonderful are the ways of God! . . . God dealt mercifully with us and gave us my dear friend, the *Gaon,* the great *Tsaddik* (righteous one), the famous one, learned in Torah and renowned for his piety, our teacher, Rabbi Esriel, head of the *Bet Din* [court] of God in Berlin. . . . And he yielded to the request of the pious congregants of Berlin and accepted their rabbinical position in order to employ his strength to fortify the pillars of religion in Germany, to magnify Torah and *to glorify his yeshiva which is a tree of life and the work of his hands.*[139]

Hildesheimer's educational ideas and the institutions founded upon them illustrate the continuities, as well as the discontinuities, between the world of rabbinical traditionalism and that of modern Jewish Orthodoxy. His departures from the pattern of Jewish education offered in the medieval European Jewish community are iconoclastic. They include the advocating of Jewish education for women; the insistence that students admitted to his seminaries in Eisenstadt and Berlin come equipped with a secular education; and his firm commitment to *Wissenschaft des Judentums* in the curricula of his seminaries, despite the protests of Hirsch and others. Yet his adherence to religious orthodoxy caused him to place limits on the conclusions that could be drawn from Jewish academic scholarship. His lasting contribution lies in the model he provided for other Orthodox educational institutions in the Western world.[140] He is one of those who helped establish the parameters for modern Jewish Orthodoxy. As such, the study of his life's labors in the field of education enables us to understand how one variety of contemporary Judaism—Orthodoxy—made its uneven passage from medievalism to modernity.

Conclusion

$\mathbf{P}$eter Berger has observed that the orthodox of all classical Western religious faiths regard themselves "as living in a tradition." For such people the tradition requires neither defense nor explanation. It provides the contours within which reality is experienced. Life in accord with the beliefs and practices of the tradition is perceived as the only proper way in which an authentic and meaningful human religious existence can be attained. The "very nature of tradition" is thus "to be taken for granted."[1]

Yet, for the acculturated Jews of the West—including the Orthodox—this notion has been compromised over the last two hundred years. For them, Jewish identity must accommodate itself to elements of consciousness and culture derived from a larger non-Jewish world in which Jews freely reside. "Jewishness" is experienced as part of what might be labeled a "hyphenated identity." Berger concludes, "This taken-for-grantedness [of tradition] is continually falsified by the experience of living in a modern society. The orthodox must . . . present to [themselves] as fate what [they] know empirically to be a choice. This is a difficult feat."[2] It is not, however, an impossible one. For if it were, then Jewish identity, practice, and belief would have atrophied and died when confronted with the ubiquity and power of Western non-Jewish culture.

Although almost a century has elapsed since Esriel Hildesheimer lived, his personal and institutional responses to the task of forging a hyphenated German-Jewish identity retain a significance that transcends the German-Jewish world in which he lived. His lasting achievement is that he created a viable Orthodox Judaism for ac-

166

culturated central European Jews. They, like most Jews of the modern world, confronted the challenges of constructing a meaningful Jewish life and faith in the face of a transformed social, religious, political, and cultural environment. Hildesheimer did achieve a German-Jewish symbiosis. This analysis of Hildesheimer's particular accomplishments thus not only provides insights into the nature of one variety of modern Jewish Orthodoxy but contributes an ecumenical model of modern Jewish identity as well.

An anecdote related by Rabbi Anton Nobel[3] illustrates Hildesheimer's synthesis of the contemporary and the traditional. Recalling his own student days at the Rabbiner-Seminar, Nobel wrote that he was asked to deliver an address at the founding ceremony of Dibbuk Haverim, the seminary's student association, in 1894. At the conclusion of his talk, he offered a student toast, a "salamander," in honor of his teacher Rabbi Hildesheimer and the other members of the Orthodox rabbinical school's faculty. According to Alexander Altmann, who remembers similar toasts offered during his student days at the Rabbiner-Seminar in the 1920s, the German student custom of the salamander, Teutonic in origin, "consisted in everybody standing up, circling their beer glasses on the table, and draining them to the last dreg."[4]

We can only speculate as to Hildesheimer's reaction to this toast. As the scion of a traditional European rabbinic family, who had been educated in the yeshiva of Rabbi Jacob Ettlinger and at the universities of Berlin and Halle, how did he feel as he sat there? He was seventy-four, and these students studying for the Orthodox rabbinate in his modern rabbinical seminary represented the culmination of his life's dreams. How did he assess his achievements as he witnessed them saluting him and the colleagues he had assembled, not with "*LeHayyim*—To Life," as tradition (*Shabbat* 67) would have it, but with the custom and rite of the German university? Was he elated or perturbed? We shall never know.

It may be that Hildesheimer simply felt that such compromise was the price that his milieu exacted for Orthodox Judaism to survive. Seen as graphic testimony to the acculturated nature of German Orthodoxy and the hyphenated nature of German-Jewish identity, however, another interpretation of the episode is more likely. For the incident bears witness to the symbiotic nature of German Judaism itself and to the consciousness of a man like Hildesheimer who shaped and lived it. After all, why should the scene have struck Hildesheimer, the product of German *Bildung*, as dissonant with tradition? The man who sang Heine to his children on Shabbat afternoons must have been pleased with the fruits of his labors. Indeed, it represented the successful synthesis between Jewish tradition and German culture. Synthesis is here understood as a syncretism between two worlds. The episode, and this interpretation of it, suggest that such synthesis succeeds when it is experienced as effective from the inside. That is, Hildesheimer, his colleagues, and his students had so completely internalized the values of the surrounding German-Jewish atmosphere that nothing struck them as discordant about this event.

An enigma remains, however. It seems that Hildesheimer was able to achieve a successful synthesis between Jewish tradition and German culture precisely because he did not examine or reflect upon his efforts too closely. This, of course, differentiated him from both the Hatam Sofer and Samson Raphael Hirsch. Although Sofer rejected modernity, his concern for the preservation of what he perceived to be an immutable tradition allowed him to promote an Orthodox Judaism which was systematic. It was clear to Sofer what belonged within the system and what belonged outside of it—"*Hadash assur min haTorah*": Everything new was forbidden. The problem was that his total rejection of secular culture made his Orthodoxy an impossible choice for most Jews, including many of the Orthodox, who lived in a world in which the option of acculturation was attractive and compelling. Conversely, Hirsch, who popularized the slogan "*Torah im Derekh Eretz*," affirmed the worth of contemporary culture perhaps to an even greater extent than did Hildesheimer. Hirsch possessed an ideological bent of mind that caused him, like Sofer, to elevate dogma to a position of paramount importance. He realized that only a secure sense of dogma could distinguish the modern Orthodox from their liberal peers in an environment where virtually all other attitudes toward non-Jewish culture that might have distinguished them had disappeared. Hirsch's emphasis on ideological consistency allowed him to be sensitive to the damaging implications that *Wissenschaft des Judentums* held for the preservation of traditional Jewish faith. Thus, unlike Hildesheimer, Hirsch could concern himself only with Jews who shared his Orthodox affirmation of Jewish faith. Hirsch could condemn the academic work of Barth and Hoffmann as "heresy," while Hildesheimer could applaud it and its authors as adornments of Jewish learning. Hildesheimer's overriding concern was to establish a faculty that could match the standards of the Hochschule and the Breslau seminary and, in so doing, create a "cultured Orthodoxy" that could rival its liberal counterparts. Hildesheimer simply did not address the problems this posed for the traditional notion that Jewish law was revealed in its totality to Moses at Sinai.

Ironically, the Emancipation liberated Orthodox Jews such as both Hirsch and Sofer from having to deal with non-Orthodox Jews, despite their radically different attitudes toward secular culture. Just as the Emancipation freed nonobservant Jews from the coercive constraints of an institutionalized and politically semiautonomous rabbinate, so it released these Orthodox rabbis from having to deal with a broad range of lay behavior that might otherwise have demanded compromise on the rabbis' part. Emancipation allowed both sides the possibility of erecting stringent boundaries and permitted both Sofer and Hirsch to create "separatist" forms of Orthodoxy. Hirsch was completely unwilling to cooperate with non-Orthodox Jews like Graetz or non-Orthodox communal institutions like the Alliance, even on matters of common concern.

Here, Hildesheimer was distinctive. Precisely because he lacked the dogmatic structure of a Sofer or a Hirsch, he could condemn Graetz for his religious views and simultaneously work with him on matters concerning the Land of Israel. He could advise his student Horovitz not to accept the post of *orthodoxer Gemeinderabbiner* in Frankfurt and yet, because he regarded him as a son, could ultimately bestow his "blessing" on Horovitz's contrary decision. He could label Frankel a *meshummad* but could also praise him as a "great scholar." He could state of the Hochschule, "Raze it to its very foundations," and still maintain close ties to nonobservant Jews such as Samuel Kristeller and work with them on matters of charity and defense. Hildesheimer's boundaries remained flexible. If it seems that he was less consistent than a Hirsch or a Sofer, it is because Hildesheimer constantly looked at matters along a continuum that was an admixture of the old and the new. This middle position, and his failure ever formally to articulate it, should not mark Hildesheimer as an opportunist or compromiser. It does mark him as human and indicates that Hildesheimer, like countless other Jews in the modern world, resolved the problem of modernity not through logic, but through creation.

A hyphenated identity or successful synthesis works not because it is logical. It works because one lives it. The synthesis inheres in the doing. It is this which allowed Hildesheimer and others to overcome the compartmentalization and fragmentation that distinguish life in the modern world, to create a modern Orthodoxy that worked. This may be why, in the end, Hildesheimer holds up a mirror to the modern Jew who is engaged in the same process of constructing and living in a pluralistic world. All Jews who affirm their identity and religion in today's world are ultimately engaged in the same task as Hildesheimer was.

Hildesheimer's enduring contribution to the Jewish world thus does not lie solely in the institutions he created. Rather, he remains a sympathetic and important figure because he underscores the possibility of a Jewish Orthodoxy, which, if not fully systematic, possesses the virtue of not being rigid. In a contemporary world, where inflexibility and division increasingly mark Jewish religious life, his model of sensitivity and integrity, fallibility and encouragement, remains instructive for Orthodox and non-Orthodox Jews alike. The significance of his life thus transcends his own death and the physical destruction of the German Jewish world that was his arena.

Notes

Preface

1. Hermann Schwab, *The History of Orthodox Jewry in Germany* (London: Mitre Press, 1950), p. 11.
2. Samuel C. Heilman, "Constructing Orthodoxy," *Transaction* (May–June 1978): 32.

1. The Man and the Challenges of His Times

1. Meir Hildesheimer, "Toward a Biography of Our Rabbi," in Esriel Hildesheimer, *The Responsa of Rabbi Esriel* (Hebrew), 2 vols. (Tel Aviv, 1969, 1976), 1:11–15.
2. Jacob Katz, *Exclusiveness and Tolerance* (New York, 1969), pp. 48–63, and *Out of the Ghetto* (Cambridge, Mass., 1973), p. 1.
3. Jacob Katz, *Tradition and Crisis* (New York, 1971), p. 33.
4. Joseph L. Blau, *Modern Varieties of Judaism* (New York, 1966), pp. 1–12, provides a discussion of the increasing participation of individual Jews in the cultural, economic, political, and social life of central Europe from the fourteenth through the seventeenth centuries. Katz, *Tradition and Crisis*, pp. 231–44, and Gershom Scholem, *The Messianic Idea in Judaism* (New York, 1971), discuss the emergence of Hasidism and the antinomian challenge posed to the Jewish community by the followers of Shabbetai Zvi and the Frankists. Especially consult Scholem's "The Crisis of Tradition in Jewish Messianism" and "Redemption through Sin," which are included in this volume. Scholem writes: "The Sabbatian 'believers' . . . represent the extreme consequence to which a Messianic crisis of tradition erupting in the very heart of Judaism could lead. The old mystical Kabbalistic symbols in

which the crisis was formulated disappeared. What remained was a wild revolt against the old traditions" (p. 77). Salo W. Baron, "Ghetto and Emancipation," *Menorah Journal* 14 (1928): 515–26.

5. Katz, *Tradition and Crisis*, pp. 87, 173. The rabbi preached in the vernacular, Yiddish or Judeo-German, on *Shabbat Hagadol*, the Sabbath preceding Passover, and on *Shabbat Shuvah*, the Sabbath preceding Yom Kippur.

6. Salo W. Baron, *The Jewish Community*, vols. 1 and 2 (Philadelphia, 1942).

7. Ibid., 2:228–36.

8. Katz, *Tradition and Crisis*, pp. 168–98.

9. Ibid., pp. 183–98, quote pp. 190–91.

10. Mordechai Eliav, *Jewish Education in Germany in the Period of Emancipation and Enlightenment* (Hebrew) (Jerusalem, 1960), pp. 35–36, 110.

11. Katz, *Tradition and Crisis*, pp. 191–92.

12. Ibid., pp. 193–96.

13. Ibid., pp. 135–48; Eliav, *Jewish Education in Germany*, p. 169.

14. Esriel Hildesheimer, *The Novellae of Rabbi Esriel on Tractates Yebamot and Ketubot* (Hebrew) (Jerusalem, 1984), p. 14.

15. M. Hildesheimer, "Toward a Biography of Our Rabbi," pp. 11–12.

16. See Jacob Katz, "Contributions toward a Biography of the Hatam Sofer" (Hebrew), in *Studies in Mysticism and Religion Presented to Gershom G. Scholem*, ed. E. E. Urbach, R. J. Werblowsky, and Ch. Wirszubski (Jerusalem, 1967), pp. 115ff. Hildesheimer's appreciation of the rabbis' lack of understanding is evidenced in several critical comments he made regarding the employment of invective and excommunication by the Orthodox rabbinate of his day against those they considered "deviants." For example, see Mordechai Eliav, ed., *Rabbiner Esriel Hildesheimer Briefe* (German and Hebrew) (Jerusalem, 1965), p. 47, 96–97 (Hebrew section). Cited hereafter as *Hildesheimer Briefe*. Also Hildesheimer's letter to Hirsch Plato, pp. 230–31 (German section), in which he similarly attacks Orthodox "extremists" who employ the weapon of excommunication in the nineteenth century.

17. Katz, *Out of the Ghetto*, pp. 197–98; *Encyclopaedia Judaica*, s.v. "Emancipation." See also Ismar Freund, *Die Emanzipation der Juden in Preussen*, vols. 1 and 2 (Berlin, 1912).

18. Isaac Unna, "Ezriel Hildesheimer," in *Jewish Leaders*, ed. Leo Jung (New York, 1953), p. 218.

19. On this law, see also Salo Baron, "Freedom and Constraint in the Jewish Community," in *Essays and Studies in Memory of Linda R. Miller*, ed. Israel Davidson (New York, 1938), pp. 9–24.

20. Moshe Samet, "Orthodox Judaism in the Modern Era," (Hebrew), in *Daat*, vol. 1, pamphlet 6, *The Haskalah and Its Impact on Jewish Philosophy in the Modern Age* (Jerusalem, n.d.), p. 278.

21. Katz, *Tradition and Crisis*, p. 266.

22. Katz, *Out of the Ghetto*, p. 157. Mendelssohn was not as extreme in the reforms he advocated as was one of his greatest students, Naftali Herz Wessely. In *Words of Peace and Truth*, his response to the Hapsburg Emperor Joseph II's Edict of Toleration, Wessely outlined a practical program for the advancement of Jewish acculturation into German intellectual society. Drawing a distinction between the Torah of Man, "educational values common to all human beings," and the Torah of God, "the content of Jewish religious tradition," Wessely sought to emphasize the rightful priority of secular knowledge. He strove thereby to elevate to first-rank status what had once been studied "merely as means and handmaidens of sacred pursuits." For a discussion of Wessely, see Katz, *Tradition and Crisis*, p. 266.

23. Katz, *Tradition and Crisis*, pp. 245–74.

24. Cited by Katz, *Out of the Ghetto*, p. 158.

25. Ibid., pp. 142–60; also discussed by Meir Hildesheimer, "Contributions toward a Portrait of Esriel Hildesheimer" (Hebrew), *Sinai* 54 (1964): 67–94.

26. Katz, *Tradition and Crisis*, pp. 245–74.

27. Eliav, *Jewish Education in Germany*, p. 157.

28. Ibid., pp. 156–57.

29. For example, Hildesheimer's brother-in-law Aaron Hirsch, a strong supporter of Orthodoxy, was the owner of the wealthiest metal firm in Germany. Emanuel Schwarzschild was one of several Frankfurt bankers who supported the Orthodox party. For a description of the social and economic status of prominent members of Hildesheimer's own Adass Jisroel congregation in Berlin, see Max Sinasohn, ed., *Adass Jisroel Berlin: Entstehung, Entfaltung, Entwurzelung, 1869–1939* (Jerusalem, 1969), p. 14. On the Frankfurt Orthodox community, see Robert Liberles, *Religious Conflict in Social Context: The Emergence of Orthodox Judaism in Frankfurt am Main* (Westport, Conn., 1985).

30. Blau, *Modern Varieties of Judaism*, pp. viii–ix.

31. Schwab, *History of Orthodox Jewry in Germany*, p. 11.

32. Eliav, *Jewish Education in Germany*, p. 157.

33. Ibid., pp. 156–57.

34. M. Hildesheimer, "Toward a Biography of Our Rabbi," pp. 11–13.

35. Meir Hildesheimer, ed., "The Rabbi and His Student" (Hebrew), *HaMaayan* 12 (1972): 41. For Ettlinger's views on education, see below, Chapter 4.

36. See Mordechai Eliav, "*Torah im Derekh Eretz* in Hungary" (Hebrew), *Sinai* 51 (1962): 128.

37. M. Hildesheimer, ed., "The Rabbi and His Student," pp. 40–41.

38. M. Hildesheimer, "Contributions toward a Portrait," p. 70.

39. Azriel Hildesheimer, ed., "Rabbi Esriel Hildesheimer on Zacharias Frankel and the Jewish Theological Seminary in Breslau" (Hebrew), *HaMaayan* (1953): 65. Hereafter cited as "Hildesheimer on Frankel."

40. M. Hildesheimer, ed., "The Rabbi and His Student," p. 40.

41. Hildesheimer, *Novellae*, p. 15.

42. Hildesheimer's method of talmudic study in the yeshiva of Rabbi Ettlinger is described as follows: "[Hildesheimer] studied *derekh hapeshat*. . . . He would first read the Gemara, then Rashi and Tosafot. . . . [He would continue by considering] difficulties raised by the Maharsha (Rabbi Samuel Eliezer ben Judah Halevi Edels, 1553–1631) and the Penei Yehoshua (Rabbi Jacob Joshua Falk, 1680–1756) on Rashi and the Tosafot. In many places, *hiddushim* [novellae] on Maimonides and various *poskim* [legal authorities] were added" (ibid., p. 11).

43. Peter Berger, *The Heretical Imperative* (Garden City, N.Y., 1979), pp. 29–30.

44. Samson Raphael Hirsch, *The Nineteen Letters* (New York, 1960), Letter 18.

45. Noah Rosenbloom, *Tradition in an Age of Reform* (Philadelphia, 1976), p. 104.

46. Ismar Schorsch, *Jewish Reactions to German Anti-Semitism, 1870–1914* (Philadelphia, 1972), p. 10.

47. Katz, *Out of the Ghetto*, pp. 157–60, and "Contributions Toward a Biography of the Hatam Sofer."

48. Katz, *Out of the Ghetto*, p. 158.

2. The Quest for Religious Authority

1. Joseph L. Blau, "Tradition and Innovation," in *Essays on Jewish Life and Thought Presented in Honor of Salo W. Baron*, ed. Blau et al. (New York, 1959), p. 95.

2. For a description of much of the legislation affecting the status of the rabbinate in Germany during this period, see *Encyclopaedia Judaica*, s.v. "The Rabbi in Germany in the Modern Period"; Samet, "Orthodox Judaism in the Modern Era," p. 278; and Jacob Katz, *Out of the Ghetto*, pp. 142–60, which describes the crisis these legislative changes caused for the German rabbinate.

3. Jerome E. Carlin and Saul H. Mendlovitz, "The American Rabbi: A Religious Specialist Responds to Loss of Authority," in *Understanding American Judaism*, ed. Jacob Neusner, 2 vols. (New York, 1975), 1:166.

4. Alexander Altmann, "The German Rabbi, 1910–1939," *Leo Baeck Institute Yearbook* 19 (1974): 31.

5. Carlin and Mendlovitz, "The American Rabbi," p. 166.

6. Ismar Schorsch, "Ideology and History in the Age of Emancipation," in Schorsch, ed., *Heinrich Graetz—The Structure of Jewish History and Other Essays* (New York, 1975), p. 10.

7. Altmann, "The German Rabbi," p. 31.

8. See Schwab, *History of Orthodox Jewry in Germany*; Mordechai Eliav,

"Rabbi Isaac Dov Halevi Bamberger—The Man and His Era" (Hebrew), *Sinai* 84 (1979): 62; Mordechai Breuer, *Jüdische Orthodoxie im Deutschen Reich, 1871–1918* (Frankfurt am Main, 1986), p. 50, for the importance of Bamberger, and p. 43, for a similar discussion of the roles of Hirsch and Hildesheimer.

9. Eliav, "Rabbi Isaac Dov Halevi Bamberger," pp. 62–63, 65–67.

10. Ibid., p. 63.

11. Katz, "Tzvi Hirsch Kalischer," in *Guardian of Our Heritage,* ed. Leo Jung (New York, 1958), p. 212.

12. Eliav, "Rabbi Isaac Dov Halevi Bamberger," p. 63.

13. Esther Calvary, "Kindheitserinnerungen," *Bulletin des Leo Baeck Instituts* 8 (1959): 187.

14. See Eliav, "*Torah im Derekh Eretz* in Hungary," p. 130; Calvary, "Kindheitserinnerungen," pp. 187–92.

15. *Der Orient* was a weekly magazine published by the famed Hebraist and Jewish scholar Julius Fuerst. *Der Israelit* was a leading Orthodox weekly established in Mainz in 1860 by Hildesheimer's former pupil Marcus Lehmann.

16. On *Die Jüdische Presse,* see Mordechai Eliav, "*Die Jüdische Presse*— The Newspaper of Rabbi Esriel Hildesheimer" (Hebrew), *Sinai* 65 (1969): 121–33.

17. Hildesheimer's responsa and novellae have been published in two volumes (*Responsa*), both in Hebrew. The first volume, containing sections of *Orah Hayim* and *Yoreh Deah,* was published in Tel Aviv in 1969. The second, in which sections of *Even HaEzer* and *Hoshen Mishpat* appear, was issued at Tel Aviv in 1976. Additional novellae are published in Hildesheimer, *Novellae.*

18. Ellis Rivkin, "Solomon Zeitlin's Contributions to the Historiography of the Inter-Testamental Period, *Judaism* 14 (1965): 358.

19. Hildesheimer, *Responsa,* Novellae to the *Orah Hayim,* p. 153.

20. Ibid., *Yoreh Deah,* no. 186. Similarly, in an involved halakhic correspondence with Rabbi Zvi Hirsch Kalischer regarding whether it was permissible for a *mohel* to circumcise a child born to a gentile mother and a Jewish father, Hildesheimer ruled negatively. He added, however, that if such an actual case came before him, he would not rely on his own opinion but would consult with Ettlinger (*Yoreh Deah,* nos. 229 and 230).

21. Ibid., Novellae to the *Orah Hayim,* p. 157.

22. Katz, *Tradition and Crisis,* pp. 192, 197.

23. M. Hildesheimer, "The Rabbi and His Student," pp. 40–48.

24. Reported in Dov Katz, *The Musar Movement* (Hebrew), 2 vols. (Jerusalem, 1969), 2:321, 1:187.

25. Eliav, "*Torah im Derekh Eretz* in Hungary," p. 140.

26. Ibid. Also see *Hildesheimer Briefe,* Letter 7 (German); M. Hildesheimer, "Contributions toward a Portrait," p. 79.

27. Hildesheimer, *Responsa, Orah Hayim,* no. 5. For a more complete

description of Hildesheimer's relations with Spektor and the esteem in which many other eastern European rabbis held Hildesheimer, see M. Hildesheimer, "Toward a History of Our Rabbi," in his introduction to *Responsa*, pp. 11–26, with special emphasis on pp. 17–18 and 24–25.

28. Zvi Benjamin Auerbach, "A Biography of Rabbi Esriel Hildesheimer in His Hometown of Halberstadt," (Hebrew), in *Festschrift for Rabbi Yehiel Jacob Weinburg*, ed. Azriel Hildesheimer and Kalman Kahana (Jerusalem, 1969), pp. 229–35. There appears to be some confusion as to the year Hildesheimer received his doctorate from Halle. Altmann, in "The German Rabbi," p. 46, quoting an 1899 edition of the *Allgemeine Zeitung des Judentums*, states that Hildesheimer received the degree in 1844. Similarly, Meier Hildesheimer, in his foreword to *Rabbiner Dr. I. Hildesheimer: Gesammelte Aufsätze* (Frankfurt, 1923), p. ix, reports that Hildesheimer received the doctorate in 1844. Monika Richarz, *Der Entritt der Juden in Die Akademischen Berufe* (Tübingen, 1974), p. 106, gives 1846 as the date. Hildesheimer's collected essays will hereafter be referred to as *Gesammelte Aufsätze*.

29. Hildesheimer, *Responsa, Orah Hayim*, no. 7.

30. Auerbach, "Hildesheimer in Halberstadt," p. 230.

31. For an excellent description and analysis of the meaning of the term *mumar*, see Jakob Petuchowski, "The *Mumar*—A Study in Rabbinic Psychology," *Hebrew Union College Annual* 30 (1959): pp. 179–91. On the specific phrase *"mumar* to the entire Torah," see p. 180.

32. Auerbach, "Hildesheimer in Halberstadt," pp. 230, 235.

33. Hildesheimer, *Responsa, Orah Hayim*, no. 7.

34. Ibid. Also see Auerbach, "Hildesheimer in Halberstadt."

35. For Philippson's role as initiator of the conference, see Auerbach, "Hildesheimer in Halberstadt," p. 235.

36. *Der Orient* (1847), pp. 357–58.

37. Ibid., p. 358.

38. Ibid., pp. 357–58.

39. Ibid., pp. 357–60 and 362–64.

40. Ibid., p. 363.

41. On this point, see the perceptive essay of Arthur Hertzberg, "Modernity and Judaism," in *Great Confrontations in Jewish History*, ed. Stanley Wagner and Allen Breck (Boulder, Colo., 1975), p. 130.

42. *Der Orient* (1847), p. 364.

43. *Hildesheimer Briefe*, Letter 2 (Hebrew).

44. Mordechai Eliav, "Rabbi Hildesheimer and His Influence on Hungarian Jewry" (Hebrew), *Zion* 27 (1962): 61.

45. Ibid. In 1836 there were 191 Jewish families and 908 Jewish individuals living in Eisenstadt. After the revolution in 1848, however, that number may have diminished. Many families are likely to have relocated to nearby Vienna. See *Encyclopaedia Judaica* s.v. "Eisenstadt."

46. Raphael Patai, "Eisenstadt," (Hebrew), in *Mother Cities among the*

People Israel, ed. Y. L. HaCohen Fishman, 4 vols. (Jerusalem, 1946), 1:64–65.

47. Eliav, "Rabbi Hildesheimer and His Influence on Hungarian Jewry," p. 61.

48. Ibid.

49. *Hildesheimer Briefe,* Letter 3 (Hebrew).

50. For example, see Hildesheimer, *Responsa, Yoreh Deah,* no. 186, and *Orah Hayim,* no. 4, for his laments concerning the nonobservance that characterized his age.

51. Ibid., *Orah Hayim,* no. 32.

52. M. Hildesheimer, "Contributions toward a Portrait," p. 76.

53. Eliav, "Rabbi Hildesheimer and His Influence on Hungarian Jewry," p. 61.

54. Patai, "Eisenstadt," p. 67.

55. Eliav, "*Torah im Derekh Eretz* in Hungary," p. 139.

56. Ibid., p. 129.

57. Patai, "Eisenstadt," p. 67.

58. Eliav, "*Torah im Derekh Eretz* in Hungary," p. 129.

59. *Hildesheimer Briefe,* Letter 3.

60. Quoted in Eliav, "*Torah im Derekh Eretz* in Hungary," p. 138.

61. Quoted in Isaiah Wolfsberg, "Rabbi Esriel Hildesheimer and Rabbi David Hoffmann" (Hebrew), *Sinai* 14 (1944): 70.

62. *Hildesheimer Briefe,* Letter 3.

63. *Allgemeine Zeitung des Judentums* (1860), pp. 489 and 498.

64. *Hildesheimer Briefe,* Letter 8 (Hebrew).

65. Ibid.

66. *Gesammelte Aufsätze,* pp. 57, 13.

67. A. Hildesheimer, "Hildesheimer on Frankel," p. 65.

68. Wolfgang Häusler, "'Orthodoxie' und 'Reform' im Wiener Judentum in der Epoche des Hochliberalismus," *Studia Judaica Austriaca* 6 (1978): 47.

69. Löw's attacks on Hildesheimer appeared in the pages of *Ben Chananjah* throughout the decade (1858–67) of his editorship.

70. Eliav, "*Torah im Derekh Eretz* in Hungary," p. 132. For Hildesheimer's views on Frankel, see A. Hildesheimer, "Hildesheimer on Frankel," and the chapters that follow below.

71. It is probable that Löw charged Hildesheimer with a poor knowledge of Hebrew so as to paint him as an obscurantist, a pious Orthodox rabbi who had no modern knowledge of Hebrew grammar. Such a charge would have brought him scorn from the acculturated members of the Jewish community of Hungary.

72. Eliav, "*Torah im Derekh Eretz* in Hungary," p. 153.

73. Joel Rembaum has provided a thorough historical survey of this controversy in his article "The Development of a Jewish Exegetical Tradition Concerning Isaiah 53," *Harvard Theological Review* 75 (1982): 289–311.

His study illustrates that there was ample precedent for Graetz's position within classic Jewish exegesis. As Hildesheimer was undoubtedly aware of this, his refusal to mention it in this instance reveals his polemical intent vis-à-vis Graetz.

74. M. Hildesheimer, "Contributions toward a Portrait," p. 78.

75. Jacob Katz, "Contributions toward a Biography of the Hatam Sofer," pp. 133–41.

76. Hildesheimer, *Responsa, Yoreh Deah,* no. 219.

77. Quoted in Häusler, "'Orthodoxie' und 'Reform' im Wiener Judentum in der Epoche des Hochliberalismus," p. 32.

78. Calvary, "Kindheitserinnerungen," pp. 187ff.

79. Eliav, "Rabbi Hildesheimer and His Influence on Hungarian Jewry," p. 72.

80. Translated by Alexander Guttmann, *The Struggle over Reform in Rabbinic Literature* (Jerusalem, 1977), pp. 290–91.

81. *Hildesheimer Briefe,* Letter 16 (Hebrew).

82. Ibid., Letter 50 (German).

83. Ibid., Letter 13 (German). See also Eliav, "Rabbi Hildesheimer and His Influence on Hungarian Jewry," pp. 71–72; Meir Hildesheimer, "Rabbi Judah Aszod and Rabbi Esriel Hildesheimer" (Hebrew), in *Festschrift for Yehiel Jacob Weinberg,* ed. Azriel Hildesheimer and Kalman Kahana (Jerusalem, 1969), p. 301.

84. Eliav, "*Torah im Derekh Eretz* in Hungary," pp. 140–41.

85. *Der Israelit* (1864), pp. 27–30, 358.

86. *Hildesheimer Briefe,* Letter 15 (Hebrew).

87. Ibid., Letter 13.

88. M. Hildesheimer, "Rabbi Judah Aszod and Rabbi Esriel Hildesheimer," p. 295.

89. Ibid., pp. 296–97.

90. Quoted in Eliav, "Rabbi Hildesheimer and His Influence on Hungarian Jewry," p. 74.

91. *Hildesheimer Briefe,* Letter 15.

92. See Alexander Guttmann's translation of Lichtenstein's responsum concerning Hildesheimer cited above in *Struggle over Reform in Rabbinic Literature,* p. 290.

93. Nathaniel Katzburg, "The Jewish Congress of Hungary, 1868–1869," *Hungarian Jewish Studies* 2 (1969): 6–7.

94. *Gesammelte Aufsätze,* pp. 24–26.

95. Ibid., p. 25.

96. Ibid., p. 13.

97. Quoted in Eliav, "Rabbi Hildesheimer and His Influence on Hungarian Jewry," p. 76.

98. Hildesheimer, *Responsa, Orah Hayim,* nos. 20 and 21.

99. Maimonides, *Hilchot Tefilah* 11:3, says the *bimah* should be placed in

the center of the synagogue. The *Kesef Mishnah* rules that it may be placed next to the ark.

100. Hildesheimer, *Responsa, Orah Hayim,* no. 20.
101. *Gesammelte Aufsätze,* p. 26.
102. Ibid., pp. 19, 27.
103. Ibid., p. 27.
104. Hildesheimer, *Responsa, Hoshen Mishpat,* no. 246.
105. *Gesammelte Aufsätze,* p. 27.
106. *Hildesheimer Briefe,* Letter 20.
107. Hildesheimer, *Responsa, Yoreh Deah,* no. 187.
108. *Hildesheimer Briefe,* Letter 20.
109. Hildesheimer, *Responsa,* "Novellae to *Yoreh Deah,*" p. 363.
110. Quoted in Eliav, "Rabbi Hildesheimer and His Influence on Hungarian Jewry," p. 77.
111. *Hildesheimer Briefe,* Letter 22 (Hebrew).
112. Ibid., Letter 18 (Hebrew).
113. Ibid., Letter 15; Katzburg, "Jewish Congress of Hungary," pp. 1–20.
114. Katzburg, "Jewish Congress of Hungary," pp. 14–15.
115. *Hildesheimer Briefe,* pp. 80ff.
116. Ibid., Letter 19.
117. M. Hildesheimer, "Rabbi Judah Aszod and Rabbi Esriel Hildesheimer," p. 295.
118. Katzburg, "Jewish Congress of Hungary," pp. 18–19.
119. Esriel Hildesheimer, *Ausführlicher Rechenschafts-Bericht der . . . 35 Mitglieder des ungarischen Israelitischen Congresses* (Prague, 1869), pp. 33–34.
120. *Hildesheimer Briefe,* Letter 17.
121. Sinasohn, *Adass Jisroel Berlin,* pp. 11–12. By 1874 the Berlin Jewish community numbered 45,464 persons.
122. Ibid., p. 13.
123. Ibid.
124. Ibid., p. 14.
125. *Hildesheimer Briefe,* Letter 14.
126. Ibid.
127. Ibid., Letter 20 (Hebrew); Eliav, "Esriel Hildesheimer and His Influence on Hungarian Jewry," pp. 83–84.
128. Agitation for Reform in the community preceded the congress, but it was not until 1868 that they established their own community. See Yuhuda Spiegel, "Ungvar" (Hebrew), in *Mother Cities among the People Israel,* ed. Y. L. HaCohen Fishman, 4 vols. (Jerusalem, 1946), 4:14, 22.
129. *Hildesheimer Briefe,* Letter 20 (Hebrew); and Eliav, "Esriel Hildesheimer and His Influence on Hungarian Jewry," pp. 83–84.
130. Breuer, *Jüdische Orthodoxie im Deutschen Reich,* p. 433.
131. Sinasohn, *Adass Jisroel Berlin,* p. 22.

132. Ibid.

133. *HaMagid* (1869), vol. 13, no. 26.

134. Meir Hildesheimer, ed., "Writings Regarding the Founding of the Berlin Rabbinical Seminary" (Hebrew) *HaMaayan* 14 (1974): 14.

135. The letter is printed in its entirety in Sinasohn, *Adass Jisroel Berlin*, pp. 17–21.

136. M. Hildesheimer, ed., "Writings Regarding the Founding of the Berlin Rabbinical Seminary," pp. 12–30.

137. Hildesheimer, *Responsa, Hoshen Mishpat*, no. 253.

138. *Hildesheimer Briefe*, Letter 55.

139. Israel Klausner, *In The Ways of Zion* (Hebrew) (Jerusalem, 1978), pp. 149ff; and Mordecai Eliav, *Love of Zion and Men of Hod: German Jewry and the Settlement of Eretz-Israel in the Nineteenth Century* (Tel Aviv, 1970), p. 405.

140. Isaac Heinemann, "Rabbi Marcus Horovitz," in *Jewish Leaders*, ed. Leo Jung (New York, 1953), p. 263.

141. *Hildesheimer Briefe*, Letters 65 and 69 (German) and 35 (Hebrew).

142. Ibid., Letter 69.

143. Ibid., Letter 36 (Hebrew).

144. A full discussion of the Law of Secession appears in the next chapter.

145. *Hildesheimer Briefe*, Letter 29.

146. Additional evidence of Hildesheimer's policy is found in a letter he wrote to a Mr. H. Mor in Pest on February 26, 1889. Hildesheimer was delighted to learn that a Sabbath Observers' Society, apart from the general community, had been formed to fight the "indifference and laxity" in religious observance of the Pest community. He recalled that he had attempted to establish such a society in 1867 but that it had failed. He was pleased that it had now come to pass and was very happy that the society had elected him to honorary membership. Hildesheimer's support of this group reveals once more his sentiment regarding Orthodox religious secession from the larger Jewish community (ibid., Letter 89).

147. Ibid., Letter 39. The Jews of Pinsk asked Hildesheimer to intervene on their behalf with the czar after a series of pogroms. Because he felt his influence, as a foreigner, would be negative, Hildesheimer refused to speak to the czar and advised them to seek out Spektor or another rabbinical authority in Russia. This letter, nevertheless, indicates the prestige and reputation he enjoyed among the Jews of Europe.

148. Ibid., Letter 84.

149. Ibid., Letter 64.

150. Abraham M. Hirsch, "Letters on Palestine from Samuel Montagu to Benjamin Hirsch," *Historia Judaica* 14 (1952): 119–32.

151. Ismar Schorsch, *Jewish Reactions to German Anti-Semitism, 1870–1914* (Philadelphia, 1972), p. 10.

152. See Hildesheimer's essay "Das biblische-talmudische Recht," in *Gesammelte Aufsätze*, pp. 27–35.

153. Jews sometimes still had to swear a humiliating oath, *more Judaico*, in the courts of Europe. See *Hildesheimer Briefe*, Letter 91.

154. Hildesheimer, "Das biblische-talmudische Recht," p. 35.

155. *Hildesheimer Briefe*, Letter 68.

156. Hildesheimer, *Responsa, Orah Hayim*, no. 48.

157. Ibid., "Novellae to the *Orah Hayim*," pp. 123–24.

158. Ibid., Letter 96.

159. Ibid., *Yoreh Deah*, no. 231.

160. Ibid., *Orah Hayim*, no. 11.

161. Ibid., *Yoreh Deah*, no. 175.

162. Ibid., *Even HaEzer*, no. 88.

163. David Hoffmann dealt with a case very similar to this and ruled in a lenient fashion on the matter. See Hoffmann, *Melamed L'Hoyil* (Frankfurt, 1927), *Yoreh Deah*, no. 82. What is most interesting is that Hoffmann, after discussing the Jewish legal sources, adds, as a final consideration, that the young man in question would go to a Liberal rabbi for conversion should the Orthodox refuse to convert him. This was a development Hoffmann wanted to avoid.

164. Hildesheimer, *Responsa, Yoreh Deah*, no. 234.

165. *Hildesheimer Briefe*, pp. 254ff.

166. Ibid., Letter 61.

167. M. A. Shulvass, "The Rabbiner-Seminar of Berlin," (Hebrew), in *Institutions of Higher Learning in Europe: Their Development and Destruction*, ed. Samuel Mirsky (New York, 1956), p. 695.

3. The Confrontations with Jewish Religious and Cultural Pluralism

1. Quoted by Auerbach, "A Biography of Rabbi Esriel Hildesheimer in His Hometown of Halberstadt," p. 232.

2. This phraseology is taken from Charles Liebman, "Orthodoxy in American Jewish Life," in *The Jewish Community in America*, ed. Marshall Sklare (New York, 1974), p. 134.

3. For example, see Leo Levi, "The Relationship of the Orthodox to Heterodox Organizations," *Tradition* 9 (Fall 1967): 95–102. Several other articles relating to this issue have appeared in *Tradition* during the last two decades.

4. M. Hildesheimer, "Contributions toward a Portrait," p. 69.

5. A. Hildesheimer, "Hildesheimer on Frankel," p. 65.

6. *Der Orient* (1847), pp. 357–60 and 362–64.

7. Judith Bleich, "Jacob Ettlinger, His Life and Works: The Emergence of Modern Orthodoxy in Germany" (Ph.D. dissertation, New York University, 1974), p. 77.

8. *Der Orient* (1847), p. 364.

9. Originally named Moses Frankfurter, Hirsch's uncle adopted the surname Mendelssohn, in the opinion of Noah Rosenbloom (*Tradition in an Age of Reform*, p. 52), to signify "his emotional and ideational kinship with the reputed mentor of the Haskalah."

10. *Hildesheimer Briefe*, Letter 2 (Hebrew).

11. This letter is printed in Sinasohn, *Adass Jisroel Berlin*, p. 18.

12. *Hildesheimer Briefe*, Letter 42.

13. Interestingly, Rabbi Eliezer Berkovits, a graduate of the Hildesheimer seminary in the early part of this century and former chairman of the Department of Jewish Philosophy at the Hebrew Theological College in Skokie, Illinois, told me in an interview in February 1979 that a codicil was added to the certificate of ordination one received from the seminary. It stipulated that if the ordinee accepted a Reform pulpit, his ordination was automatically rescinded. The origin of this codicil obviously harkened back at least to the turn of the century. Professor Lou Silberman was kind enough to show me the certificate of ordination which his teacher Jacob Lauterbach received from the Rabbiner-Seminar. The certificate, issued at the turn of the century, warns the ordinee not to serve a congregation or community where there is a mixed choir of men and women or where an organ is played in the synagogue. Should the ordinee serve such a community, his ordination was to be retroactively rescinded. I thank Professor Silberman for sharing this document with me.

14. Bleich, "Jacob Ettlinger," p. 89.

15. Sinasohn, *Adass Jisroel Berlin*, p. 18. For a Hebrew translation of this piece see M. Hildesheimer, ed., "Writings Regarding the Founding of the Berlin Rabbinical Seminary," p. 13.

16. In assuming this stance, Hildesheimer obviously relied on Maimonides, *Mishneh Torah, Hilchot Teshuva* 3:8, which states that one who denies either the divine authorship of the Torah or the divine authorship of the Oral Law was to be identified as a *kofer ba'ikar*, a heretic who denies a basic principle of Jewish faith.

17. *Hildesheimer Briefe*, Letter 16. Häusler also discusses this episode and the Neologues' response to it in "'Orthodoxie' und 'Reform' im Wiener Judentum in der Epoche des Hochliberalismus," pp. 48–49.

18. Ibid.

19. A. Hildesheimer, ed., "Hildesheimer on Frankel," p. 66.

20. Ibid.; *Hildesheimer Briefe*, Letter 5.

21. Fischer's article appeared in *Jeschurun* 4 (1861): 196–214 and 241–52.

22. A. Hildesheimer, ed., "Hildesheimer on Frankel," p. 68.

23. Ibid., p. 67. Also see *Hildesheimer Briefe*, pp. 67–68.

24. A. Hildesheimer, ed., "Hildesheimer on Frankel," p. 67. Also see *Allgemeine Zeitung des Judentums* (1839), Supplement 96.

25. A. Hildesheimer, ed., "Hildesheimer on Frankel," pp. 67–68.

26. Hildesheimer, *Responsa, Yoreh Deah*, no. 238.

27. *Hildesheimer Briefe*, Letter 46.

28. M. Hildesheimer, ed., "Writings Regarding the Founding of the Berlin Rabbinical Seminary," p. 29.

29. A. Hildesheimer, ed., "Hildesheimer on Frankel," p. 69.

30. Ibid., pp. 70–71.

31. Ibid., pp. 69, 71.

32. Ibid., p. 70.

33. Here, of course, the validity of Frankel's scholarship is denied on the grounds of religious faith. Given Hildesheimer's own engagement in the academic study of Judaism, this attitude regarding Frankel reflects something of Hildesheimer's own position vis-à-vis *Wissenschaft des Judentums*. It will be discussed more completely in the next chapter.

34. Ibid., p. 71.

35. Ibid., p. 73.

36. *Hildesheimer Briefe*, Letter 5.

37. A. Hildesheimer, ed., "Hildesheimer on Frankel," p. 73.

38. Ibid., pp. 72–73.

39. *Hildesheimer Briefe*, Letter 66 and note, p. 259. On this point see also Schorsch, *Jewish Reactions to German Anti-Semitism*, p. 73.

40. Schwab, *History of Orthodox Jewry in Germany*, pp. 95–96.

41. Baron, "Freedom and Constraint in the Jewish Community," p. 12.

42. Schwab, *History of Orthodox Jewry in Germany*, p. 60.

43. Baron, "Freedom and Constraint in the Jewish Community," pp. 12–13.

44. Ibid., p. 14. For a fuller discussion of this matter against the background of the times, see Uriel Tal, *Christians and Jews in Germany: Religion, Politics, and Ideology in the Second Reich, 1870–1914*, trans. Noah Jacobs (Ithaca, 1975), chap. 2.

45. Ibid.

46. Quoted in Schwab, *History of Orthodox Jewry in Germany*, pp. 68–69.

47. Schorsch, *Jewish Reactions to German Anti-Semitism*, p. 10.

48. Quoted in Baron, "Freedom and Constraint in the Jewish Community," p. 15.

49. *Hildesheimer Briefe*, Letter 29.

50. Ibid., Letter 36.

51. Ibid., Letter 37 and pp. 164–65.

52. See Saemy Japhet, "The Secession from the Frankfurt Jewish Community under Samson Raphael Hirsch," *Historia Judaica* 10 (1948): 99–122.

53. *Hildesheimer Briefe*, Letter 30.

54. Liebman makes these sociological observations in his "Orthodoxy in American Jewish Life," p. 136.

55. Unna, "Ezriel Hildesheimer," p. 226.

56. Isaiah Wolfsberg, "Rabbi Esriel Hildesheimer and Rabbi David Hoffmann," p. 70.

57. Quoted in M. Hildesheimer, "Contributions toward a Portrait," p. 72.

58. *Hildesheimer Briefe*, Letter 12.

59. Azriel Hildesheimer, ed., "A Selection of Letters between Rabbi Esriel Hildesheimer and Rabbi Samson Raphael Hirsch and His Supporters" (Hebrew), in *Yad Shaul*, ed. J. J. Weinberg and P. Biberfeld (Tel Aviv, 1952–53), p. 236.

60. Japhet, "The Secession from the Frankfurt Jewish Community," pp. 114–16.

61. Ibid.; *Hildesheimer Briefe*, Letter 35 and pp. 161–62.

62. A. Hildesheimer, ed., "Letters between Hildesheimer and Hirsch," p. 238.

63. Ibid., p. 233.

64. *Hildesheimer Briefe*, Letter 36.

65. See Eliav, "Rabbi Isaac Dov Halevi Bamberger."

66. Isaac Heinemann, "Supplementary Remarks on the Secession from the Frankfurt Community under Samson Raphael Hirsch," *Historia Judaica* 10 (1948): 125–26.

67. Quoted by Heinemann, "Rabbi Marcus Horovitz," p. 265.

68. A. Hildesheimer, ed., "Letters between Hildesheimer and Hirsch," p. 240.

69. In 1751, Rabbi Jacob Emden (1697–1776) charged Rabbi Jonathan Eibeschütz (1695–1764), then of Altona, with leanings toward Shabbateanism. This controversy dragged on for years and divided German Jewry, particularly the rabbis, into two camps. One effect of this dispute was that the prestige of rabbinical institutions diminished throughout central Europe.

70. *Hildesheimer Briefe*, Letter 36.

71. Marcus Horovitz, *Matte Levi* (Frankfurt, 1881), p. i.

72. Isaac Heinemann, "Rabbi Marcus Horovitz and His Approach to Judaism" (Hebrew), *Sinai* 7 (1944): 165.

73. *Hildesheimer Briefe*, Letter 37.

74. Quoted by Heinemann, "Rabbi Marcus Horovitz," p. 263.

75. Japhet, "The Secession from the Frankfurt Jewish Community," p. 120.

76. *Hildesheimer Briefe*, p. 165.

77. Japhet, "The Secession from the Frankfurt Jewish Community," p. 120.

78. *Hildesheimer Briefe*, Letter 47.

79. Ibid., Letter 48.

80. Unna, "Ezriel Hildesheimer," p. 227.

81. *Hildesheimer Briefe*, Letter 12 (Hebrew).

82. Ibid., Letter 43 (Hebrew).

83. Schorsch, *Jewish Reactions to German Anti-Semitism*, p. 10. For the attitude of the "Old Orthodox" toward Emancipation, see Jacob Toury "Deutsch Juden im Vormärz," *Bulletin des Leo Baeck Instituts* 8 (1965): 65–82.

84. M. Hildesheimer, "Contributions toward a Portrait," p. 80.

85. Azriel Hildesheimer, ed., "An Exchange of Letters between Esriel Hildesheimer and Samson Raphael Hirsch on Matters Relating to the Land of Israel" (Hebrew), *HaMaayan* 2 (1954): 48–49.

86. Ibid., pp. 48–50.

87. *Hildesheimer Briefe*, Letter 54.

88. Ibid., p. 260.

89. Ibid., Letter 67.

90. Ibid., Letter 23 and p. 150.

91. Ibid., Letter 70. Also see Schorsch, *Jewish Reactions to German Anti-Semitism*, p. 35.

92. Four books in English have appeared recently which deal with the relations between Jews and Christians in Germany during the last decades of the nineteenth and the beginning of the twentieth centuries. The most comprehensive is Tal, *Christians and Jews in Germany*. Schorsch, *Jewish Reactions to German Anti-Semitism*, and Sanford Ragins, *Jewish Responses to Anti-Semitism in Germany, 1870–1914* (Cincinnati, 1980), are devoted to description and analysis, though from different perspectives, of Jewish defense efforts in light of the rise of anti-Semitism in Germany during this era. Jehuda Reinharz, *Fatherland or Promised Land* (Ann Arbor, 1975), also discusses much of this material, again from another perspective.

93. Ragins, *Jewish Responses to Anti-Semitism in Germany*, p. 96.

94. Schorsch, *Jewish Reactions to German Anti-Semitism*, p. 35.

95. Ibid., p. 109.

96. Quoted in *Hildesheimer Briefe*, p. 280.

97. Ibid., Letter 94.

98. Ibid., Letter 42 (Hebrew).

99. Ibid., Letter 70.

100. Ibid., Letter 51.

101. Ibid., Letter 95.

102. Ibid., Letter 53.

103. Ibid., Letter 85.

104. Samet, "Orthodox Judaism in the Modern Era," p. 280.

105. *Hildesheimer Briefe*, Letter 40.

106. *Shehitah* is the Jewish method of slaughtering animals permitted for food. It is a religious rite. "The method of slaughter consists of a single rapid cut of the neck by means of a knife of adequate length, set to exquisite sharpness . . . free from the slightest notch or flaw." The ritual involves one swift movement of the knife, which causes no pain and takes a fraction of a second. This description is found in Michael L. Munk and Eli Munk, eds., *Shehitah: Religious and Historical Aspects*, 2 vols. (Jerusalem, 1976), 2:12, 16.

107. Ragins, *Jewish Responses to Anti-Semitism in Germany*, p. 93.

108. *Hildesheimer Briefe*, p. 271.

109. Quoted by Tal, *Christians and Jews in Germany*, pp. 239–40. Also see Tal, pp. 83, 85, 104, 106–8, and 136, for further discussions of Wind-

thorst. For a concise analysis of the relationship between the Jews and Catholics in Germany at this time and the role played by Windthorst in this relationship, see Alfred D. Löw, *Jews in the Eyes of Germans* (Philadelphia, 1979), pp. 390–95.

110. A. Hildesheimer, ed., "Letters between Hildesheimer and Hirsch," pp. 246–47.

111. *Hildesheimer Briefe*, p. 271. All halakhic authorities agree that striking an animal before *shehitah* is impermissible. Rabbi Yehiel Yaakov Weinberg, in "The Use of Electricity in the Stunning of Animals prior to *Shehitah*," *Seridei Eish* (Hebrew) (Jerusalem, 1977), 1:9–172, provides an excellent summary of the Jewish legal material on the matter of striking an animal before the act of *shehitah*.

In the situation under discussion here, the problem concerns only the retention of blood after the act of *shehitah*. In this case, the argument centers around two of the categories of forbidden blood: (1) *Dam hanefesh*—the primary life force of the animal. *Dam hanefesh* is the blood that spurts forth from the animal during the moment of slaughter in a jet as the animal dies. Consumption of this blood is absolutely forbidden (an *issur karet*). (2) *Dam haeivarim*—blood retained in the meat or muscle. *Dam haeivarim* is forbidden only when it has moved from its original location to another location—*dam hapeiresh*.

The question is, how does striking the head of the animal immediately after the *shehitah* affect the flow of *dam hanefesh*? (*Yoreh Deah* 67). The *Siftei Cohen*, Rabbi Shabbetai ben Meir HaCohen (1621–62), argues that it has virtually no effect. Most authorities follow him on this issue, and Hildesheimer is clearly among them. The *Turei Zahav*, Rabbi David ben Samuel Halevi (1586–1667), however, disagrees and sees the spurt of blood as the last effort of life, which ends the life. Knocking on the head, in his opinion, would disrupt this process and result in the *dam hanefesh* being soaked up by the *dam haeivarim*. Although most authorities do not agree with the *Turei Zahav*, nonetheless his argument is significant, and Jewish custom follows his advice—it is usual not to hit the animal following *shehitah*.

It may be that Hirsch disagreed with Esriel Hildesheimer because he found the *Turei Zahav's* legal arguments so compelling. He may also have felt that compliance with this request would have been tantamount to supporting the idea that *shehitah* was inhumane and therefore needed this additional consideration. The sources do not explain Hirsch's reasons for holding this position. Both men had solid halakhic grounds for their views. There is no doubt, however, that in this case, Hildesheimer's was the position Windthorst and others wanted.

112. *Hildesheimer Briefe*, p. 271.

113. A. Hildesheimer, ed., "Letters between Hildesheimer and Hirsch," p. 248.

114. Ibid., p. 249.

115. *Hildesheimer Briefe*, Letter 79.

116. Ibid., p. 272.
117. A. Hildesheimer, ed., "Letters between Hildesheimer and Hirsch," p. 250.
118. *Hildesheimer Briefe*, p. 273.
119. Ibid., Letter 81.
120. Ibid., Letter 95.
121. Eliav, *Love of Zion and Men of Hod*, p. 93.
122. *Hildesheimer Briefe*, Letter 24.
123. Eliav, *Love of Zion and Men of Hod*, p. 107.
124. Quoted in Eliav, "Die Jüdische Presse," p. 123.
125. *Hildesheimer Briefe*, Letter 95.
126. Eliav, *Love of Zion and Men of Hod*, p. 107.
127. Hildesheimer's views on this matter appear to be typical of the stance adopted by several German Orthodox leaders regarding the Land of Israel and modern Zionism. On this point, see the views of his teacher Ettlinger in Bleich, "Jacob Ettlinger," and two of his students, Marcus Horovitz and Sinai Schiffer, who served as a rabbi in Karlsruhe. For Horovitz see Heinemann, "Rabbi Marcus Horovitz and His Approach to Judaism." Schiffer's attitudes are explicated by Aryeh Weil in "Sinai Schiffer: Portrait of an Orthodox German Rabbi, 1880–1920" (M.A. thesis, Yeshiva University, 1980). These studies demonstrate the ambivalent, if not negative, attitude Hildesheimer and his party had toward modern Zionism.
128. *Hildesheimer Briefe*, pp. 249–50.
129. Ibid., Letter 56.
130. *Die Jüdische Presse* (1881), p. 223.
131. Eliav, *Love of Zion and Men of Hod*, p. 101.
132. *Hildesheimer Briefe*, Letter 71 (emphasis added).
133. This report is found in J. Meisl, *Heinrich Graetz* (Berlin, 1917), pp. 101–5 and 142–51.
134. See Hildesheimer's remarks on the *Haluka* in his essay "Die Palästinafrage und ihre Geschichte," in *Gesammelte Aufsätze*, pp. 195ff.
135. *Hildesheimer Briefe*, p. 146; and Eliav, *Love of Zion and Men of Hod*, pp. 96–98.
136. A. Hildesheimer, ed., "Hildesheimer and Hirsch on Israel," p. 41.
137. *Hildesheimer Briefe*, Letter 24 (Hebrew).
138. Ibid., Letters 25 and 27 and p. 150.
139. A. Hildesheimer, ed., "Hildesheimer and Hirsch on Israel," p. 45.
140. *Hildesheimer Briefe*, Letter 22. For a further discussion of Hildesheimer's struggles with Graetz, see above, Chapter 3.
141. Eliav, *Love of Zion and Men of Hod*, p. 98.
142. *Hildesheimer Briefe*, Letter 24.
143. Ibid., Letter 23 (Hebrew).
144. A. Hildesheimer, ed., "Hildesheimer and Hirsch on Israel," p. 44.
145. Ibid., p. 51.
146. *Hildesheimer Briefe*, Letter 22 (Hebrew).

147. Katz, *Out of the Ghetto*, p. 216.

4. The Tasks of Education

1. George L. Mosse, *German Jews beyond Judaism* (Cincinnati and Bloomington, 1985), p. 3.
2. Esriel Hildesheimer, *Erster Bericht-Lehranstalt für Rabbinats-Kandidaten zu Eisenstadt* (Vienna, 1858).
3. Mosse, *German Jews beyond Judaism*, p. 3.
4. Ibid., p. 4.
5. Eliav, "Rabbi Esriel Hildesheimer and His Influence on Hungarian Jewry," p. 82.
6. *Hildesheimer Briefe*, Letter 24.
7. Ibid., Letter 18 (Hebrew).
8. Ibid., Letter 11.
9. Ibid., Letter 23.
10. For a discussion of Hasharat Zvi, see above, Chapter 1.
11. See Katz, *Tradition and Crisis*, pp. 183–98; Raphael Schneller, "Continuity and Change in Ultra-Orthodox Education," *Jewish Journal of Sociology* 22 (June 1980): 35–45.
12. For a full discussion of the Orthodox position regarding the education of women and girls in Germany at that time, see Breuer, *Jüdische Orthodoxie im Deutschen Reich*, pp. 116–20.
13. See Chapter 1.
14. Bleich, "Jacob Ettlinger," p. 80. On the development of this new genre of sermons, see Alexander Altmann, "The New Style of Preaching in 19th Century German Jewry," in *Studies in 19th Century German Jewish Intellectual History*, ed. Altmann (Cambridge, Mass., 1964), pp. 65–116.
15. Bleich, "Jacob Ettlinger," pp. 264–65.
16. Ibid., pp. 265–66.
17. Ibid., pp. 187–88. See also *Die Jüdische Presse* (1872), pp. 165–66.
18. Bleich, "Jacob Ettlinger," p. 251.
19. Bleich writes: "Ideally, he [Jacob Ettlinger] saw elements of secular culture utilized for the enhancement of the sacred" (ibid., p. 250).
20. Ibid., pp. 268–69 (emphasis added).
21. Quoted in M. Hildesheimer, "Contributions toward a Portrait," p. 72 (emphasis added).
22. Hildesheimer, *Erster Bericht*, pp. 30, 32–33.
23. *Hildesheimer Briefe*, Letter 1 (Hebrew).
24. Hildesheimer, *Erster Bericht*, pp. 30, 32–33.
25. E. Hildesheimer, *Dritter Bericht über die öffentliche Rabbinatsschule* (Halberstadt, 1869), p. 9.
26. Mordechai Breuer, *The Torah-im-Derekh-Eretz of Samson Raphael Hirsch* (Jerusalem, 1970), pp. 11–12, 7.

27. Ibid., pp. 23–24. Also see Breuer, *Jüdische Orthodoxie im Deutschen Reich*, p. 125.

28. Mordechai Eliav, "Different Approaches to *Torah im Derekh Eretz*," (Hebrew), in *Sefer Aviad—Articles and Researches in Memory of Isaiah Wolfsberg Aviad*, ed. Isaac Raphael (Jerusalem, 1986), p. 81.

29. *Hildesheimer Briefe*, p. 277.

30. Esriel Hildesheimer, *Etwas über den Religionsunterricht der Mädchen* (Berlin, 1871), pp. 8, 14.

31. *Hildesheimer Briefe*, Letter 86.

32. For other descriptions of this distinction between the views of Hildesheimer and Hirsch, see Eliav, "Rabbi Esriel Hildesheimer and His Influence on Hungarian Jewry," pp. 84–86, and Breuer, *Jüdische Orthodoxie im Deutschen Reich*, pp. 125ff. For another exposition of Hirsch's views on *Torah im Derekh Eretz*, see Rosenbloom, *Tradition in an Age of Reform*, pp. 351–53.

33. A. Hildesheimer, ed., "Hildesheimer and Hirsch on Israel," p. 42.

34. *Gesammelte Aufsätze*, p. 205.

35. Eliav, *Love of Zion and Men of Hod*, p. 99.

36. Hildesheimer described his attitude in an article published in *Die Jüdische Presse* (1889), p. 21.

37. Eliav, *Love of Zion and Men of Hod*, p. 99.

38. *Hildesheimer Briefe*, Letter 23 (Hebrew).

39. *Die Jüdische Presse* (1879), pp. 5–7.

40. Eliav, *Love of Zion and Men of Hod*, p. 103.

41. *Hildesheimer Briefe*, p. 99 (Hebrew).

42. Ibid., Letter 24 (Hebrew).

43. Ibid.

44. Hildesheimer, *Responsa, Orah Hayim*, no. 48.

45. Hildesheimer, *Responsa, Even HaEzer*, no. 58.

46. Ibid.

47. Eliav, "Rabbi Esriel Hildesheimer and His Influence on Hungarian Jewry," p. 61.

48. *Hildesheimer Briefe*, Letter 24.

49. Eliav, "*Torah im Derekh Eretz* in Hungary," pp. 127–42.

50. *Hildesheimer Briefe*, Letter 11.

51. Hildesheimer, *Erster Bericht*, p. 18.

52. Ibid., pp. 26–29.

53. Ibid., p. 29.

54. Esriel Hildesheimer, *Bericht der öffentliche Rabbinats-Schule zu Eisenstadt* (Halberstadt, 1868), pp. 32–34. For a full report of the exchange between Hildesheimer and Löw, see Eliav, "*Torah im Derekh Eretz* in Hungary," p. 132.

55. See A. Kober, "The Breslau Rabbinical Seminary" (Hebrew), in *Institutions of Higher Learning in Europe: Their Development and Destruction*, ed. Samuel Mirsky (New York, 1956), p. 610.

56. Hildesheimer, *Erster Bericht*, pp. 29–33.

57. Hildesheimer, *Bericht der öffentliche Rabbinats-Schule*, pp. 49–51, 32, 34.

58. Kober, "The Breslau Rabbinical Seminary," pp. 610–33.

59. Hildesheimer, *Dritter Bericht*, p. 6. Perhaps by offering these courses, Hildesheimer aimed to establish himself as a model of a *Torah im Derekh Eretz* personality for his students and others.

60. Ibid., pp. 10–13.

61. Ibid. See also the Introduction above.

62. Ibid., pp. 19–20.

63. Quoted in Eliav, "*Torah im Derekh Eretz* in Hungary," p. 138.

64. Quoted in Wolfsberg, "Rabbi Esriel Hildesheimer and Rabbi David Hoffmann," p. 70.

65. *Hildesheimer Briefe*, Letter 27 (Hebrew).

66. Sofer could not totally succeed in hermetically sealing off his yeshiva and the world of his students from external influences. He himself apparently knew German, and students at his yeshiva sometimes went on to earn doctorates at secular universities. For example, the career of Rabbi Bernard Illowy, an ordinee of the Pressburg yeshiva, who received a doctorate from the University of Prague, is reported in David Ellenson, "A Jewish Legal Decision by Rabbi Bernard Illowy of New Orleans and Its Discussion in Nineteenth Century Europe," *American Jewish History* 69 (1979): 174–95. Another Pressburg ordinee, Kaufmann Kohler, ultimately became president of the Hebrew Union College. See Kohler, "Personal Reminiscences of My Early Life," *Hebrew Union College Monthly*, May 1918, pp. 224–33.

67. *Hildesheimer Briefe*, Letter 27.

68. Ibid., Letter 14 (German).

69. Meier Hildesheimer, ed., "Aus dem Briefwechsel Israel Hildesheimers," in *Festschrift zum vierzigjährigen Amtsjubiläum des Herrn Rabbiners Dr. Salomon Carlebach* (Berlin, 1910), pp. 243–45.

70. *Hildesheimer Briefe*, Letter 38.

71. Shulvass, "The Rabbiner-Seminar of Berlin," pp. 692–93.

72. The report of this letter is found in *Das Rabbiner-Seminar zu Berlin: Bericht über die ersten fünfundzwanzig Jahre seines Bestehens (1873–1898)* (Berlin, 1898), pp. 7–8.

73. Ibid., pp. 6, 8.

74. Shulvass, "The Rabbiner-Seminar of Berlin," p. 695.

75. Jacob Rosenheim, *Zichronot* (Tel Aviv, 1955), pp. 35–36.

76. Shulvass, "The Rabbiner-Seminar of Berlin," p. 693.

77. *Der Israelit* (1873), p. 882.

78. Ibid. (1872), nos. 16–18 and 22.

79. A recent article describing diverse nineteenth-century Orthodox efforts in and attitudes toward *Wissenschaft des Judentums*, including Hildesheimer's and Hirsch's, can be found in Mordechai Breuer, "*Wissenschaft des Judentums*—Three Orthodox Approaches" (Hebrew), in *Jubilee Volume*

in Honor of Rabbi Joseph Dov Halevi Soloveitchik, 2 vols. (Jerusalem, 1984), 2:856–65.

80. M. Hildesheimer, ed., "Writings Regarding the Founding of the Berlin Rabbinical Seminary," pp. 22–24.

81. *Erster Jahresbericht des Rabbiner-Seminars* (Berlin, 1874), pp. 61–62.

82. See Hirsch, *The Nineteen Letters*, Letter 18.

83. A. Hildesheimer, ed., "Letters between Hildesheimer and Hirsch," p. 242.

84. *Hildesheimer Briefe*, Letter 23 (Hebrew) and p. 163 (German).

85. Asher Reichel, ed., *Letters of Rabbi Isaac Halevy* (Jerusalem, 1972), pp. 158, 194, 132.

86. Rosenheim, *Zichronot*, p. 49.

87. Jacob Rosenheim, *Erinnerungen* (Frankfurt, 1970), pp. 54–55.

88. Rosenheim, *Zichronot*, p. 50.

89. Hoffmann, *Melamed L'Hoyil, Orah Hayim*, p. 2.

90. *Das Rabbiner-Seminar zu Berlin*, pp. 36–48.

91. The report issued by the seminary in 1898 included an extensive list of the students' publications, of which the following is a random sampling: Aron Ackerman, rabbi in Brandenburg A.H., *Das Hermeneutische Element der biblischen Accentuation: Ein Beitrag zur Geschichte der hebr. Sprache* (Berlin, 1893); Isaac Auerbach of Rogasen, *Die französische Politik der päpstlichen Kurie von Tode Leo's IX bis zum Regierungsantritt Alexander's II* (Halle, 1893); Eduard Ferber, *Der philosophische Streit zwischen J. Kant und Johann Aug. Eberhard* (Berlin, 1894); Salomon Goldschmidt, *Geschichte der Juden in England im 11. und 12. Jahrhundert* (Berlin, 1886); Paul Grunbaum, *Die Priestergesetze bei Flavius Josephus, eine Parallele zu Bibel und Tradition* (Halle, 1887); Hartwig Hirschfeld, *Jüdische Elemente im Koran* (Berlin, 1878); Marcus Petuchowski, *Mischnajoth, Text mit Punktation nebst deutscher Uebersetzung und Erklärung. Teil III Seder Naschim* (Berlin, 1896–97). See *Das Rabbiner-Seminar zu Berlin*, pp. 36–44.

92. Altmann, "The German Rabbi," pp. 31–49.

93. *Hildesheimer Briefe*, Letter 26 (Hebrew).

94. *HaLevanon* (1876), p. 312.

95. *Erster Jahresbericht*, p. 62.

96. On the Hochschule's admission requirements, see *Erster Bericht über die Hochschule für die Wissenschaft des Judentums* (Berlin, 1874), p. 22. On the Breslau Seminary, see Kober, "The Breslau Rabbinical Seminary," p. 610.

97. For example, see *Hildesheimer Briefe*, Letters 63 and 92 (German) and 38 (Hebrew).

98. Shulvass, "The Rabbiner-Seminar of Berlin," p. 697.

99. A Hildesheimer, ed., "Letters between Hildesheimer and Hirsch," p. 242.

100. Rosenheim, *Zichronot*, p. 50.

101. A. Hildesheimer, ed., "Letters between Hildesheimer and Hirsch," p. 242.

102. Ibid. (emphasis added).

103. *Hildesheimer Briefe*, pp. 208–9.

104. As quoted in Zevi Weinberg's "Jacob Barth's Lectures on the Book of Isaiah Delivered in the Berlin Rabbinerseminar" (Hebrew), in *Studies in Scripture and Commentary in Honor of Aryeh Weig*, ed. Uriel Simon and Moshe Goshen-Gottstein (Ramat Gan, 1980), pp. 229–41.

105. David Hoffmann, *Das Buch Leviticus: Übersetzt und erklärt*, 2 vols. (Berlin, 1905), 1:v, 6–7.

106. Ibid., p. 1.

107. Ibid., p. 9. An English translation of Hoffmann's "Introduction" to *Leviticus* can be found in Jenny Marmorstein, "David Hoffmann—Defender of the Faith," *Tradition* 7–8 (1966): 91–101.

108. Julius Wellhausen, *Prolegomena to the History of Israel* (New York, 1957), p. 35.

109. Hoffmann, *Das Buch Leviticus*, 2:29.

110. Meyer Waxman, "Professor David Tzvi Hoffmann," (Hebrew), in *The Science of Judaism in Western Europe*, ed. Simon Federbush (Jerusalem, 1958), 1:207.

111. Alexander Altmann, "Theology in Twentieth Century German Jewry," *Leo Baeck Institute Yearbook* 1 (1956): 210–11.

112. David Hoffmann, *Mar Samuel* (Leipzig, 1873), p. 58.

113. David Hoffmann, *The First Mishna and the Controversies of the Tannaim*, trans. Paul Forchheimer (New York, 1977), pp. 1–2.

114. See Judah Rosenthal, "The Hochschule für die Wissenschaft des Judentums" (Hebrew), in *Institutions of Higher Learning in Europe: Their Development and Destruction*, ed. Samuel Mirsky (New York, 1956), p. 668, and Kober, "The Breslau Rabbinical Seminary," p. 610.

115. *Das Rabbiner-Seminar zu Berlin*, pp. 32–33.

116. Ibid., p. 36.

117. Ibid., p. 10.

118. Ibid.

119. Ibid., pp. 10–11.

120. Ibid., pp. 32–33.

121. Shulvass, "The Rabbiner-Seminar of Berlin," pp. 699–700.

122. Altmann, "The German Rabbi," pp. 31–49.

123. See Rosenthal, "The Hochschule für die Wissenschaft des Judentums," p. 662, and Kober, "The Breslau Rabbinical Seminary," p. 610.

124. *Program zur Eröffnung des jüdisch-theologisches Seminars zu Breslau*, August 10, 1854, p. 2. On the Hochschule, see Rosenthal, "The Hochschule für die Wissenschaft des Judentums," p. 662.

125. *Program*, p. 2.

126. Quoted in Kober, "The Breslau Rabbinical Seminary," p. 608.

127. *Erster Bericht über die Hochschule für die Wissenschaft des Judentums*, pp. 25–26, 22.

128. Rosenthal, "The Hochschule für die Wissenschaft des Judentums," pp. 662–68.

129. For a list of the Breslau seminary's graduates and their publications, see Kober, "The Breslau Rabbinical Seminary," pp. 610–33. On the *Hochschule* and some of its outstanding students see Rosenthal, "The Hochschule für die Wissenschaft des Judentums," pp. 678–80. The Rabbinerseminar published a list of its graduates and their academic publications in *Das Rabbiner-Seminar zu Berlin*, pp. 36–48.

130. *Hildesheimer Briefe*, Letter 57.

131. Schorsch, "Ideology and History in the Age of Emancipation," in *Heinrich Graetz*, pp. 10–11.

132. Samuel Klein, "Einiges über die Tätigkeit Dr. I. Hildesheimer's in Ungarn," *Jeschurun* 7 (1920): 256.

133. Quoted in Marmorstein, "David Hoffmann," p. 91.

134. See M. Hildesheimer, "Contributions toward a Portrait," p. 81.

135. *Das Rabbiner-Seminar zu Berlin*, p. 35.

136. *Hildesheimer Briefe*, Letter 84.

137. Ibid., Letter 52 and pp. 245–46.

138. Chaim Tchernowitz, *Chapters of a Life* (Hebrew) (New York, 1954), p. 108.

139. M. Hildesheimer, ed., "Writings Regarding the Founding of the Berlin Rabbinical Seminary," pp. 34–36 (emphasis added).

140. See Aaron Rothkoff, *Bernard Revel* (Philadelphia, 1972), p. 243.

Conclusion

1. Berger, *Heretical Imperative*, p. 30.

2. Ibid.

3. Rabbi Nobel (1871–1922) succeeded Marcus Horovitz as the *orthodoxer Gemeinderabbiner* of Frankfurt. He was also the teacher of Franz Rosenzweig, and it was he who bestowed the title of *haver* upon him.

4. Altmann, "The German Rabbi," p. 47.

Bibliography

Periodicals

Allgemeine Zeitung des Judentums. 1839 and 1860.
Ben Chananjah. 1858–67.
Der Israelit. 1864 and 1873.
Jeschurun. 1861.
Die Jüdische Presse. 1872–89.
HaLevanon. 1876.
HaMagid. 1869.
Der Orient. 1847.

Primary Sources

Berkowitz, Eliezer. Interview. February 1979.
Calvary, Esther. "Kindheitserinnerungen." *Bulletin des Leo Baeck Instituts* 8 (1959): 187–92.
Eliav, Mordechai, ed. *Rabbiner Esriel Hildesheimer Briefe.* (German and Hebrew). Jerusalem: Verlag Rubin Mass, 1965.
Erster Bericht über die Hochschule für die Wissenschaft des Judentums. Berlin: G. Bernstein, 1874.
Erster Jahresbericht des Rabbiner-Seminars. Berlin: Itzkowski, 1874.
Hildesheimer, Azriel, ed. "Harav Azriel Hildesheimer al Zechariah Frankel u'veit hamidrash b'Breslau" (Rabbi Esriel Hildesheimer on Zacharias Frankel and the Jewish Theological Seminary in Breslau). *HaMaayan* 1 (1953): 65–73.
––––––. "Hiluf mikhtavim bein harav Azriel Hildesheimer u'vein harav

Shimshon Rafael Hirsch al inyanay eretz yısrael" (An Exchange of Letters between Esriel Hildesheimer and Samson Raphael Hirsch on Matters Relating to the Land of Israel). *HaMaayan* 2 (1954): 41–52.

––––––. "Mitokh hiluf hamikhtavim bein maran harav Azriel Hildesheimer u'vein maran rabbi Shimshon Rafael Hirsch" (A Selection of Letters between Rabbi Esriel Hildesheimer and Rabbi Samson Raphael Hirsch and His Supporters). In *Yad Shaul,* edited by J. J. Weinberg and P. Biberfeld, pp. 233–51. Tel Aviv: [s.n.], 1952 or 1953.

Hildesheimer, Esriel. *Ausführlicher Rechenschafts-Bericht der . . . 35 Mitglieder des ungarischen Israelitischen Congresses.* Prague: Brandeis, 1869.

––––––. *Bericht der öffentliche Rabbinats-Schule zu Eisenstadt.* Halberstadt, 1868.

––––––. *Dritter Bericht über die öffentliche Rabbinatsschule.* Halberstadt, 1869.

––––––. *Erster Bericht-Lehranstalt für Rabbinats-Kandidaten zu Eisenstadt.* Vienna, 1858.

––––––. *Etwas über den Religionsunterricht der Mädchen.* Berlin: M. Driesner, 1871.

––––––. *Hiddushei rabbi Azriel al m'sachtot yevamot-ketubot* (The Novellae of Rabbi Esriel on Tractates Yebamot and Ketubot). Jerusalem: Mifal Torat Hachmei Ashkenaz, 1984.

––––––. *She'elot u'teshuvot rabbi Azriel* (The Responsa of Rabbi Esriel). 2 vols. Tel Aviv: Chaim Gittler, 1969 and 1976.

Hildesheimer, Meir, ed. "Harav v'talmido" (The Rabbi and His Student). *HaMaayan* 12 (1972): 40–48.

––––––. "Ketavim b'devar yesod beit hamidrash l'rabbanim b'Berlin" (Writings Regarding the Founding of the Berlin Rabbinical Seminary). *HaMaayan* 14 (1974): 12–37.

––––––. "Rabbi Yehuda Assad v'rabbı Azriel Hildesheimer" (Rabbi Judah Aszod and Rabbi Esriel Hildesheimer). In *Festschrift for Yehiel Jacob Weinberg,* edited by Azriel Hildesheimer and Kalman Kahana, pp. 285–302. Jerusalem: Feldheim, 1969.

Hildesheimer, Meier, ed. "Aus dem Briefwechsel Israel Hildesheimers." In *Festschrift zum vierzigjährigen Amtsjubiläum des Herrn Rabbiners Dr. Salomon Carlebach,* edited by M. Stern, pp. 243–307. Berlin: "Hausfreund," 1910.

––––––. *Rabbiner Dr. I. Hildesheimer: Gesammelte Aufsätze.* Frankfurt, 1923.

Hirsch, Abraham M. "Letters on Palestine from Samuel Montagu to Benjamin Hirsch." *Historia Judaica* 14 (1952): 119–32.

Hirsch, Samson Raphael. *The Nineteen Letters.* New York: Feldheim, 1960.

Hoffmann, David. *Das Buch Leviticus: Übersetzt und erklärt.* 2 vols. Berlin: M. Poppelauer, 1905.

––––––. *The First Mishna and the Controversies of the Tannaim.* Translated by Paul Forchheimer. New York: Publication of Congregation Kehillat Yaakov, 1977.

_____. *Mar Samuel*. Leipzig: O. Leiner, 1873.

_____. *Melamed L'Hoyil*. Frankfurt: Hermon, 1927.

Horovitz, Marcus. *Matte Levi*. Frankfurt, 1881.

Marmorstein, Jenny. "David Hoffmann—Defender of the Faith." *Tradition* 7–8 (1966): 91–101.

Program zur Eröffnung des jüdisch-theologisches Seminars zu Breslau. August 10, 1854.

Das Rabbiner-Seminar zu Berlin: Bericht über die ersten fünfundzwanzig Jahre seines Bestehens (1873–1898). Berlin: H. Itzkowski, 1898.

Reichel, Asher, ed. *Letters of Rabbi Isaac Halevy*. Jerusalem: Mossad Harav Kuk, 1972.

Rosenheim, Jacob. *Erinnerungen*. Frankfurt: Kramer, 1970.

_____. *Zichronot*. Tel Aviv: Agudat Yisrael, 1955.

Tchernowitz, Chaim. *Pirkei Hayim* (Chapters of a Life). New York: Ogen, 1954.

Weinberg, Yehiel Yaakov. *Seridei Eish*. Jerusalem: Mossad Harav Kuk, 1977.

Secondary Sources

Altmann, Alexander. "The German Rabbi, 1910–1939." *Leo Baeck Institute Yearbook* 19 (1974): 31–50.

_____. "The New Style of Preaching in 19th Century German Jewry." In *Studies in 19th Century German Jewish Intellectual History*, edited by Alexander Altmann, pp. 65–116. Cambridge, Mass.: Harvard University Press, 1964.

_____. "Theology in Twentieth Century German Jewry." *Leo Baeck Institute Yearbook* 1 (1956): 193–216.

Auerbach, Zvi Benjamin. "Toledot hayav shel rabbi Azriel Hildesheimer b'ir moladeto Halberstadt" (A Biography of Rabbi Esriel Hildesheimer in His Hometown of Halberstadt). In *Festschrift for Rabbi Yehiel Jacob Weinberg*, edited by Azriel Hildesheimer and Kalman Kahana, pp. 229–35. Jerusalem: Feldheim, 1969.

Baron, Salo W. "Freedom and Constraint in the Jewish Community." In *Essays and Studies in Memory of Linda R. Miller*, edited by Israel Davidson, pp. 9–24. New York: Jewish Theological Seminary, 1938.

_____. "Ghetto and Emancipation." *Menorah Journal* 14 (1928): 515–26.

_____. *The Jewish Community*. Vols. 1–3. Philadelphia: Jewish Publication Society, 1942.

Berger, Peter. *The Heretical Imperative*. Garden City, N.Y.: Anchor Books, 1979.

Blau, Joseph L. *Modern Varieties of Judaism*. New York: Columbia University Press, 1966.

———. "Tradition and Innovation." In *Essays on Jewish Life and Thought Presented in Honor of Salo W. Baron*, edited by Joseph Blau et al., pp. 95–104. New York: Columbia University Press, 1959.

Bleich, Judith. "Jacob Ettlinger, His Life and Works: The Emergence of Modern Orthodoxy in Germany." Ph.D. dissertation, New York University, 1974.

Breuer, Mordechai. "Hochmat yisrael—shalosh gishot ortodoxiyot" (*Wissenschaft des Judentums*—Three Orthodox Approaches). In *Sefer yovel lichvod moreinu hagaon rabbi Yoseph Dov Halevi Soloveitchik* (Jubilee Volume in Honor of Rabbi Joseph Dov Halevi Soloveitchik). 2 vols. 2:856–65. Jerusalem, 1984.

———. *Jüdische Orthodoxie im Deutschen Reich, 1871–1918*. Frankfurt am Main: Jüdischer Verlag bei Athenäum, 1986.

———. *The Torah-im-Derekh-Eretz of Samson Raphael Hirsch*. Jerusalem: Feldheim, 1970.

Carlebach, Alexander. "The Rabbi in Germany in the Modern Period." *Encyclopaedia Judaica*, 13:1453–55. Jerusalem, 1971.

Carlin, Jerome E., and Saul H. Mendlovitz. "The American Rabbi: A Religious Specialist Responds to Loss of Authority." In *Understanding American Judaism*, edited by Jacob Neusner, 2 vols. 1:165–214. New York: Ktav, 1975.

Dinur, Benzion. "Emancipation." *Encyclopaedia Judaica*, 6:696–718. Jerusalem, 1971.

Eliav, Mordechai. *Ahavat tzion v'anshei hod* (Love of Zion and Men of Hod: German Jewry and the Settlement of Eretz-Israel in the Nineteenth Century). Tel Aviv: Hakibbutz Hameuchad, 1970.

———. "Gishot shonot l'torah im derekh eretz" (Different Approaches to *Torah im Derekh Eretz*). In *Sefer Aviad—Articles and Researches in Memory of Isaiah Wolfsberg Aviad*, edited by Isaac Raphael, pp. 77–84. Jerusalem: Mossad Harav Kuk, 1986.

———. *Hahinukh ha-yehudi b'Germania bimei hahaskalah vehaemantzipatziah* (Jewish Education in Germany in the Period of Emancipation and Enlightenment). Jerusalem: Sivan Press, 1960.

———. "Ha-Jüdische Presse—ittono shel harav Azriel Hildesheimer" (*Die Jüdische Presse*—The Newspaper of Rabbi Esriel Hildesheimer). *Sinai* 65 (1969): 121–33.

———. "Harav Yitzhak Dov Halevi Bamberger—Haish u'tekufato" (Rabbi Isaac Dov Halevi Bamberger—The Man and His Era). *Sinai* 84 (1979): 61–71.

———. "Mekomo shel harav Azriel Hildesheimer bema'avak al demuttah shel yahadut Hungariyah" (Rabbi Hildesheimer and His Influence on Hungarian Jewry). *Zion* 27 (1962): 59–86.

———. "Torah-im-derekh-erets be-Hungariyah" (*Torah im Derekh Eretz* in Hungary). *Sinai* 51 (1962): 127–42.

Ellenson, David. "A Jewish Legal Decision by Rabbi Bernard Illowy of New

Orleans and Its Discussion in Nineteenth Century Europe." *American Jewish History* 69 (1979): 174–95.

_____. "Modern Orthodoxy and the Problem of Religious Pluralism: The Case of Rabbi Esriel Hildesheimer." *Tradition* 17 (1979): 74–89.

Freund, Ismar. *Die Emanzipation der Juden in Preussen.* Vols. 1 and 2. Berlin, 1912.

Fuerst, Aharon, and Yehouda Marton. "Eisenstadt." *Encyclopaedia Judaica,* 6:546–48. Jerusalem, 1971.

Guttmann, Alexander. *The Struggle over Reform in Rabbinic Literature.* Jerusalem: World Union for Progressive Judaism, 1977.

Häusler, Wolfgang. "'Orthodoxie' und 'Reform' im Wiener Judentum in der Epoche des Hochliberalismus." *Studia Judaica Austriaca* 6 (1978): 29–56.

Heilman, Samuel C. "Constructing Orthodoxy." *Transaction* 15 (May–June 1978): 32–40.

Heinemann, Isaac. "Rabbi Marcus Horovitz." In *Jewish Leaders,* edited by Leo Jung, pp. 259–72. New York: Bloch, 1953.

_____. "Rabbi Mordechai Horovitz u'tefisat hayahadut shelo" (Rabbi Marcus Horovitz and His Approach to Judaism). *Sinai* 7 (1944): 162–71.

_____. "Supplementary Remarks on the Secession from the Frankfurt Community under Samson Raphael Hirsch." *Historia Judaica* 10 (1948): 123–34.

Hertzberg, Arthur. "Modernity and Judaism." In *Great Confrontations in Jewish History,* edited by Stanley Wagner and Allen Breck, pp. 123–35. Boulder, Colo.: University of Colorado and Ktav, 1975.

Hildesheimer, Meir. "Kavim li'dmuto shel Azriel Hildesheimer" (Contributions toward a Portrait of Esriel Hildesheimer). *Sinai* 54 (1964): 67–94.

Japhet, Saemy. "The Secession from the Frankfurt Jewish Community under Samson Raphael Hirsch." *Historia Judaica* 10 (1948): 99–122.

Katz, Dov. *Tnuat hamusar* (The Musar Movement). 2 vols. Jerusalem: Beitan Hasefer, 1969.

Katz, Jacob. *Exclusiveness and Tolerance.* New York: Oxford University Press, 1969.

_____. "Kavim le-biographiyah shel ha-Hatam Sofer" (Contributions toward a biography of the Hatam Sofer). In *Studies in Mysticism and Religion Presented to Gershom G. Scholem,* edited by E. E. Urbach, R. J. Werblowsky, and Ch. Wirszubski, pp. 115–48. Jerusalem: Magnes Press, 1967.

_____. *Out of the Ghetto.* Cambridge, Mass.: Harvard University Press, 1973.

_____. *Tradition and Crisis.* New York: Schocken, 1971.

_____. "Tzvi Hirsch Kalischer." In *Guardians of Our Heritage,* edited by Leo Jung, pp. 207–28. New York: Bloch, 1958.

Katzburg, Nathaniel. "The Jewish Congress of Hungary, 1868–1869." *Hungarian Jewish Studies* 2 (1969): 1–33.

Klausner, Israel. *B'darchei Tzion* (In the Ways of Zion). Jerusalem: Ruben Mass, 1978.

Klein, Samuel. "Einiges über die Tätigkeit Dr. I. Hildesheimer's in Ungarn." *Jeschurun* 7 (1920): 256–70.

Kober, A. "The Breslau Rabbinical Seminary." In *Mosadot torah be'Airopah b'vinyanam u'v-hurbanam* (Institutions of Higher Learning in Europe: Their Development and Destruction), edited by Samuel Mirsky, pp. 605–34. New York: Ogen, 1956.

Kohler, Kaufmann. "Personal Reminscences of My Early Life." *Hebrew Union College Monthly,* May 1918, pp. 224–33.

Levi, Leo. "The Relationship of the Orthodox to Heterodox Organizations." *Tradition* 9 (Fall 1967): 95–102.

Liberles, Robert. *Religious Conflict in Social Context: The Emergence of Orthodox Judaism in Frankfurt am Main.* Westport, Conn.: Greenwood Press, 1985.

Liebman, Charles. "Orthodoxy in American Jewish Life." In *The Jewish Community in America,* edited by Marshall Sklare, pp. 131–74. New York: Behrman, 1974.

Löw, Alfred D. *Jews in the Eyes of Germans.* Philadelphia: Institute for the Study of Human Issues, 1979.

Meisl, J. *Heinrich Graetz.* Berlin, 1917.

Mosse, George L. *German Jews beyond Judaism.* Cincinnati and Bloomington: Hebrew Union College and Indiana University Presses, 1985.

Munk, Michael L., and Eli Munk, eds. *Shehitah: Religious and Historical Aspects.* 2 vols. Jerusalem: Feldheim, 1976.

Patai, Raphael. "Eisenstadt." In *'Arim v'imahot b'Yisrael* (Mother Cities among the People Israel), edited by Y. L. HaCohen Fishman, 4 vols. 1:41–79. Jerusalem: Mossad Harav Kuk, 1946.

Petuchowski, Jakob. "The *Mumar*—A Study in Rabbinic Psychology." *Hebrew Union College Annual* 30 (1959): 179–91.

Ragins, Sanford. *Jewish Responses to Anti-Semitism in Germany, 1870–1914.* Cincinnati: Hebrew Union College Press, 1980.

Reinharz, Jehuda. *Fatherland or Promised Land.* Ann Arbor: University of Michigan Press, 1975.

Rembaum, Joel. "The Development of a Jewish Exegetical Tradition Concerning Isaiah 53." *Harvard Theological Review* 75 (1982): 289–311.

Richarz, Monika. *Der Entritt Der Juden in Die Akademischen Berufe.* Tübingen: J. C. B. Mohr, 1974.

Rivkin, Ellis. "Solomon Zeitlin's Contributions to the Historiography of the Inter-Testamental Period." *Judaism* 14 (1965): 354–65.

Rosenbloom, Noah. *Tradition in an Age of Reform.* Philadelphia: Jewish Publication Society, 1976.

Rosenthal, Judah. "The Hochschule für die Wissenschaft des Judentums." In *Mosadot torah be'Airopah b'vinyanam u'v-hurbanam* (Institutions of

Higher Learning in Europe: Their Development and Destruction), edited by Samuel Mirsky, pp. 655–88. New York: Ogen, 1956.

Rothkoff, Aaron. *Bernard Revel.* Philadelphia: Jewish Publication Society, 1972.

Samet, Moshe. "Hayahadut haharedit baz'man hehadash" (Orthodox Judaism in the Modern Era). In *Daat,* vol. 1, pamphlet 6, *Hahaskalah v'hashlachoteyha al hafilosofiyah hayehudit ba-et hahadashah (The Haskalah and Its Impact on Jewish Philosophy in the Modern Age),* pp. 276–82. Jerusalem: Hebrew University, n.d.

Schischa, A. "Hildesheimer Correspondence." *Journal of Jewish Studies* 19 (1967): 79–89.

Schneller, Raphael. "Continuity and Change in Ultra-Orthodox Education." *Jewish Journal of Sociology* 22 (June 1980): 35–45.

Scholem, Gershom. *The Messianic Idea in Judaism.* New York: Schocken, 1971.

Schorsch, Ismar, ed. *Heinrich Graetz—The Structure of Jewish History and Other Essays.* New York: Jewish Theological Seminary, 1975.

_____. *Jewish Reactions to German Anti-Semitism, 1870–1914.* Philadelphia: Columbia University Press and Jewish Publication Society, 1972.

Schwab, Hermann. *The History of Orthodox Jewry in Germany.* London: Mitre Press, 1950.

Shulvass, M. A. "The Rabbiner-Seminar of Berlin." In *Mosadot torah be'Airopah b'vinyanam u'v-hurbanam* (Institutions of Higher Learning in Europe: Their Development and Destruction), edited by Samuel Mirský, pp. 689–714. New York: Ogen, 1956.

Siegel, Seymour. *Conservtive Judaism and Jewish Law.* New York: Ktav, 1977.

Sinasohn, Max, ed. *Adass Jisroel Berlin: Entstehung, Entfaltung, Entwurzelung, 1869–1939.* Jerusalem, 1969.

Spiegel, Yehuda, "Ungvar." In *'Arim v'imahot b'Yisrael* (Mother Cities among the People Israel), edited by Y. L. HaCohen Fishman, 4 vols. 4:5–54. Jerusalem: Mossad Harav Kuk, 1946.

Tal, Uriel. *Christians and Jews in Germany: Religion, Politics, and Ideology in the Second Reich, 1870–1914,* translated by Noah Jacobs. Ithaca: Cornell University Press, 1975.

Toury, Jacob. "'Deutsche Juden' im Vormärz." *Bulletin des Leo Baeck Instituts* 8 (1965): 65–82.

Unna, Isaac. "Ezriel Hildesheimer." In *Jewish Leaders,* edited by Leo Jung, pp. 213–32. New York: Bloch, 1953.

Waxman, Meyer. "Professor David Tzvi Hoffmann." In *Hochmat Yisrael b'maarav Airopah* (The Science of Judaism in Western Europe), edited by Simon Federbush, 3 vols. 1:199–209. Jerusalem: Ogen, 1958.

Weil, Aryeh. "Sinai Schiffer: Portrait of an Orthodox German Rabbi, 1880–1920." M.A. thesis, Yeshiva University, 1980.

Weinberg, Zevi. "Hahartsaot shel Yaakov Barth al sefer Yeshiyahu b'veit midrash b'Berlin" (Jacob Barth's Lectures on the Book of Isaiah Delivered in the Berlin Rabbinerseminar). In *Iyunay mikra u'farshanut lichvod Aryeh Weig* (Studies in Scripture and Commentary in Honor of Aryeh Weig), edited by Uriel Simon and Moshe Goshen-Gottstein, pp. 229–41. Ramat Gan: Bar Ilan University Press, 1980.

Wellhausen, Julius. *Prolegomena to the History of Israel.* New York: Meridian Books, 1957.

Wolfsberg, Isaiah. "Harav Azriel Hildesheimer v'harav David Hoffmann" (Rabbi Esriel Hildesheimer and Rabbi David Hoffmann). *Sinai* 14 (1944): 65–74.

Index

Danish. *See* Denmark
Darmstadt, 77
Deaf-mutes, 127–28
Decorum. *See* Aesthetics; Civility
Delitzsch, Franz, 104
Democracy, 34–35, 55
Denmark, 8, 118
Derekh Eretz. See Bildung; Humanities
Deutsch, Abraham David, 47, 52
Deutsch, Joel, 127
Deutsch-Israelitischer Gemeindebund, 101–2
Disputes. *See* Communal relations; Polemics; Rabbinical relations
Divorce, 68–69, 160
Dress, 43, 71. *See also* Clerical robes
Düsseldorf, 140

Eastern Europe, 26–27, 60–62, 70, 80, 109–10, 145–48, 159, 163–64, 180
Eberhard, Johann Augustus, 147
Economic life, 4, 12–13, 53, 57, 61, 63, 88–89, 96, 110, 120–21, 124–26, 138, 140–41, 173
Education, xii, 1, 3–7, 9–11, 13, 18–19, 23, 35–37, 40, 44, 55, 57–58, 64, 71, 74, 98–99, 111, 115–19, 122–26, 128–29, 131, 133, 135, 138, 140, 142, 146–47, 156–57, 164–65; for women, 6, 13–14, 18, 58, 117–18, 122–24, 128, 135, 138, 164. *See also Bildung; Gymnasium;* Schools, Seminaries; Study; Universities; Yeshivot
Eger, Akiva, 6, 36
Eger, Lev, 6
Egypt, 98
Ehrmann, Herz, 106–7
Eibeschütz, Jonathan, 93, 184
Eisenstadt, Hungary, 2, 27, 36–37, 43, 54, 56, 76–77, 94, 109, 115, 121, 128–35, 140, 145, 164, 176
Eliav, Mordechai, xi, xiii, 23
Emancipation. *See* Citizenship
Emden, Jacob, 93, 184
Engel, Moshe Lev, 49–50
England, 63, 97
Enlightenment, 104, 115, 133. *See also* Haskalah; Modernity
Ethics. *See* Morality

Ethiopia, 97–98
Ettlinger, Jacob, 1, 8, 14–15, 26, 39, 49, 74–76, 94, 101, 118–22, 133, 167, 174
Excommunication, 2–3, 8, 11, 29, 32, 43, 125, 172
Exile, 3, 12, 29, 31, 141
Extremism, 37–39, 53, 56, 108. *See also* Antimodernism

Falasha Jews, 97–98
Family, 4, 36, 68–69, 99, 103, 121, 123, 133. *See also* Hildesheimer, Esriel: family
Feilchenfeld, Wolf, 37, 54, 78–80, 83
Fenner, Ferdinand, 105
Fischer, Gottlieb, 78, 80
Formstecher, Solomon, 77
France, 99, 147
Frankel, Zacharias, 40, 78–80, 82, 84, 130–31, 140, 149, 154–55, 160, 162, 169
Frankfurt-am-Main, ix, 18–19, 35, 37, 75, 87–88, 90, 93–94, 96–97, 102, 141–42, 169, 173
Frankfurter, Menahen Mendel, 121
Franz Joseph, Hapsburg monarch, 44–46
Freedom, religious, 34, 86–87, 102, 105, 107–8. *See also* Citizenship
Freethinkers, 9, 12, 61, 67–68, 73, 101, 109, 120, 139, 144
French language, 13
Fulda, 70

Galia, Lev, 6–7, 13–14, 27–28, 117
Galia, Moses, 6
Ganzfried, Solomon, 56–58
Geiger, Abraham, 55, 76–78, 84, 109, 139, 145, 154–55, 160, 162
Geography, 121, 130–32, 157
Geometry, 15
German language, x–xi, 10–14, 18–19, 23–24, 28, 30, 37–38, 43, 49, 117–118, 130–33
Germany, 8–9, 62–65, 71–74, 76, 80–81, 85–86, 89–90, 92, 98, 101–3, 105–9, 117, 126, 138–39, 141–42, 145–46, 148, 157, 159, 161, 164, 166, 173. *See also* Altona; Berlin; Bonn; Breslau; Darmstadt; Düsseldorf; Frankfurt;

Koran, 147
Kosher laws, 51, 81, 98, 102, 105–8, 158.
    See also Shohet
Krauss, Sigmund, 53
Kristeller, Samuel, 101, 169
Kroner, Theodore, 81–84
Ktav Sofer, 27, 47, 51
Kulturkampf, 87

Laity, 3, 11–12, 53, 55, 77, 88–89, 96,
    100, 128, 133, 138, 140–41, 169, 173
Landau, Ezekiel, 11
Landau, Samuel, 11
Landsberger, Moses, 77
Languages, non-Jewish, 13, 16, 47, 49,
    118, 121, 132. *See also* French; German; Hungarian
Lasker, Eduard, 9, 86–87
Latin, 13, 16, 121, 130–33
Law. *See* Courts; Halakha; Tradition
Laxity in observance, 67–69, 81–82, 84,
    92, 100, 109, 120, 134, 169, 177, 180
Lazarus, Moritz, 103–4
Lehmann, Marcus, 80, 111
Lehren, Akiba, 109, 111–12, 125–26
Leipzig, 75
Lemberg, 109
Levian, Mattathias, 28–32, 71
Levinson, Elijah, 26
Lewisohn, Sally, 141
Lewy, Gottschalk, 101, 110, 112
Lewy, Israel, 160
Liberalism, 14, 18, 36, 41, 45, 52, 55, 60,
    63, 69, 75, 84–86, 92, 100–5, 123, 130,
    134, 139, 142, 147, 162, 168–69
Lichtenstein, Hillel, 43, 47
Lieberman, Benjamin, 55
Lipkin, Israel, 26
Literalism, 66–67
Literature, German, 24, 115, 130
Liturgy. *See* Prayer; Reform of religion
Löw, Leopold, 40, 42, 45–46, 130–31,
    133, 177

Magdeburg, 32–35, 75
Maimonides, Moses, 123, 157–58
Mainz, 55
Mainz, Lippman, 88

Mainz, Moshe, 90
Mannheim, 100
Marcuse, J., Berlin, 55
Marienwerder, Germany, 104
Marriage, 29, 32, 48, 50, 68–69, 77, 99–
    100, 157, 160
Mar Samuel, 149, 155
Mathematics, 15, 121, 130–32
Mendel, Moses Menachem, 35
Mendelssohn, Moses, 18th-century
    Berlin, 10–11, 173
Mendelssohn, Moses, 19th-century
    Frankfurt, 75, 182
Mendlovitz, Saul, 21
Messianism, 18, 41, 171
Methodology, 160. *See also* Study
Midrash, 121, 123, 155, 157–58, 160
Mihalowitz, Hungary, 47–50, 53
Mishnah. *See* Talmud
Modernity, ix, 1, 10–12, 14, 16–18, 20,
    22–24, 26, 29, 31–32, 35, 39, 43–44,
    46, 63, 67, 71–72, 115–19, 121, 125,
    127–28, 131–33, 138, 164–66, 169.
    See also Acculturation; *Bildung*; Liberalism; Secular patterns;
    Wissenschaft
Mohel (circumciser), 67, 69, 175
Montagu, Samuel, 62–63
Morality, 63–64, 67, 85, 100, 104, 121,
    123, 160. *See also* Musar
Moses, Moritz, 61
Mosse, George L., 115
Munk, Elijah, 88, 102
Musar literature, 138
Musar movement, 26
Museums, 58
Music, 18, 24, 48, 50–51, 55, 168. *See
    also* Choirs

Nationalism, 7. *See also* Zionism
Natural science, 132
"Necessity of Protest against the Actions of the Reformers" (pamphlet), 75
Neologues, 36, 39–42, 43–54, 56–57, 71
Neo-Orthodoxy. *See* Orthodoxy
Noahide commandments, 85
Nobel, Anton, 167, 193
Nobel, Joseph, 104

Nonconformists, 160–61
Novellae, rabbinic, 23–24, 175

Oaths, 64, 181
Offenbach, Hesse, 77
Ordination, 130, 158–60, 182
Organs, 48, 51, 55
Orphans, 110–13, 124
Orthodoxy, modern, ix–xiii, 2, 11–12,
  14, 19, 22, 36, 39, 42, 46, 53–60, 62,
  71–72, 90, 98, 105, 113–14, 118–19,
  129, 164–70

Palestine. See Jerusalem; Zionism
Paris, 99
Patriotism, 32, 109
Pedagogy. See Study
Peoplehood, Jewish. See Community of
  Israel
Periodicals, 15, 24, 28, 34–35, 39–40,
  45–46, 74–75, 78–79, 103, 107–9,
  111, 124, 130, 142–43, 147, 175
Pest. See Budapest
Petitions, 38–39, 45–48, 55, 64, 85,
  101–3, 107–8, 124
Philanthropy, 12–13, 42, 59, 63–64, 70,
  76, 99–100, 108–11, 124, 140–42,
  169. See also Orphans
Philippson, Ludwig, 28, 32–35, 42, 75
Philology, 139
Philosophy, 14–15, 18, 23, 67, 104, 116–
  17, 121–22, 126, 138–39, 147, 157–
  58, 160–62
Physics, 15
Pinsker, Leon, 60–61
Pluralism, 11–12, 29, 33, 41, 57, 59–60,
  62, 71–72, 74–75, 78, 84, 86, 88, 101–
  5, 107, 111–13, 142, 170. See also
  Communal secession
Pogroms, 70, 109–10, 180
Poland. See Eastern Europe
Polemics, 24, 28, 31, 35, 39–43, 54, 71,
  75, 78–80, 83, 111–12, 130, 134, 139–
  40, 145–46, 149, 153, 155, 168
Politics, 33–34, 38, 46, 53, 61, 85–87,
  93, 98, 102–3, 105–6, 112, 140, 147,
  169. See also Government
Poskim, 138, 144, 159, 164

Prague, 11
Prayer, 4, 18, 23–24, 29, 32–33, 48, 55,
  65–68, 79, 104, 123, 127, 135, 143
Prejudice, anti-Jewish, 64, 66, 70, 85,
  101–10, 169–70, 185
Pressburg, 19–20, 27, 47, 133
Propaganda, 9, 41, 85, 101–2, 106. See
  also Polemics
Prussia, 1, 8, 62, 64, 86–87. See also
  Berlin

Rabbiner-Seminar, Berlin, x, 2, 26, 59,
  62, 66, 80, 83, 96, 105, 141–49, 154,
  156–64, 167–69, 182, 191
Rabbinic courts, x, 6, 8, 63–64, 66–68,
  77–79, 98, 134, 164
Rabbinical functions, 3–5, 7, 9–10, 17,
  21, 23–25, 28–29, 31–32, 38, 47–48,
  57, 65–67, 77, 98, 103, 133, 157, 159,
  169. See also Authority; Education
Rabbinical organizations, 85
Rabbinical relations, 24, 26, 38–40, 43–
  47, 56–58, 61, 78–80, 84–85, 88, 90,
  93–94, 96–97, 101–4, 107, 111–12,
  119, 130, 133–35, 139, 142–43, 145–
  46, 148–50, 155, 162, 168. See also
  Hildesheimer, Esriel: disputes with
  Orthodox Jews; Polemics
Rabbis. See Culture, rabbinic; Semi-
  naries; Yeshivot
Rabinowitz, Saul, 61
Ragins, Sanford, 101, 106
Rappoport, Shlomo Judah Leib, 97, 154
Rashi, 4, 158
Rationalism, 16, 18, 44, 104, 153, 163
Reform of religion, 19, 33, 47, 53–55,
  65–66, 68, 74–75, 103, 129, 173
Refugees. See Pogroms
Religion: nature of, 21, 76, 89, 168
Religionsgesellschaft, Frankfurt. See
  Hirsch, Samson Raphael; Breuer,
  Solomon
Religions-Wissenschaft, 154, 160
Responsa, x, 14, 23–24, 26, 29–32, 42,
  49–50, 67, 80, 89, 94, 127, 157–58,
  175
Revelation, 42, 73, 76–78, 82–84, 113,
  145, 149–51, 155–56, 158, 162–63, 169

Revolutions, 13, 44, 176
Ritual. *See* Ceremonies
Rivkin, Ellis, 24
Röhling, August, 104
Rokeach, Eleazar, 79
Rosenfeld, Josef, 123
Rosenheim, Jacob, 142, 146, 149, 156
Rosenstein, Elchanan, 55
Rothschild, Wilhelm Karl von, 80
Russia. *See* Eastern Europe

Sabbath, 4, 48, 51, 64–66, 68–69, 105, 126–27, 158, 168, 172
Sachs, Michael, 54
Sacrifices, 55, 66–67
Samet, Moshe, 105
Sanhedrin, 144–45
Saxony, 1, 28, 32–35, 75. *See also* Halberstadt
Schick, Maharam, 26, 47, 127–28
Schleiermacher, Friedrich, 23
Schlesinger, Akiba Yoseph, 43
Scholarship, 40, 76, 82, 84, 119, 139, 141, 145, 151, 154–55, 161, 163, 165, 169. *See also* Education; *Wissenschaft des Judentums;* Yeshivot
Schools, 13, 18, 28, 37, 40, 44, 52, 56, 58–60, 64–66, 110–12, 116, 118, 121–22, 124, 126–28, 142, 148, 163. *See also* Seminaries; Yeshivot
Schorsch, Ismar, 18, 22, 63, 101–2, 161–62
Schreiber, Emanuel, 76
Shrenzel, M., Lemberg, 109
Schwab, Hermann, ix, 12
Schwarzschild, Emanuel, 96–97, 141, 148, 173
Schwerin, 141
Science. *See Wissenschaft des Judentums*
Scripture, 1, 4–6, 10, 13, 15, 23, 41, 46, 51, 76–77, 82, 85, 121, 123–24, 131–32, 135, 138–39, 142, 144, 146, 149–51, 153–58, 160–63
Secular patterns, 4–5, 8, 10–11, 13–14, 18–19, 23, 37–38, 40–44, 51, 53, 55, 57, 60, 63, 71, 73, 100–2, 105, 109, 111, 116–30, 133–34, 144–45, 159, 161, 164, 167, 169. *See also*

Freethinkers; *Gymnasium;* Humanities
Seminaries, 44–47, 51, 53, 59, 76, 78, 80, 90, 116, 119, 129–35, 138–41, 165. *See also* Breslau; Hochschule; Rabbiner-Seminar
Semitic languages, 15, 149, 160. *See also* Hebrew
Separation of sexes, 48, 51, 134
Separatism. *See* Communal secession
Sephardim, 98–99. *See also* Bernays, Isaac
Septuagint, 1, 15
Sermons, 3, 18, 47, 49, 56, 71, 118, 131, 138, 157–58, 160–61, 172
Shochrei Deah, Amsterdam, 38
Shohet (ritual slaughterer), 51, 56–57, 185–86. *See also* Kosher laws
Shulhan Aruch. See Codes
Shulvass, M. A., 71
Silesia. *See* Breslau; Kattowitz
Simon, J., Berlin, 55
Society for the Support of Eretz Yisrael, 108
Sociology, xiii, 17, 19, 21, 47, 49, 60, 65–66, 68–71, 113–14, 149, 160, 163
Sofer, Abraham. *See* Ktav Sofer
Sofer, Eliezer Zusman, 134–35
Sofer, Haim, 43, 47
Sofer, Moses. *See* Hatam Sofer
Sofer, Samuel, 47
Sofer family, 133
Soldiers, 38
Spektor, Isaac Elchanan, 27, 61, 163–64, 176
Staadecker, Dr., Mannheim, 100
Status, legal, 16–17, 19, 86–87
Stein, Pinchas, 46
Steinthal, Hermann, 139
Stern, Ludwig, 90
Sternheim, L., Berlin, 55
Struck, D., Berlin, 55
Study: methods of, 15–16, 18, 37, 133, 138, 160, 174
Switzerland, 64
Synagogue, 2, 4, 9, 18, 28–29, 33, 38, 47–51, 55, 65, 68, 71, 88, 96, 100, 104–5, 135, 138
Synthesis. *See* Acculturation

About the Author

David Ellenson is Professor of Jewish Religious Thought, Hebrew Union College-Jewish Institute of Religion, Los Angeles. He received a bachelor's degree from The College of William and Mary and masters degrees from the University of Virginia, Hebrew Union College-Jewish Institute of Religion, New York, and Columbia University. His doctorate is from Columbia University. He is author of *Tradition in Transition: Orthodoxy, Halakha, and the Boundaries of Modern Jewish Identity* (1989).